All Things Bright & Beautiful
California Impressionist Paintings from The Irvine Museum

ESSAYS BY   *William H. Gerdts*   *Jean Stern*   *Harvey L. Jones*   *David Dearinger*

GUEST CURATOR

William H. Gerdts

ALL THINGS BRIGHT & BEAUTIFUL

California Impressionist Paintings from The Irvine Museum

THE IRVINE MUSEUM

PUBLISHED BY
The Irvine Museum
Twelfth Floor
18881 Von Karman Avenue
Irvine, California 92612

Library of Congress catalog card no. 97-077984
ISBN 0-9635468-2-1 (cloth)
ISBN 0-9635468-9-9 (paper)
Printed in Italy

COVER: Colin Campbell Cooper (1856–1937),
Pergola at Samarkand Hotel, Santa Barbara,
c. 1921, oil on canvas, 29 x 36 inches,
Joan Irvine Smith Fine Arts, Inc.

PLATE 1 (page 2): E. Charlton Fortune (1885–1969),
Study of Monterey Bay, c. 1918, oil on canvas,
12 x 16 inches, The Irvine Museum

Contents

ALL THINGS BRIGHT & BEAUTIFUL
CALIFORNIA IMPRESSIONIST PAINTINGS
FROM THE IRVINE MUSEUM

is an Allied Activity of the
California Sesquicentennial, 1850–2000

GOVERNOR PETE WILSON

May, 1998

Gayle and I are delighted to introduce *All Things Bright and Beautiful*.

As Californians, we take special pride in the Golden State's preeminent status in the arts and by our role as a vital source of cultural enrichment and sheer enjoyment for people worldwide.

The skill and creativity reflected in artistic expression has inspired people for many ages, and the paintings in this exhibit are exemplary of California's rich historical art tradition. Painted between 1890-1930, these Impressionist masterpieces show our state as it was, about one hundred years ago, when California entered the twentieth century confident in the promise of tremendous growth in agriculture, commerce and population.

It is indeed fitting and timely that this magnificent exhibition is on tour as California celebrates its Sesquicentennial. I congratulate Joan Irvine Smith, president of the Irvine Museum, as well as director Jean Stern and his staff, for their tremendous efforts on behalf of this exhibit and adding to California's historic renown for artistic excellence.

To exhibition spectators and participants alike, please accept our best wishes for every future success.

Sincerely,

PETE WILSON

Foreword

The Board of Directors and the staff of The Irvine Museum take great pride and pleasure in presenting this exhibition of California Impressionist paintings. The mission of The Irvine Museum is to preserve and display California art of the Impressionist period, and it is our goal to present these magnificent works of art not only to our constituents in California but also to people throughout the United States and the world over. The paintings in *All Things Bright and Beautiful: California Impressionist Paintings from The Irvine Museum* reflect the highest standards of American art. Furthermore, those that focus on the landscape encapsulate the unique qualities of California Impressionism by combining great beauty with historical significance and, most of all, a deep reverence for nature.

Landscape painting is a time-honored tradition that is inseparable from the spirit of American art. In the early 1800s, at the time of the Industrial Revolution, a group of dedicated landscape painters who became known as the Hudson River school ventured into what was then the "wilderness" of the Hudson River Valley, where they painted virgin and unspoiled countryside. These artists were in awe of the beauty and grandeur of nature and developed a popular and long-lived style that centered on landscape as primary subject. In a very real sense, they were the environmental activists of their day.

In California, a similar group of spiritually aware painters working in the early 1900s recorded the beauty of nature. William Wendt believed that nature was a manifestation of God and viewed himself as nature's faithful interpreter. His feelings for the land were so profound that only rarely did he include people or animals in his landscapes. Maurice Braun was affiliated with the Theosophical Society, whose tenets included a form of transcendentalism and the belief that every natural object has a spiritual presence. Theosophy had a profound influence on Braun's art. His paintings were loving expressions of the moods of nature, not mere descriptions.

With the coming of the 1930s, art no longer paid homage to nature, as artists turned to the cities and the material attributes of the modern age for inspiration. It is said that art mirrors society, and when we supplanted our regard for nature, we placed our trust in technology and undervalued the importance of our natural environment.

PLATE 2
William Wendt (1865–1946)
The Silent Summer Sea, 1915
Oil on canvas, 40 x 50 inches
Joan Irvine Smith Fine Arts, Inc.

Now, the perils of environmental ignorance have become painfully clear to people the world over.

The splendor of nature fascinated artists in the past and compelled them to make beautiful paintings. Today, with the renascence of the glorification of nature in art, that spirit is motivating enlightened people in the same way it energized artists of nearly a hundred years ago. The common bond is a deep reverence for nature and the common goal is the preservation of our environment—no statement is more eloquent than the silent testament of these magnificent paintings. Each generation, in its turn, is the steward of the land and the water. Our time is now. I sincerely hope that the message these paintings impart will inspire us all to action in this most pressing obligation.

Joan Irvine Smith
President, The Irvine Museum

Prefaces

Rarely does an East Coast museum have the opportunity to show paintings of the variety and quality included in this exhibition of California Impressionists. In fact, students of American art history are seldom taught about the art of the West except as it is depicted by Albert Bierstadt and other eastern artists who ventured past the Rocky Mountains. Therefore, for us at the National Academy Museum and School of Fine Arts as well as for audiences in the greater New York metropolitan area, this show is a refreshing awakening.

The development of western art as illustrated in this exhibition actually followed a similar path to that of the East, beginning with an interest in nature that shifted from topographical to monumental images, like those of the Hudson River school, to more subjective, poetic landscapes that reflected French Barbizon influences. Ultimately, American artists studying in Munich and Paris transported to this country variations of the high-keyed palette and stubby brushstroke of the French Impressionists, which permeated western as well as eastern art at the turn of the century.

Cross-pollination took place not only between Europe and the United States but also between the two coasts. There were Americans from both New York and California who worked in Giverny in the circle of Monet; there were those who studied with William Merritt Chase in New York and some who took his classes in California in 1914; and there were others who maintained bicoastal friendships. The intermingling of work from eastern and western states was furthered at various exhibitions like the 1915 Panama-Pacific International Exposition in San Francisco. Such a mix was also apparent at the National Academy of Design's annual exhibitions, as David Dearinger relates in his essay. The separation of the art of the West from that of the East is therefore an art-historical contrivance that is now being corrected. What is truly different, regional if you will, is the light and landscape of California. It is as unique and as recognizable as that of Italy, England, or Holland, and it is what sets California Impressionism apart from eastern or midwestern Impressionism.

It is appropriate that the National Academy, whose annual exhibitions have been taking place for one hundred and seventy-two years, host this exhibition organized by

Jean Stern, executive director of The Irvine Museum, since the work of California artists was shown here from the Academy's inception. We are grateful to Joan Irvine Smith, who was ahead of her time in collecting these works, and to the Board of The Irvine Museum. Professor William H. Gerdts, a member of our Advisory Board, is to be congratulated for curating the exhibition, and Dr. David Dearinger, chief curator at the Academy, for coordinating it at our venue. We are also indebted to Mr. and Mrs. Thomas B. Stiles and Mr. and Mrs. Paul Bagley, noted New York collectors of California Impressionism, for insuring that the exhibition would be presented at the Academy. Such bicoastal cooperation today continues the spirit of the interaction between the artists whose work is herein represented.

Annette Blaugrund
Director, National Academy Museum and School of Fine Arts

On behalf of the Terra Museum of American Art, I would like to extend thanks to the Board and staff of The Irvine Museum for making it possible to present *All Things Bright and Beautiful: California Impressionist Paintings from The Irvine Museum,* perhaps Chicago's first exposure to many of these plein-air painters from California.

The Irvine Museum has established this early twentieth-century legacy as a special focus for scholarly research. This dedication has now helped to fill in our knowledge of yet another, earlier generation's response to the region's breathtaking light and natural beauty, an awesome if fragile environment that inspires artists to the present day. These visions of California, both north and south, should remind those for whom the notion "Impressionism" denotes French landscapes that Impressionism as a style spread across the planet, no less to Maine and Long Island than to New South Wales, Argentina, Japan, and many other places where the immediacy of fugitive light and color evoked the artist's like response.

We are very pleased that the American Impressionists collected by Ambassador Daniel J. Terra will be briefly complemented by these glowing paintings of Laguna Beach, Point Lobos, Monterey, and San Juan Capistrano.

John Hallmark Neff
Director/Chief Curator, Terra Museum of American Art

The Dixon Gallery and Gardens is honored to present this extraordinary exhibition, *All Things Bright and Beautiful: California Impressionist Paintings from The Irvine Museum.* The beautiful paintings included are not only exceptional examples of regional American Impressionism but they also represent the spirit of The Dixon Gallery and Gardens and of our founders, Margaret and Hugo Dixon. The main focus of The Dixon Gallery and Gardens has always been the collection and presentation of French and American Impressionism, Post-Impressionism, and related schools. Showing this collection of California Impressionist paintings from The Irvine Museum exemplifies our mission.

We welcome the opportunity to make these works of art available for the education, enjoyment, and enrichment of the entire Memphis and mid-South communities.

Jack Blair
Chairman, Board of Trustees, The Dixon Gallery and Gardens

When the opportunity arose to exhibit this group of California Impressionist paintings, we enthusiastically seized it. We have had the pleasure of collaborating with The Irvine Museum on previous projects and so knew them to be successfully executed and well received by the public. We have also worked with Professor William H. Gerdts, the guest curator of the present exhibition, and respect his eye and expertise. And, we value the privilege of again working with Joan Irvine Smith, whose vision in assembling her own collection, in creating The Irvine Museum, and in supporting this exhibition and publication show tremendous foresight; she is to be highly commended.

The Oakland Museum of California has a well-known tradition of collecting and exhibiting the work of California's finest Impressionist painters. Our collections are among the best. But only a relatively small audience can venture into the San Francisco Bay Area to see the collection, and even then not all is on display—we must exhibit works of artists who have gone before and those who come after the great era of California Impressionism. Contemporary California artists, and those working in photography, sculpture, and the decorative arts, too, all must have their place in the Oakland Museum. We therefore did not want to pass up the rare opportunity to have this group of works displayed in our museum for the people of the Bay Area to enjoy.

It has not gone unnoticed that we are approaching the sesquicentennial of California—a significant anniversary of the discovery of gold in 1848, of the Gold Rush in 1849, and of statehood in 1850. It seems fitting that California will share some of its artistic "gold" one hundred and fifty years after these defining moments in the history of our state. We are pleased and honored to be part of this celebration of brightness, beauty, and one of California's most-loved artistic traditions.

Dennis M. Power
Director, Oakland Museum of California

Acknowledgments

This book and the exhibit it accompanies are the culmination of the dedicated efforts of a number of individuals. First and foremost, our guest curator, William H. Gerdts, professor of art history at the Graduate School of the City University of New York, inspired this project and guided it from inception through completion. David Dearinger, chief curator of the National Academy Museum, played a key role in planning the traveling exhibit. Joining Professor Gerdts and Dr. Dearinger as authors are Harvey L. Jones, senior curator of art at the Oakland Museum of California, and our own executive director, Jean Stern. Each of these scholars has given generously of their talent, effort, and enthusiasm in the preparation of the catalogue.

A number of others have made less visible, but important, contributions. Paul and Kathy Bagley, Mort and Donna Fleischer, De McCall, Ray Redfern, George and Irene Stern, and Tom and Barbara Stiles all have allowed us to use images of their paintings in this volume. Pam Ludwig, director of Joan Irvine Smith Fine Arts, Inc.; Bolton Colburn, director of the Laguna Art Museum; Ruth Westphal, noted author in the field; Barbara Pieper, director of the California Arts Council: Lilli Colton, our graphic designer; Joseph N. Newland, our editor; and Christopher Bliss and Casey Brown, our photographers have all given of their knowledge, judgment, and professional skills. Merika Adams Gopaul, Janet Murphy, and Brenda Negri, from our staff, also have assisted with the catalogue and with the organization and logistics of the exhibit.

We are honored to open this exhibit at the National Academy Museum in New York City, and we look forward to sharing it with the patrons of the Terra Museum of American Art in Chicago, The Dixon Gallery and Gardens in Memphis, and the Oakland Museum of California. We appreciate the support and assistance of the director and staff at each venue.

In closing, I would like to acknowledge the inspiration of our founders, Joan Irvine Smith and Athalie R. Clarke; the financial support of the Joan Irvine Smith & Athalie R. Clarke Foundation; and the continuing guidance and generosity of our president, Joan Irvine Smith, for making the Museum possible.

James I. Swinden
Vice President, The Irvine Museum

PLATE 3
Paul Lauritz (1889–1975)
Poinsettias, c. 1925
Oil on canvas, 32 x 36 inches
The Irvine Museum

Images of "The Land of Sunshine":
California Impressionism

William H. Gerdts

"The Land of Sunshine" is an almost ubiquitous expression bestowed upon California at the turn of the century and after, deriving both from the poem by C. R. Pattee and from the magazine of that title, in the first issue of which the poem was published.[1] Soon after it was founded in 1894, the magazine's editorship was taken over by Charles Fletcher Lummis, probably the most ardent and effective booster of the attractions of Southern California, which included the physical beauties that are pictorially extolled in almost every painting in this exhibition.[2] Lummis himself wrote only occasionally about California artists, authoring articles on Ed Borein and Alexander Harmer, but the magazine frequently included pieces on California painters, some by George Wharton James, Lummis's great rival as a cultural arbiter, and the circle who gathered around Lummis in the Garvanza–Arroyo Seco district of Pasadena and eastern Los Angeles, which included pioneering California Impressionists such as Elmer Wachtel, William Wendt, Granville Redmond, and Hanson Puthuff as well as critical champions of the movement such as Antony Anderson and Everett Maxwell.

Reference to California as "The Land of Sunshine" is more specifically directed toward *Southern* California, but Impressionist painting first appeared in the state in San Francisco in the 1890s.[3] A number of pictures by Guy Rose, Evelyn McCormick, and Ernest Peixotto, which probably demonstrated a tentative Impressionism, appeared in exhibitions held at the San Francisco Art Institute and the Mechanics' Institute in that city in 1892 and 1893. These works depicted scenes in Claude Monet's home village of Giverny, France, where those painters were among the earliest Californians to join the artists' colony that was established there in 1887. Both Rose and Peixotto returned to Giverny in 1894, and the latter subsequently exhibited additional Giverny scenes in San Francisco at the Guild of Arts and Crafts in 1896 and at the Bohemian Club in 1897.

Still, these works by native Californians probably had less impact than the pictures on display by leading French Impressionist painters and by eastern American artists. In March of 1891, and again in 1893 and 1895, William Kingston Vickery[4] supervised a series of loan exhibitions held as benefits for San Francisco orphanages and hospitals, while in November of 1891, another show was mounted at the San Francisco Art Association

Notes for this essay begin on page 152.

PLATE 4
Guy Rose (1867–1925)
Provençal Olive Orchard
(In the Olive Orchard)
Oil on canvas, 15 x 18 inches
The Joan Irvine Smith Collection

to support the San Francisco Polyclinic; these exhibits first introduced Impressionism to California in the form of paintings by Monet, Eugène Boudin, Camille Pissarro, Pierre Renoir, and Edgar Degas.[5] These pictures were lent by Mrs. William H. Crocker, the leading, if not the only, California patron of French Impressionist art at the time. And in 1894, paintings by Monet, Pissarro, Renoir, Boudin, and Alfred Sisley were on view in the city at the California Midwinter International Exposition, in which McCormick and Peixotto were also represented.

The critical reaction to such innovative work was varied. John A. Stanton, himself an exhibitor of Breton and Parisian subjects and the chief administrator of the Exposition, noted that "never since Corot's time has there been a man of so much prominence in art as Claude Monet" and describing his works as "so full of atmosphere and color that it really dazzles you, and makes you catch your breath. The work may not be appreciated or understood by the masses.... Pizzarro [sic], Renoir, and Sisley, are pronounced impressionists, and their works can be carefully considered by those who are interested in the new school."[6] Even the Tonalist painter Arthur Mathews, the most influential artist in San Francisco and director of the California School of Design, was at least equivocal about the paintings by Monet (identified incorrectly as "Manet" by him), concluding: "For myself I feel that this particular phase of art sacrifices too much for a problem—the vibration of light and color; but I am not prepared to discuss the issue."[7] The Californians, though not specifically named, fared less well, with Lesley Martin noting "several specimens of daymares in landscape, resulting from the swallowing of camels in the effort to paint vibrations and see purple in every condition of the atmosphere. In excuse for these outbursts it may be said they have most of them been done in France at a time when the waves of Impressionism and Symbolism met the conflicting stream of the Vibrationists in full flood. As these painters are young they will have time to repent them of their deeds."[8]

If Martin was not receptive to Impressionist art, another critic received the new strategies with tremendous enthusiasm when a show of Maurice Prendergast's watercolors and monotypes appeared at the Vickery Gallery in May of 1900, sent on from the Macbeth Gallery in New York, where it had been shown two months earlier. These were scenes of Italy, primarily Prendergast's magnificently colorful watercolors of Venice, painted in 1898–99. The reviewer from the *San Francisco Chronicle* recognized in these pictures the essential modern-life concerns of Impressionism, believing that the show "marks an epoch in the art records of the West. This is, in fact, the first time that the stay-at-home local painters and patrons of the beautiful have had an opportunity to study not the exaggerated, but the legitimate impressionist.... In the first place, every picture teems with life, of the gayest and brightest. It gives the opportunity for action and nuance of color...."[9]

But despite the ardent welcome accorded Impressionism, the art world of San Francisco remained mostly dominated by French-influenced Barbizon and Tonalist aesthetics associated especially with Arthur Mathews. Although it was obviously the poetic mood and spiritual resonances that nourished the Tonalist approach, Mathews also found naturalistic underpinnings to support his formal strategies, noting that "Our sun is not so clear or our colors so intense.... The atmosphere here is thicker and richer for that reason."[10] At the turn of the century, Mathews was the city's most influential figure, while William Keith—earlier the most renowned painter of the panoramic grandeur of the California landscape—had, since the 1880s, turned increasingly to more broadly rendered and densely packed scenes of scrub and oak forests, abandoning not only the specificity of his earlier work, but also the topographical celebration implicit therein. Keith's later work bears a close similarity to that of the eastern master George Inness, at the time esteemed the country's finest landscape specialist, and this affinity was enhanced by Inness's visit to California in 1891 when he and Keith painted together and formed a firm friendship. One of the earliest American Impressionists to visit and paint in California was the Indiana painter Theodore Steele, recognized as the leading figure of the so-called Hoosier school; Steele was on the West Coast in 1892. On his way from Oregon to Redlands, where he was to paint some of the earliest Impressionist scenes of Southern California, Steele stopped in San Francisco and visited Keith. Steele reported that Keith found the grandeur of the California landscape no longer paintable. By and large, this view remained held strongly by San Francisco landscapists for some time, though Steele himself, presciently, decided:

> I do not think his conclusions that these subjects are unpaintable is correct, but they will be painted by artists of the Monet type, for one can see Monets everywhere. The same color charged air, the same scintillating radiance that Monet finds in the south of France, though with nobler forms and greater compositions than one usually finds in his pictures. I have no shadow of a doubt that some day there will develop a school of painters on this western coast, that can fully interpret these great subjects, and give to the world a new and powerful school of art.[11]

In actuality, this new and powerful school of Impressionism had just begun to form, but it did so in Southern, not Northern, California.[12]

Nancy Dustin Wall Moure, the brilliant scholar of Southern California art, has posited the names of William Wendt, Granville Redmond, and Elmer Wachtel as the leading landscape painters of Los Angeles, each working "in his own particular variation of the Impressionist style," by the turn of the century.[13] It may not be coincidental that these painters of the region formed part of Charles Lummis's circle in the Arroyo Seco. Unfortunately, few of Wachtel's pictures painted at this time can be securely identified, while Redmond's works of this period appear to be overwhelmingly tonal. In any case, it was William Wendt who emerged then, and remains recognized now, as the first outstanding figure in the development of California Impressionism; he was identified, ultimately, as both the "Painter Laureate" of California[14] and the "Dean of Southern California artists."[15]

At the turn of the century, Wendt was still a resident of Chicago; though he had begun visiting Southern California in 1896, he only moved permanently to Los Angeles a decade later. Even as late as 1916, John E. D. Trask opined of Wendt that his "recognition in the East has perhaps exceeded that which he has received in his own home."[16] Wendt began exhibiting depictions of the California landscape at the Art Institute of Chicago as early as 1897, and they were a component of what amounted to a one-artist invitational show there in 1899. To what degree these paintings from the end of the nineteenth century partook of Impressionist strategies is difficult to determine, but in these years Wendt appears to have adopted the coloration and scintillating brushwork of the movement, celebrating the brilliant light distinctive of the region. For instance, *A Poppy Field, California,* lent to the Art Institute in 1897 by Dr. A. J. Ochsner, and *The Scarlet Robe* (also a poppy field painting) shown in 1899, must have utilized Impressionist chromaticism. What the exhibition records also establish is that Wendt, even before he settled in California in 1906, traveled throughout the state, for he exhibited scenes of Monterey, Montecito, Catalina Island, and Point Loma during these years.

Yet, Wendt increasingly abandoned specific place names in the titles of his pictures, favoring rather those that offered temporal and seasonal identification as well as recognition of natural variations of tree and topography—eucalyptus, oak, sycamore, and pine; pastures, woodlands, canyons, mountains, and foothills. The titles also began, by 1899 with *The Earth Yields Its Gold,* to suggest the moralistic, even spiritual implications of the goodness and bounty of Nature, and especially the "spirit of California."[17] Wendt himself suggested as early as 1898 that in such an environment, "One feels that he is on holy ground, in Nature's Temple."[18] Wendt has been identified, rightly, as the primary representative of the *paysage moralisé* in California, and I would go further and suggest that this may even be true for the Impressionist movement generally.[19]

A prime example of this is Wendt's *There is no Solitude [Even] in Nature,* painted in 1906 (plate 55), the year Wendt settled in Los Angeles, and shown at the Art Institute of Chicago in 1907. This is a view of Laguna Canyon, near El Toro Road, but the specifics of a locale are no longer the artist's concern; the ability to locate beauty and interest in the essentially commonplace was a hallmark of Impressionism. By this time, also, Wendt had begun to abandon those Impressionist strategies that allowed for the emphasis upon transience in favor of more structural and blocky forms, concentrating upon mass and solidity as he sought the true vitality of Nature. Antony Anderson even posited a possible alliance between Wendt's work and the modern idiom of Cubism when he asked, "Has the lesson of the cubists been conned by William Wendt?… I saw—or thought I saw—cubic signs in the shape of his clouds and the modelling of his live oaks."[20] As his title indicates, Nature is very much alive here, resplendent in California light, with Wendt's favorite color contrasts of green and gold. His *Ranch in the Valley* (plate 5) is a much later painting of about 1928, in which even the trees assume an almost cubic, stylized form, and Impressionist light is of little concern, while the artist explores the topographical variations of the rolling hills and winding roads in a manner not so dissimilar to that of his eastern counterpart Willard Metcalf, an artist who painted throughout his beloved New England. Like Metcalf, Wendt recognized the human presence not only in the establishment of the roadways but in the ranch buildings in the middle distance, but in these works, as in all his paintings, the figure itself is definitively omitted.

PLATE 5
William Wendt (1865–1946)
Ranch in the Valley, c. 1928
Oil on canvas, 30 x 40 inches
Joan Irvine Smith Fine Arts, Inc.

PLATE 6
Hanson Puthuff (1875–1972)
Monarch of the Malibu
Oil on canvas, 32 x 40 inches
Joan Irvine Smith Fine Arts, Inc.

Nancy Moure has denied the suggestion of any stylistic influence of Wendt on other artists of his time, and it is true that his own strategies seem nearly unique.[21] Likewise, the spiritual essence that Wendt sought and revealed in Nature appears more fully realized in his art than in the paintings of any of his contemporaries except, perhaps, for Maurice Braun, and Braun's metaphysical underpinnings were derived from a very different source, that of Theosophy. Yet, I believe one can discern a similar pantheistic celebration of Nature in the work of some of the other California painters often categorized as "Impressionists," particularly when they exalted the soaring mountain forms of the state. This seems especially true of the work of Hanson Puthuff, not coincidentally another figure in Charles Lummis's Arroyo Seco set, and a frequent companion of Wendt's on his painting trips into the California landscape. In his painting *Monarch of the Malibu* (plate 6), which was exhibited in Los Angeles at the annual exhibition of the Painters and Sculptors of Southern California in 1924, Puthuff presents a darkened valley foreground from which arises the lofty mountain form in the brilliant light that scholars then and now have found unique to California.[22] The rugged mountain form also seems particularly suitable for the stronger brushwork that Puthuff utilized here, closer than that of many of his contemporaries to the blocky, cubic strategies employed by Wendt, though still more delicate, more "Impressionist." Puthuff, a decade younger than Wendt, had settled in Los Angeles in 1903, but like his older colleague he had Chicago connections; Puthuff is said to have studied there in the 1890s at the Academy of Fine Arts, and he returned to live in Chicago for a year or two, beginning in 1906. Puthuff was a true plein-air painter, usually completing his work out-of-doors. He excelled in the depiction of soaring mountain forms, from the Malibu range and the Verdugo Mountains just beyond his Los Angeles home on La Crescenta, to the Sierras in the north; in 1915 he painted the Sierras in a series of ten decorative murals commemorating *The Spirit of California* for the Laughlin Theater in Long Beach.[23]

Perhaps the other California Impressionist most noted for his depictions of mountain grandeur is Edgar Alwin Payne, though Payne's overall oeuvre is far more extensive, encompassing not only many coastal scenes, especially at Laguna Beach, and a large production of pictures painted in Arizona, but also harbor views in Brittany and Venice, as well as Swiss Alpine landscapes. Whereas Wendt and Puthuff favored the California mountain ranges closer to the coastal regions, Payne concentrated on the Sierras, such as in his magnificent picture of *The Sierra Divide,* painted in 1921 (plate 7); indeed, he was christened "The God of the Mountains" in 1927 in a review of his show at the Stendahl Art Galleries.[24] Using somewhat slablike pictorial strategies not totally unrelated to those introduced by Wendt, Payne offers the viewer less of an inviting foreground than does Puthuff. The great peaks rise immediately above the lake

in the lower left, while the eye is directed diagonally up at the right by the row of ascending trees and then swiftly back toward the mountain peak, along the flat contrasting diagonal of stone. Payne eschewed the brilliant California light exploited by Puthuff, preferring instead the coloristic contrast of the verdant bit of ground in the lower right and the pure white of the snow filling the mountain crevasses. This was a favorite compositional form of Payne's, and can be seen again in such pictures as the magnificent *Rugged Slopes and Tamarack* (Mr. and Mrs. Thomas B. Stiles II collection).

While Payne stressed majesty rather than poetry in his paeans to California mountain scenery, he shared Wendt's awe before the grandeur of Nature, and attempted to reveal his spiritual response. Many Californians detected the spiritual resonances in the great mountains—the "Mother Mountains" as the Sierra Madre were named, with their great peaks rearing up from the flat-breasted earth, as noted by Charles Lummis.[25] The artist also expressed clearly his preference for the Sierras over the Alps. Payne told Fred Hogue:

> When one goes into the Swiss Alps he does not get the feeling of communion with nature that one experiences here in California. Even on the peaks, one finds there shelter huts. The slopes are cultivated to the snow line. The hotels follow you everywhere. Here it is different. The California Sierras are not yet fully explored. I have stood on the banks of fifty mountain lakes that are neither charted nor named. I have sketched in the shadow of mountains that would be famous in Europe, but that are known here only as units of the Sierra range…. There is more color in the high Sierras than in the Alps, and more atmosphere. The rocks of the Alps are granite, of a uniform gray. In the Sierras one finds mineral ledges everywhere. There is a diversity of color. There are reds and greens not to be found anywhere in Europe. One finds here the mountains of Switzerland under the skies of Italy.[26]

PLATE 8
Edgar Payne (1883–1947)

Sycamore in Autumn, Orange County Park, c. 1916

Oil on board, 32 x 42 inches

Joan Irvine Smith Fine Arts, Inc.

What may seem strange is that the California Impressionists appear to have deliberately avoided those natural monuments with which the state had hitherto been distinctly and pictorially associated, Mts. Shasta and Tamalpais, and especially Yosemite and the Big Trees. There were exceptions, of course, but these appear to have been few.[27] This may be, in part, because the artists considered such motifs hackneyed by the early twentieth century, and also because they believed that a new, more modern aesthetic required a different set of motifs, and in this case, one that generally faced west toward the limitless expanse of ocean, the better to express the paradisiacal metaphor intrinsic to their conceptions. Interestingly, the previously popular Yosemite region would find new appeal among selected early Modernists of the next artistic generation, such as Marguerite and William Zorach.

Of course, all of the California Impressionists also painted more intimate landscapes, such as Payne's *Sycamore in Autumn, Orange County Park* (plate 8). Here, the play of light through the golden leaves and flickering on the ground is of primary concern; such emphasis offers an interesting contrast with similar compositions painted earlier in Northern California by William Keith, and exhibits a clear distinction between the soulful lyricism of American Barbizon painting and the clear, more colorful veracity of Impressionism. Payne was yet another artist who had studied in Chicago, at the Art Institute, before making his first trip to California in 1909, when he visited Laguna Beach; he was back in Laguna in 1911, painting there with Hanson Puthuff. Though maintaining a Chicago address through 1923, Payne settled in California in 1917, first in Glendale, and then in Laguna Beach.[28]

Elmer Wachtel was another California Impressionist whom Moure has posited as one of the region's earliest painters involved with the strategies of Impressionism, but the chronology and development of his work is extremely difficult to chart. Wachtel, born a year earlier than Wendt, was one of the first generation of California Impressionists; he was also one of the earliest to settle in the state, moving to Los Angeles in 1882. He was among the earliest professional painters in the city and was involved in the founding of the Los Angeles Art Association in 1890. In 1894 Wachtel sought training in New York City, and in 1896–97 he was in Europe before settling permanently in Los Angeles, where he worked as an illustrator while pursuing his calling of landscape painting. In 1904 Wachtel had his house and studio in the Arroyo Seco and was one of the circle of Charles Lummis. Basically independent, Wachtel was one of the few major painters in the region who did not join the California Art Club when it was founded in Los Angeles in 1911, though he was an exhibitor in the early shows of the Del Monte Art Gallery in Monterey in 1907–9; in Los Angeles he held exhibitions of his work in his studio and at commercial galleries.[29]

Wachtel was noted in 1914 as "the first exponent of the landscape of California."[30] His paintings, almost always undated, reflect the idyllicism to which many California artists resorted. He traveled widely throughout California as well as to Arizona and New Mexico for his subject matter. It would probably be correct to assume that his more tonal and Barbizon-related paintings are earlier than his lighter and more colorful Impressionist pictures. The breadth and freedom of *Golden Autumn, Cajon Pass* (plate 9) is typical of the latter. Unlike Puthuff, who utilized a flat foreground plane as a preliminary to his exaltation of the Malibu Mountains, Wachtel emphasizes the sinuous trees and the underbrush sparkling in the light of California, while presenting the distant mountain range as a backdrop. Canyons and valleys were his preferred subject matter—Santa Anita Canyon, Topanga Canyon, Monrovia Canyon, San Fernando Valley, Santa Paula Valley, Ojai Valley, Montecito

PLATE 9
Elmer Wachtel (1864–1929)
Golden Autumn, Cajon Pass
Oil on canvas, 22 x 30 inches
Joan Irvine Smith Fine Arts, Inc.

PLATE 10
Marion Kavanagh Wachtel (1876–1954)
Landscape with Oak Trees
Watercolor and pastel, 20 x 16 inches
Joan Irvine Smith Fine Arts, Inc.

Valley—and harmonized with Wachtel's emphasis on the foreground. Edgar Hunt noted that Wachtel did not use broken brushstrokes, but rather tended to paint "in large flat colors, the gauze of atmosphere superimposed upon the primary colors. In this he is an Impressionist."[31] Cajon Pass, between San Bernardino and Barstow, is formidable territory, but here the overlapping purple-hued mountain ranges seem inviting and easily traversed, although there is no human presence to roam through this landscape, no desecration of pristine Nature.

Elmer Wachtel was as proficient in watercolor as in oils, and in his early years in Los Angeles he was probably better known for his work in the former medium.[32] He was one of the earliest professional watercolor painters in Los Angeles, and probably *the* first to devote himself to landscape painting in that medium. He was joined in this preference by his wife, Marion Kavanaugh Wachtel (she dropped the "u" after her marriage, and was recognized as Marion Kavanagh Wachtel). Elmer never abandoned watercolor, but appears to have emphasized oils in his later years. In contrast, Marion achieved renown for her work in watercolor, becoming a member of the New York Water Color Club in 1911. She also exhibited watercolors at the Chicago Art Institute in 1911–14, and throughout the 1920s with the California Water Color Society, which had been founded in 1921; she resumed oil painting after Elmer's death. She had been a student at the Art Institute of Chicago and of William Merritt Chase in New York, and was briefly in San Francisco in 1903 as a pupil of William Keith, who advised her to go south and contact Elmer Wachtel; the following year they were married.[33]

Marion Wachtel's emphasis was on tree-filled landscapes, concentrating upon oaks and eucalyptus, such as her *Landscape with Oak Trees* (plate 10). This painting avoids the simplification and stylization that characterize many of her watercolors, and which

led to the disparaging and controversial designation by Merle Armitage in 1928 of many of the California Impressionists as "the eucalyptus school," at a time when the Impressionist movement had begun to lose its vitality.[34] This approach was defended and championed by Arthur Millier, the leading Los Angeles critic of the time;[35] both Marion and Elmer Wachtel were credited by Millier for developing "a type of decorative composition from which many a younger painter has borrowed the framework."[36] As in Elmer's paintings, Marion here emphasizes the foreground, with two sinuous oaks emerging from the rocky terrain, their foliage silhouetted against the sky. The artist carries the eye back into the distance on the trails that lead through the hilly landscape to the far mountains, all rendered in her favorite colored washes of green-blue-purple. The vertical composition, echoing the upward spiral of the trees, was one often favored by Marion Wachtel, but was unusual among her colleagues, who generally preferred an expansive horizontal layout.

Granville Redmond has also been identified as one of Southern California's earliest artists to investigate Impressionist strategies, but Redmond's pictures from the first decade of the century appear overwhelmingly tonal, with little vibrancy or chromatic brilliance, though he appears to have worked with more vivid colors between 1903 and 1905.[37] Subsequently, Antony Anderson, in reviewing Redmond's one-artist show at Steckel's Gallery in Los Angeles in July 1907, noted that his "color, however, is seldom rich and suave—often, indeed, it is rather thin and dry. His bent is very much toward tonal pictures, so called, by which is meant, it would seem, the partial negation of color. Some of these pictures are very pleasing, though they are seldom alive or vibrant."[38]

Redmond, a deaf-mute, was born in Philadelphia but grew up in Northern California, studying at the Institution for the Deaf, Dumb, and Blind in Berkeley. He subsequently studied at the

California School of Design in San Francisco, where Arthur Mathews was one of his teachers, but he also worked in 1893 with Ernest Peixotto, who had been in Giverny; at the end of that year, Redmond himself was studying in Paris. By 1898 he had returned to California and opened a studio in Los Angeles. Subsequently, Redmond divided his time between Southern California, where he painted at Laguna Beach and Catalina Island, and the north, working around Monterey, where he lived for two years beginning in 1908, before moving to San Mateo. In 1918, Redmond was back permanently in Los Angeles.[39]

Redmond's overall artistic drive is fairly complex, for unlike many other American painters, he appears not to have moved from a Tonalist to an Impressionist manner but rather to have varied the two, according to his subject matter, his own temperament, and to the marketable qualities of the works themselves. It would appear that his personal preference may have been for the more muted, quite lyrical aesthetics generally identified with Arthur Mathews and Northern California landscape painting, while the heightened colorism of Impressionism was preferred by collectors. In 1931 Arthur Millier stated that "Redmond likes best of all to paint pictures of solitude and silence. 'Alas,' he wrote, 'people will not buy them. They all seem to want poppies.'"[40] Yet, the explanation for the diversity of his art may not be that simple. His beautiful dark blue *Nocturne* (plate 11) certainly partakes of a dominant single hue, a hallmark

PLATE 11
Granville Redmond (1871–1935)
Nocturne
Oil on canvas, 30 x 40 inches
Joan Irvine Smith Fine Arts, Inc.

of Tonalism, but the brilliance of the coloration with its shining reflections of moonlight suggests rather an Impressionist nocturne, however much that might appear to be an oxymoron. Such an identification is strengthened through consideration of other nocturnes Redmond painted, such as his 1920 *Moonlight Seascape (Catalina Island)* (California School for the Deaf, Fremont).

Redmond's fame both in his own time and today rests principally upon his mastery of the theme of fields of wild flowers, above all, golden yellow poppies; *California Landscape with Flowers* (plate 12) is one of the most monumental of these, the expansive horizontal spread of the canvas echoing the vastness of the state itself.

In such pictures, the tapestry of bright colors covering the rolling hillside glows in the light of California, a paean to its unique natural qualities. Probably dating from the 1920s, as does its near mate, *Poppy Field Landscape* (Laguna Art Museum), such pictures inevitably conjure up the aesthetics of Impressionism. They call to mind Claude Monet's own paintings of poppies in Giverny and elsewhere, and the works of American artists working in a similar fashion—Childe Hassam on the island of Appledore, Julian Onderdonk in the bluebonnet fields of Texas. Redmond was painting and exhibiting scenes featuring fields of poppies at least as early as 1912.

Despite the fact that some critics labeled Redmond's poppy pictures as "potboilers,"[41] his choice of subject matter here is, itself, a tribute to and celebration of California, where the poppy is the state flower. In California at the turn of the century, poems were written and legends were recalled extolling the poppy, designated the "Queen flower of them all."[42] And writers such as Charles Lummis declared such fields of wild flowers "The Carpet of God's Country," referring not only to the poppies, but to the "forty million flowers" of all species and all colors that covered the landscape—the field, not of the "Cloth of Gold," but "of the cloth of all the jewels and all the colors and all the ores in the treasury of the universe."[43] In addition, the cultivation of the poppy, otherwise a wild flower, was considered by gardeners worthy of celebration.[44]

Almost all of the state's landscape painters joined Redmond in choosing to paint such subject matter; it would probably be simpler to list those who did not. Several, however, made fields of poppies, sometimes contrasted with purple lupine, as their specialty, pictures on which their entire reputation rests. One of these is William Franklin Jackson, probably the most significant artist in Sacramento at the turn of the century. In 1863 the Jackson family had settled in Sacramento, where William grew up, before entering the first class at the California School of Design in San Francisco, in 1874, and also studying with the portrait painter Benoni Irwin. Jackson returned to Sacramento in 1880 where, in 1885, he became director of the Crocker Art Gallery there, and then a year later became director of the Sacramento School of Design associated with the museum.[45] At the School, Jackson introduced his students to plein-air painting, which underlies his own work, such as his poppy and lupine picture *Radiant Valley* (plate 46). The flower fields that Jackson recorded were located in the San Joaquin valley and around Sacramento and Rosedale.[46] Except for some early portraits,

Jackson's oeuvre was almost totally devoted to landscape; the one major exception was his controversial *Suite of the Army* of 1903, a representation of nude young ladies bathing, which has long hung in the Men's Bar in Sacramento's Sutter Club.[47]

A painter of greater renown was John Gamble, one of the best-known painters in the thriving artistic community in Santa Barbara, where by the mid-twentieth century he was considered the dean of Santa Barbara artists. The great majority of Gamble's mature production would appear to be poppy and lupine pictures such as his *Santa Barbara Landscape* (plate 53). Gamble had been in San Francisco, where he studied at the California School of Design, before going on to Paris; his art began to attract attention as early as 1885. Gamble's involvement with the wild flower theme may have begun as early as 1897, when his *Wild Mustard* elicited special notice and was perceived as "out of the ordinary" in the spring exhibition of the San Francisco Art Institute.[48] By 1903, he was noted as having made attractive studies of Southern California poppies, "one of which he calls 'The Golden Poppy,' and which shows a mountain gorge, lined with California's wonderful eschscholtzias, is a most striking and attractive thing."[49] Gamble sent *The Golden Poppy* to the Louisiana Purchase Universal Exposition in St. Louis in 1904, and received a commission that year to paint a large scene of California poppies for the lobby of the Saint Francis Hotel in San Francisco. He arrived in Santa Barbara in 1906 as a result of the San Francisco earthquake and fire, in which his studio was destroyed and which led so many artists to abandon that city, some of whom headed further south. Gamble worked in a soft, painterly manner emphasizing the chromatic range

John Gamble painting near Santa Barbara, c. 1920.
Courtesy of the Santa Barbara Historical Society.

of golden poppies, blue and purple lupine, and sometimes the pink buckeye, along with wild lilac, wild mustard, and wild buckwheat, often framed, as here, against the Santa Barbara mountains.[50]

The painters discussed so far, who were among the dominant figures in Southern California art at the end of the nineteenth century and in the first decade of the twentieth, may not have considered themselves as belonging to the Impressionist movement, nor did critics specifically identify them as such.[51] Certainly those who spent time abroad early in their careers, such as Wendt, Redmond, and Gamble, could not have helped being exposed to what was still, for Americans, a radically advanced aesthetic, while these artists may also have become aware of Impressionism through works seen in San Francisco in the 1890s, or in New York and Chicago in that decade. Still, their celebration of the light and colors of California would appear to have been basically home-grown.

The actual identification of California artists as "Impressionist" would appear to have begun no earlier than 1909, and became more common by 1911. The problem here is that the critical reception, by and large extremely positive, was directed not toward Wendt, Puthuff, or Redmond, but toward a group of painters almost totally forgotten today: Jack Gage Stark seems to have been the first, followed by Detlef Sammann, Helena Dunlap, and Ernest Browning Smith. Antony Anderson, the very perceptive art critic for the *Los Angeles Times*, unquestionably the major critical force on the local scene and one who would champion the local Impressionist faction until his retirement in the mid-1920s, noted in December 1911, that "by now we are getting accustomed to impressionism in Los Angeles. Few of us dare laugh at it, for fear that we may become the butt of our own jokes. We are beginning to take it seriously, to study it, to enjoy it. We've had [Jack Gage] Stark, [Detlef] Sammann, Helena Dunlap, [Ernest] Browning Smith…."[52]

It was at this time also that a group of works painted in Pasadena by Frederick Frieseke, an artist who was then becoming one of the best-known American painters working in Giverny, France, and who was visiting his parents in California, was seen by Anderson at the Kanst Art Gallery in Los Angeles in December of 1911. They were not on public view but were being framed there. Anderson "had stepped into the Kanst studio, to find five wonderful paintings of gardens under sunlight by Frederick C. Frieseke, who had run out from New York to visit his parents here, and who painted these five impressions of gardens with figures on his brief stay…. They would be eye-openers to our Los Angeles public— educational skyrockets. Yet, Frieseke was a perfectly proper and academic painter a year or two ago, just as Sammann was."[53] It is not known whether Anderson's comments drew local artists to study these pictures before they were shipped back to Frieseke's New York dealer, William Macbeth, but Kanst did hold an exhibition of Frieseke's work, though the date of the show has not been identified.[54]

Thus, Impressionism was "in the air" in Los Angeles when one of the state's native sons, Guy Rose, returned in 1914 from a long sojourn in Giverny and New York. Born in San Gabriel, Rose was another artist who had trained in San Francisco at the California School of Design before going on for further study in Paris, in 1888. He must have become aware of Impressionism there, and found further exposure when he joined the art colony in Giverny in 1890–91; Rose included several Giverny landscapes among his pictures on view in Los Angeles at Sanborn, Vail, & Co. in October of 1891, and several were shown at the San Francisco Art Association the following year. After this visit to California, Rose was in New York, and in 1894 returned to Paris and Giverny. Beginning in 1895, Rose taught for four years at Pratt Institute, Brooklyn, before returning to Paris and Giverny in 1899, and then purchasing a house in the latter in 1904. Having had to abandon his art almost completely owing to lead poisoning around 1897, Rose resumed painting in 1908, and became one of the most successful of Frieseke's many associates, like him painting colorful figural pictures of lovely young women outdoors, as well as several nudes in interiors. Much more than Frieseke, however, Rose concentrated on pure landscapes, utilizing the high-key colorism and painterly brushwork of Impressionism, undoubtedly influenced by Claude Monet himself; Rose and his wife, Ethel, were among the very few American painters of his generation in Giverny who actually came to know Monet personally.[55]

Presumably the majority of Rose's French pictures were painted in and around Giverny, but Rose traveled quite extensively in France, both to the northern coast at Honfleur, and in the south to Toulon, Antibes, and Cannes. It must have been during such a trip that he painted *In the Olive Orchard (Provençal Olive Orchard)* (plate 4) in southern France, a sparkling, light-filled landscape utilizing all the strategies of orthodox Impressionism. Rose here, and in several similar pictures of groves of tamarisk trees in the region that were probably painted in the same period, revels in the undulating forms, each tree almost rhythmically dancing, while casting transparent shadows over the glistening colored ground. A work called *Olive Trees,* presumably this painting, was exhibited at the Macbeth Gallery in New York in April of 1917.

Having enjoyed a tremendously successful group show late in 1910 at the Madison Gallery in New York along with his fellow Givernyites Frieseke, Richard Miller, and Lawton Parker, Rose returned to that city two years later. He painted in New York and in Wickford, Rhode Island, while teaching an outdoor sketch class at Narragansett; several figural works depicting lovely young women in the landscape painted at Wickford have recently come onto the art market.[56] Two years later, in October of 1914, Rose returned to Los Angeles, and the following year he began exhibiting with the California Art Club and teaching at the Stickney Memorial School in Pasadena, where he became director in 1918, while enjoying one-person shows over the next decade at the Steckel, Kanst, and Cannell and Chaffin galleries in Los Angeles, and from 1920 on at the Stendahl Galleries in that city—as well as at the Elizabeth Battey Gallery, Pasadena, the Friday Morning Club in Los Angeles, the Shakespeare Club in Pasadena, and the Los Angeles Museum of History, Science, and Art. He also established representation at the Macbeth Gallery in New York, where he exhibited from 1913 to 1918. At his death, in 1926, Rose was deemed "unquestionably the greatest landscape painter of the Impressionist school that California has produced."[57]

Southern California appears to have become immediately aware that a major artistic personality had returned to Los Angeles. Antony Anderson noted that "the return of Guy Rose…was an event of importance to Los Angeles…."[58] Anderson also recognized immediately that Rose's paintings represented unqualified Impressionism, referring to him in a review of Rose's first Los Angeles show at the Steckel Gallery in February 1915 as a "frank disciple of Monet and his school…. Like them, he paints the out-of-doors, its colors broken into beauty by brooding sunlight, caressing air and moving winds. Needless to add that he paints much in the 'high key,' which is the key of nature."[59] Anderson was later, however, to distinguish Rose's work from that of Monet, finding the former's paintings more poetic, more architectonic, and more pictorial.[60] Edgar Hunt noted in 1916 that Rose was "modern in every respect."[61] At the same time, Rose was seen as championing the California landscape; when his pictures were on view in February of 1916, Anderson noted that "charming as are the pictures from Giverny and

Toulon, they have not the grasp of the solidities that we find in those from Laguna and La Jolla. They are not so translucently poetic. Perhaps the painter has always needed the sunlight of his boyhood."[62]

Rose gave a new boost to the spreading of the tenets of Impressionism in the region, first through the exhibition of his Giverny paintings, and then of his newer work painted along the coastline at Laguna Beach and La Jolla in late 1914, 1915, and 1916, in the High Sierra in the summer of 1916, as well as in his home area of San Gabriel. *Indian Tobacco Trees, La Jolla* (plate 58), is one of these. Here, the trees sway almost voluptuously, as had his olive and tamarisk trees in southern France, but are positioned against the rich blue of the Pacific Ocean, while casting purple shadows on the undulating hilly coast, and with the oceanside cliffs behind. All Nature seems alive and animated, forms glowing in the rich warm California sunlight. His *San Gabriel Road* (plate 13) is a more structured picture, the shadowed foreground bounded by the low-lying buildings at the left, and the rustic bench, the fence, and the row of receding thick trunks of the pepper trees at the right, compressing space. Purple shadows, the distinguishing color of Impressionism, fill the picture. The eye is led to the wall of the San Gabriel Mission, which Rose also painted separately, appearing above and behind the shacks, symbolic of both stability and history in the region. If Rose had been primarily a landscape painter in Giverny, the paintings he created in California are almost totally figureless,[63] though human presence is occasionally acknowledged in the form of walls, buildings, and seaside staircases among the rocks.

Rose was one of the few California Impressionists to have had direct contact with a major European Impressionist. Perhaps the only other such painter was Arthur Grover Rider, a disciple of the greatest of the Spanish Impressionists, Joaquín Sorolla. Just as Sorolla was a later master than Monet, so Rider appeared in California only in the 1920s, possibly as early as 1924, when the Impressionist movement was already entrenched in the state.[64] He lived in Los Angeles and painted at Laguna Beach, where he established a studio in the early 1930s. Like so many of the California Impressionists, Rider came from Chicago and trained there at the Academy of Fine Arts before going to Paris. Rider is said to have become a disciple of Sorolla when the latter was teaching at the Art Institute of Chicago in 1911, after which Rider followed him back to Spain;[65] other reports have them meeting while Rider was painting on the beach at Valencia, Spain. Rider worked there for nine summers, exhibiting in Valencia at the Circulo des Bellas Artes; and he was a part of Sorolla's funeral cortege in 1923.[66] Following Sorolla's lead in both subject and pictorial mode, Rider became intensely interested in Spanish fishing boats with their billowing sails, painting in broad areas of bright colors such subjects as *The Spanish Boat* (plate 14), a theme

he began exhibiting at the Art Institute of Chicago in 1921 and which he repeated many times. The emphasis here is upon the play of white and brilliant blue, contrasted with the keel of the boat and the figure in dark shadow; the picture gains tremendous immediacy in the unrestrained movement of boat, figure, and water directly toward the viewer.[67]

Guy Rose advanced the aesthetics of Impressionism in Southern California not only by his own example, but by attracting to the region a number of his Giverny colleagues, several of whom joined him teaching at the Stickney Memorial School. Richard Emil Miller, primarily a figure painter in the Frieseke mold, was the first of these. Miller arrived in Pasadena in July of 1916 and gave weekly criticisms there beginning in October; he remained through March of 1917, while living on Arroyo Drive among the art colony, and painting in the garden of Mrs. Adelbert Fenyes (Eva Scott Fenyes), herself an artist.[68] Miller had had a work on view in Los Angeles in 1913 at the opening show of the Museum of History, Science, and Art, and Rose included Miller's *Scarlet Necklace* (Hevrdejs collection) in a show he organized for the Museum early in 1916; it was acquired by the Museum, but deaccessioned in 1966.

Miller seems to have had an influence on the local art scene, but more lasting was the later appearance in the Los Angeles area of John Frost and Alson Clark. John ("Jack") Frost was the son of the great illustrator, Arthur B. Frost; he and his brother, Arthur Jr., had been taken to France by their father for Parisian training in 1906. Frost and his family lived in Giverny for several years beginning in 1907, during which Arthur Sr.'s closest friend and fishing companion was Guy Rose; John Frost studied there and in Paris with Richard Miller. After returning to America following three years in a Swiss sanitarium for tuberculosis from 1911–14, John Frost settled in Pasadena in the beginning of 1919, and was soon followed

PLATE 15
John Frost (1890–1937)
The Flowering Desert, 1922
Oil on canvas, 27 x 32 inches
Joan Irvine Smith Fine Arts, Inc.

by his parents, all of them undoubtedly attracted both by the favorable climate, given young John's frail health, and by Rose's presence.

Indeed, the health-promoting effects of the climate of California had long been touted as one of the major attractions for both visitors to and settlers in Southern California, particularly for those suffering from pulmonary ailments.[69] California was regarded as "The Summerland of America" for the ever-salubriousness of its climate.[70] In 1892, Dr. Walter Lindley was promoting the elevated valleys of Southern California as winter resorts for those with pulmonary diseases, while in the summer the same sites served as vacation hostels.[71] Yet, many warnings were issued against over-optimistic expectations of recovery; as early as 1895, Dr. Norman Bridge warned against the notion that a three months' vacation would be restorative.[72] Henry Kingman later pointed out that the region was not suited to those suffering from tuberculosis owing to the dampness, and recommended instead the neighboring southwestern states.[73] Nevertheless, John Frost thrived in the Southern California climate. Recollecting his years in Giverny with Rose, John Frost was quoted in 1927 as stating that "he now finds ten minutes outside of Pasadena, all the atmosphere Guy Rose and he found abroad in those days."[74] Arthur B. Frost, Sr., lived in Pasadena until his death in 1928, and John remained only long enough to close out his father's affairs, and then returned east.[75]

John Frost appears to have been totally devoted to landscape and, not surprisingly, his style is quite close to Rose's, as seen in his 1923 *The Pool at Sundown* (plate 57). The bright sunlight, the strong coloration combining greens, golds, and purples, and the flickering brushwork are all hallmarks of Impressionism, and the scene reflects the popular motif of the pollarded willows of Giverny (one of Frost's trees appears to be similarly pollarded), although the mountain background is characteristically California. Frost does not appear to have been particularly attracted either to coastal or Sierra subjects, however, in clear distinction to Rose; rather, his most characteristic subjects were the cottonwood tree and the desert landscape, seen here in *The Flowering Desert* of 1922 (plate 15). The desert, of course, would have had special attraction for one suffering from tuberculosis. In 1926 a critic noted that "when John Frost looked toward our mountains and our desert he found exactly the subjects suited to his training and temperament."[76] Frost's palette is his alone, a pale reflection of Impressionist chromatics, though still relying on color rather than tone. The artist enjoyed the great flat expanse, enlivened by the tufts of green foliage and patches of pink verbena, with a gnarled desert tree at the right, and backed by the almost spectral snow-topped mountains in the distance.

Arriving in Pasadena for a visit in 1919, the same year as Frost, and settling there in the Arroyo Seco the following year, the otherwise peripatetic Alson Skinner Clark remained in Southern California for the rest of his career. As with so many of his colleagues there, Clark had been born and had trained in Chicago, at the Art Institute, before going on to study first in New York and then in Paris. Clark then led a nomadic life, mostly abroad, though he continued to exhibit extensively at the Art Institute through the mid-1920s, even after he was resident in California; he also enjoyed the first of several one-person shows there in 1906.

Alson S. Clark in his Paris studio, 1910. Courtesy of Carol Clark and the estate of Alson S. Clark.

In the summer of 1907, Clark painted a series of pictures, subsequently exhibited in America, of French châteaux, and afterwards he was in Giverny for a visit in the autumn of 1910. While his stay there was short, he re-established earlier connections with Frieseke, Rose, and Lawton Parker, and joined the rest of the colony there, including Miller and the Frosts. Clark subsequently painted a much-heralded series of eighteen pictures of the building of the Panama Canal in 1913, which were exhibited at the Panama-Pacific International Exposition in San Francisco in 1915. After settling in California, he joined Rose on the faculty of the Stickney Memorial School (shortly before the latter's debilitating stroke), and in the same year had his first one-person show in the state at Stendahl Galleries in

A photograph by Alson S. Clark of the tennis court of the Hotel Baudy, Giverny, France, 1910. From left to right: Frederick Frieseke, Guy Rose, and two unidentified men. Courtesy of Carol Clark and the estate of Alson S. Clark.

Los Angeles. Even in his later years, Clark did not abandon his travels, making numerous painting trips to Mexico, the first time in 1923, and he may have returned to Charleston in 1933, having painted there previously in 1917. In addition, in 1902, Clark painted murals in the Mancel Talcott School in Chicago. He later accepted mural commissions in California, such as the seven panels done for the Carthay Circle Theatre in 1926, four for the First National Bank of Pasadena in 1929, eight oval paintings for the Women's Dining Room of the California Club in Los Angeles also in 1928, and in 1932 eight sepia murals for the Teatro Leo Carillo in Los Angeles. He also painted the curtain for Pasadena's Community Playhouse in 1925.[77]

Among the more significant artists active during the later years of the Giverny colony, Clark was one of the painters there devoted almost solely to landscape. He occasionally painted the figure, including a group of portraits created in the middle of the decade of the 1900s, before he adopted the strategies of Impressionism; later, one of his first California pictures and one of his best-known works is a depiction of his wife, *Reverie (Medora on the Terrace)* (Rose Family Foundation) of 1920. Nevertheless, his focus subsequently remained the exploration of the scenery of Southern California, although, unlike the painting of many of his colleagues, small figures occasionally enliven his scenes, providing a human dimension. Clark traveled throughout the beaches, deserts, and mountains of the state, working especially on Catalina Island and at La Jolla and San Diego, where he painted such works as his 1924 *The Weekend, Mission Beach* (plate 16), using an extremely high key, with an exceedingly low horizon, and with a tremendous expanse of sky, which allowed him to highlight exuberant, moving cloud formations. The low-lying tents on the beach offer no interference to the contemplation of the limitless sunlit landscape, but rather

PLATE 16

Alson S. Clark (1876–1949)

The Weekend, Mission Beach, 1924

Oil on canvas mounted on board, 25¼ x 32 inches

The Irvine Museum

PLATE 17
Guy Rose (1867–1925)
Laguna Eucalyptus, c. 1916
Oil on canvas, 40 x 30 inches
The Irvine Museum

testify to the harmony of human enjoyment of Nature in California.

Without meaning to denigrate the many other professional painters working with Impressionist-related strategies and objectives, William Wendt and Guy Rose would seem to have been the most significant and original painters in Southern California in the first three decades of the twentieth century. Rose may have had more direct influence on some of his contemporaries, but Wendt was active there far longer, and both artists realized critical acclaim as well as significant patronage, not only in California but elsewhere—Wendt in Chicago particularly and Rose in New York.[78] Though the two do not appear to have been especially close, there is no indication of any sense of rivalry between them, or that most contemporaries regarded them as representative of opposing or competing "schools."[79] They were both active in the California Art Club, and, along with Puthuff, Payne, and the Wachtels, among others, both Wendt and Rose were also members of the Ten Painters Club of California, a primarily Impressionist group not unlike its namesake in New York, the Ten American Painters; the short-lived California association held exhibitions in 1919, at the Kanst Art Gallery, at which each of nine members succeeded one another with one-artist shows held between March and July (that for Jack Wilkinson Smith remained unscheduled). Rather, Wendt and Rose seem to have been two of the brightest stars in a glowing firmament shining upon and celebrating the California landscape.

Both artists were also active painting at Laguna Beach. Wendt had been there as early as 1905, and was one of the founders of the Laguna Beach Art Association in 1918, the year he built his studio there. Rose exhibited with the Association in August and September of 1918, May and June of 1919, and, after his stroke, his work was shown during all three summer months in 1922. With its year-round temperate climate, along with the natural beauty of its broad swath of cliff-crested beaches and its nearby canyons, Laguna Beach had served as one of the earliest painting grounds for Southern California landscape painters, even in the late nineteenth century, and by the second decade of the twentieth, it had become a well-known art colony, the most celebrated one west of the Mississippi.[80] Edgar Payne was the guiding figure in the establishment of the Art Association, leading his colleagues to adopt the abandoned town hall and remodel it under his direction; Payne became the Association's first president. The colony there differed from many other art communities in that, unlike, say, Giverny, it did not revolve around one major figure, nor did it, as did Old Lyme, Connecticut, or Provincetown, Massachusetts, foster a significant summer art school.[81]

Around 1917, Rose painted one of his seminal images of California there, his *Laguna Eucalyptus* (plate 17), perhaps the supreme achievement of Rose's fascination with trees, which led him to show the distinguishing characteristics of many varieties both abroad and in America. Eucalyptus trees, imported from Australia, were planted in the 1890s in response to the Timber Culture Act, as an improvement to legalize land claims in the area. They probably came from the seedbeds along the railroad tracks where the trees were raised by A. C. Carle of El Toro. Carle had been hired by Dwight Whiting, owner of the Rancho de Los Alisos; about forty to fifty thousand trees were grown by him.[82]

The eucalyptus was celebrated not only in paint but also in poetry, as in Harry Noyes Pratt's "The Eucalyptus."[83] In Rose's picture, the trees are seen from a worm's-eye view, their incredibly tall and thin trunks snaking upward, and their masses of foliage framed against the sky, their shapes echoed in the billowing clouds. The work, sent by the artist late in 1917 to his New York dealer, William Macbeth, who exhibited and sold it early the following year,[84] offers a succinct rebuttal to the implicit denigration associated with the expression "the eucalyptus school."

Laguna Eucalyptus is unusual among Rose's pictures painted in that community. Most of his other known Laguna pictures are bright, sunlit coastal scenes that emphasize the steep, craggy rock formations plunging directly into the Pacific. Indeed, the ocean and the coast understandably figure in almost all the landscapes painted by the many members of the Laguna art colony; the California coastline had long been recommended as one of the most enticing features of the region, above all because "its beauties and attractions may be enjoyed during every month of the year."[85] William Wendt's *The Silent Summer Sea,* painted in 1915 (plate 2), is a stark, terse, but brilliantly lighted coastal scene, set abruptly above the rocks, with only a precarious toe-hold in the yellow-brown hillside grasses before the visual plunge into the blue waters. Wendt, typically, emphasizes the structural solidity of the rocks with slablike brushstrokes, relieved against the intense blue of the ocean, made all the more immediate through the high horizon. Thus, the viewer senses the tremendous breadth of the sea, while at the same time, without any coloristic amelioration or atmospheric haze, the high horizon validates the picture's basic flatness. *The Silent Summer Sea* was exhibited with the California Art Club in October of 1915, when it gathered such encomiums as the one

Guy Rose in his Paris studio, 1902. Courtesy of Roy C. Rose and the Rose Family Photo Collection.

PLATE 18

Jack Wilkinson Smith (1873–1949)

Crystal Cove State Park, 1923

Oil on canvas, 52 x 70 inches

Joan Irvine Smith Fine Arts, Inc.

that appeared in the *Graphic:* "[Wendt] seems to have captured the spirit of 'The Silent Summer Sea.' I believe Mr. Wendt will one day paint marines which will win him world renown. There is a direct understanding for flowing elements, a fine interpretation of texture and glory in the composition."[86]

Another of Wendt's finest paintings done along the coast, some miles north of Laguna Beach, is *Crystal Cove* (Joan Irvine Smith Fine Arts), painted in 1912, three years earlier than *The Silent Summer Sea.* The site also was the setting for Jack Wilkinson Smith's *Crystal Cove State Park* (plate 18), a ravishing juxtaposition of cliffs, rocks, ocean, and cloud-filled sky, all tinged with myriad touches of alternating prismatic colors. Despite the ruggedness of the scenery, the painting exudes a sense of peace and harmony, in an unspoiled natural paradise; indeed, California itself was deemed "An Artist's Paradise" by the earlier California painter-sculptor, Gutzon Borglum.[87] When Smith's picture was on view at Cannel and Chaffin Gallery in Los Angeles in the autumn of 1920, it was reproduced in *California Southland* with the caption: "Calm and serene, infinite in its power to solace, this picture speaks to us of Peace."[88] Smith too had grown up in Chicago, where he studied at the Art Institute and was influenced by Wendt. He was first in California in 1906, later becoming active in the California Art Club as well as the Laguna Beach Art Association. In California, Smith specialized in two themes, both of which highlighted rocky masses—craggy sunlit coastal scenes and views in the High Sierra.[89]

The artist who displayed singular devotion to the painting of the coast at Laguna was Frank Cuprien, whose *An Evening Symphony* (plate 19) is characteristic of his stock theme—a quiet panorama of waves rolling into shore. "Shore" itself is almost absent here, and the picture consists of two horizontal bands of water and sky, enlivened by the glint of sunlight on the water and a soft atmospheric haze in the distance. Cuprien's format is a very traditional one, depicting slow, incoming tides in opalescent colors, and recalls the eastern shore pictures painted by William Trost Richards in the 1870s and after, but Cuprien infused a gentle chromaticism into these compositions that allied them with Impressionism. Evening scenes appear to have held special attraction for the artist. Cuprien had studied in New York and in Philadelphia—where he had received criticism from Richards, an artist whom he greatly admired—before studying in Munich and Paris. After returning to the United States, he was in Florida and Texas before moving to California around 1912, living in Santa Monica, on Catalina Island, and in 1914 building a studio in Laguna Beach on a bluff off the Pacific Coast Highway, overlooking the ocean. A founder of that town's Art Association, Cuprien served as president in 1921.[90]

PLATE 19
Frank Cuprien (1871–1948)
An Evening Symphony
Oil on canvas, 18 x 26 inches
Joan Irvine Smith Fine Arts, Inc.

PLATE 20
Karl Yens (1868–1945)
America the Beautiful, 1918
Oil on canvas, 40 x 50 inches
The Irvine Museum

Opposite:
PLATE 21
Anna Hills (1882–1930)
The Spell of the Sea (Laguna Beach, Near Moss Point), 1920
Oil on canvas, 30 x 40 inches
Joan Irvine Smith Fine Arts, Inc.

More painterly and more replete with movement than the work of Smith or Cuprien, is Karl Yens's *America the Beautiful* (plate 20), which takes its name from the American flag seen in the distance among the houses atop the cliffs. Both sea and rocks are boldly painted, but structure is sacrificed both to vivacious brushwork and to the bright sunlight swathing the foreground boulders. The buildings, though only in the mid- and far ground, offer more of a sense of habitation than most Laguna landscapes, which are generally devoid of human presence. The German-born Yens came to America in 1901, and in 1911 migrated to California, settling in South Pasadena and teaching at the University of Southern California before moving to Laguna Beach in 1918, the year he helped found the Art Association. Yens also created a sizable number of figural works in the studio, and his somewhat more expressive style is consonant with his role in 1916 in founding the Los Angeles Modern Art Society, some members of which were at least mildly attracted to the strategies of Post-Impressionism; he was later one of the members of the Modern Art Workers, founded in 1925.[91]

Anna Althea Hills was one of the most active members of the Laguna Beach art colony and the Art Association. In 1912 Hills moved to California, having previously studied at the Art Institute of Chicago and in New York at the Cooper Union and with Arthur Wesley Dow before going on to Paris. During those years she had been a figure painter, but once in California, she appears to have become totally devoted to landscape. She settled in Laguna Beach in 1913, and played a dominant role in the organization of the Art Association, of which she was president from 1922 to 1925 and again from 1927 to 1930.[92] Hills's paintings, both interior scenes of valleys and mountain formations, and coastal views such as *The Spell of the Sea (Laguna Beach, Near Moss Point)* of 1920 (plate 21), make use of the smaller, often broken brushwork and variegated coloration of orthodox Impressionism, reflecting, perhaps, some influence of Guy Rose. Like Rose, also, she delighted in the undulation of the eucalyptuses' sinuous trunks supporting their feathery foliage. Small figures of several women appear in the lower left, in beneficent Nature.

The sea appears only in the distance in Jean Mannheim's *Arch Beach, Laguna Beach* of 1920 (plate 22); the artist concentrated instead on the rolling hillside with lush green foliage and a patch of golden poppies, though some buildings appear through the grove of trees at the far right. At the time, Mannheim had three studios, a home studio and a garden studio in Pasadena and a summer studio at Arch Beach.[93] Mannheim was not a painter of the sea, in particular; he was equally involved with the figure and the landscape, the former earlier in his career, but he increasingly painted the scenic beauty of California, and figures out-of-doors in bright sunlight. Born in Germany, Mannheim began studying in Paris in 1882, and then came to the United States in 1885, settling in Chicago. In 1895 he moved to Decatur, Illinois, for seven years, and then, after a brief trip to Europe, he settled in Denver, where he remained and taught for five years. In 1907–8 he worked in London with Frank Brangwyn and then returned to the United States. Mannheim settled in the Arroyo Seco in Pasadena and taught at the Stickney Memorial School; he became active in the California Art Club and was equally involved with the Laguna Beach Art Association.[94]

Another Laguna Beach painter who was secure in painting both the figure and the landscape was the Hungarian-born Joseph Kleitsch, who had studied in Munich before immigrating to the United States in late 1901 or early 1902, when he settled in Cincinnati. By 1906 he was painting in Denver (while Jean Mannheim was there), and in 1907–9 he was in Mexico City; much of the following decade was spent in Chicago. In 1920 Kleitsch went to California, wintering in Laguna Beach, where he maintained a home for his final decade. Kleitsch was one of the founders of the Painters and Sculptors Club, which originated in his studio in 1922; in the Club's first exhibition, Kleitsch showed a work entitled *The Flower Garden*.[95] While he had earlier been known primarily as a portraitist,

PLATE 22

Jean Mannheim (1862–1945)
Arch Beach, Laguna Beach
Oil on canvas, 34 x 39 inches
The Irvine Museum

and this continued to provide his main source of income in Southern California, Kleitsch painted both studio models and outdoor scenery there, including such garden pictures as his *Bougainvillea, Mission San Juan Capistrano* of 1923 (plate 23), utilizing a completely Impressionist approach and coloration. This may be the painting entitled *The Garden of Capistrano* exhibited in Kleitsch's one-person show in Los Angeles in June of 1926 at the Stendahl Galleries, with which he had signed an exclusive contract in 1922. Here, concentrating on the lush surrounding blooms, painted in full sunlight, Kleitsch dispensed with the Mission itself, which appears with its garden in another work by Kleitsch, *San Juan Capistrano* of 1924 (Joan Irvine Smith collection). The subject of these pictures is a Spanish Colonial Revival garden, planted with old-fashioned perennials and vines, that was cultivated at the Mission at the turn of the century.[96] The missions housed the best-known gardens in the state, and not surprisingly attracted many painters. It was noted that "the gardens about the Missions as we see them today must be accepted as of comparatively recent planting, though an old-time flavor is given by the setting."[97]

Cultivated garden paintings are not unknown among the California Impressionists, but they are not nearly as common as they are among their counterparts on the East Coast, perhaps because the westerners favored the unconfined expansiveness of the wild flower fields.[98] As Charles Howard Shinn had written in 1888, "When our wild flowers are almost gone, I suppose that people will begin to want them to plant in gardens."[99] As we have seen, Frederick Frieseke painted garden scenes in Los Angeles on a visit to his parents in 1911, and it is possible that these provided inspiration for local artists to undertake this theme. One of the closest equivalents to the garden pictures favored by Childe Hassam and many of the painters working in such eastern art colonies as Old Lyme and Cragsmoor is *The Joyous Garden* (plate 24) by Benjamin Brown, who also was one of the many painters of fields of poppies and other wild flowers. This picture is of a rare formal garden; the alternating red, pink, and white flowers front a well-manicured lawn, bordered by box hedges, before the white walls of a substantial house. Brown, who first studied in St. Louis and then in Paris, was one of the earliest of the Impressionists to reside in the state, settling in Pasadena in 1895. His early landscapes were painted in a

PLATE 23
Joseph Kleitsch (1882–1931)
Bougainvillea, Mission San Juan Capistrano, 1923
Oil on canvas, 30 x 24 inches
Joan Irvine Smith Fine Arts, Inc.

PLATE 24

Benjamin Brown (1865–1942)

The Joyous Garden, c. 1910

Oil on canvas, 30½ x 40½ inches

Joan Irvine Smith Fine Arts, Inc.

more tonal mode, but shortly after the turn of the century he began to adopt the high-keyed color of Impressionism, which he applied to all the subjects favored by the California Impressionists—both coastal and mountain scenes, blossoming trees, and floral subjects. Given Brown's preference for saturated color, it is interesting to note that he was also one of the California Impressionists most inclined toward the depiction of snow scenes. Brown's approach to Impressionism is, in fact, perhaps the closest to that of Childe Hassam among the artists of Southern California. Brown was also the most active printmaker among the artists discussed here, and with his brother, Howell, organized The Print Makers of Los Angeles in 1914.[100]

In the East, artists depicted both formal gardens and the increasingly popular informal cultivations of flowers—the "grandmother's gardens" popularized in the late nineteenth century as more truly American and as reflecting earlier, sounder cultural values.[101] The creation of such gardens found favor in California, fueled both by the climate and by the popularity of the Arts and Crafts movement, which promoted outdoor life and the use of indigenous materials. But, artists in the state do not seem to have responded strongly to this potential subject, though it did attract several painters in Northern California. A number of colorful pictures by Theodore Wores, one of San Francisco's leading painters and teachers, depict the old adobe church in Saratoga, California, that the artist had remodeled into a Mission Revival house with a patio garden, while one of the finest paintings by Anne Bremer, another respected San Francisco painter of the early twentieth century, is entitled *An Old Fashioned Garden* (Mills College, Oakland). Colin Campbell Cooper rendered some of the most beautiful paintings of gardens in Southern California. Cooper had established his artistic identity at the turn of the century with pictorial homages to European Gothic architecture, but on his return to America in 1902 he transferred his interest to modern city life and especially the skyscraper, which he painted in Chicago, Philadelphia, and particularly New York, while the somewhat low-keyed tones of his earlier work exploded into Impressionist light and color. In 1915, Cooper painted some fine architectural images at San Francisco's Panama-Pacific International Exposition, where he received a Gold Medal for his six oil paintings shown there. The following winter of 1915–16, Cooper visited and painted in Los Angeles, San Diego, and Santa Barbara,[102] and six years later he moved to Santa Barbara, becoming dean of the School of Painting at the Santa Barbara School for the Arts. While he maintained his formal strategies, Cooper abandoned the urban theme when he moved to Santa Barbara, where he became, with John Gamble, one of the two most prominent Impressionist painters in the quite distinct and well-recognized art colony there.[103] His new architectural images, ranging from his own modest bungalow on Anacapa Street to the Kimberly Crest mansion in Redlands and including the San Juan Capistrano Mission, were all accompanied by garden plantings and colorful surroundings of flowering vines and trees. Some of Cooper's most exuberant settings are views painted at Santa Barbara's elegant hostelries, the El Encanto and Samarkand hotels, for example, *Pergola at Samarkand Hotel, Santa Barbara* (plate 25), a fully Impressionist, sun-dappled scene.[104]

It is not surprising that some of the Southern California Impressionists produced floral still lifes in so lush a land; Cooper was one, but the preeminent flower painter was Franz Bischoff. His *Peonies* (plate 26) is typical of his art, a riot of brilliantly colored and lighted growing flowers, which nevertheless seem almost disembodied from the soil from which they spring. Peonies, chrysanthemums, and roses seem to have been

Opposite:

PLATE 25

Colin Campbell Cooper (1856–1937)

Pergola at Samarkand Hotel, Santa Barbara, c. 1921

Oil on canvas, 29 x 36 inches

Joan Irvine Smith Fine Arts, Inc.

Right:

PLATE 26

Franz A. Bischoff (1864–1929)

Peonies, c. 1912

Oil on canvas, 30 x 40 inches

Joan Irvine Smith Fine Arts, Inc.

Bischoff's preferred blossoms, which are sometimes shown, as here, still in cultivation and thus in plein-air pictures, while others are already cut and placed indoors in vases. Bischoff was equally adept at floral still lifes and landscape, and in both themes his expressive brushwork allies him to some degree with Post-Impressionism, somewhat akin to the direction of Yens's art, and perhaps influenced by the work of Vincent van Gogh, whose painting he is known to have copied.[105] Bischoff was born in Bohemia and came to New York in 1885, first working as a decorator in a china factory, a vocation he subsequently pursued in Detroit. He achieved recognition as a china painter specializing in floral motifs. Bischoff visited Los Angeles in 1900 and five years later purchased land in the Arroyo Seco, moving to California the following year and completing his studio-home in 1908. It was about the time of his move to California that he turned to easel painting, and then he broadened his artistic horizons to include landscapes in addition to floral work, the latter especially remaining in the realm of the decorative.[106]

Since the mid-nineteenth century, American landscape painters have been drawn to painting the occasional still life, since so much of that theme is drawn from Nature. This is understandable in California artists, since their celebration of the lush floral output of the region coincides with their exaltation of the land itself, though a few of the state's painters opted, alternatively, for recording man-made still-life forms (the most notable of which are Armin Hansen's figureless studio interiors). One such still-life painting landscapist is Paul Lauritz, here represented by his gorgeously colored *Poinsettias* of about 1925 (plate 3), the flowers' spiky petals casting purplish shadows in rhythmic patterns against a light wall. The Norwegian-born Lauritz was early influenced by the Norwegian Impressionist, Fritz Thaulow, and was encouraged by Christian Krogh, the dean of his native country's artists.[107] Lauritz immigrated to Canada and worked in commercial art in Vancouver, British Columbia, before migrating to Portland, Oregon, where he began to create easel paintings. He was active in Alaska before arriving in Los Angeles in 1919. Lauritz is otherwise known as a significant teacher as well as an important regional landscape painter, working in a mode not unlike that of Puthuff.[108] Whatever Lauritz's subject matter, *Poinsettias* substantiates Arthur Millier's assertion that "color has always been his forte." [109]

A notable distinction between the work of the California Impressionists and that of their eastern counterparts is the dearth of images of the man-made environment by the western artists. Excepting the paintings of Los Angeles by Frank Coburn,[110] Southern California painters generally avoided the urban subjects that so occupied such painters as Childe Hassam, Colin Campbell Cooper, and William Merritt Chase in New York and which were painted occasionally by other artists of the movement, such as Willard Metcalf and Theodore Robinson.[111] But it was not only the large cities that the California painters generally avoided; they seldom dealt, at least obviously, with their own environmental construct—the suburbs and towns in which they lived; the resort hotels that populated the beaches they otherwise depicted as empty expanses[112] (those at Santa Barbara painted by Colin Campbell Cooper excepted); and their homes and studios vis-à-vis the landscape that they so glorified, themes that preoccupied many eastern artists, John Twachtman and J. Alden Weir, for example.[113] The principal exceptions here are the colorful paintings by Joseph Kleitsch and Clarence Hinkle[114] of the town and buildings of Laguna Beach, and those by Franz Bischoff and John Christopher Smith of the small coastal town of Cambria, located between Santa Barbara and Monterey, near William Randolph Hearst's castle at San Simeon. Close friends, Bischoff and Smith painted there together, perhaps on their way to Monterey, in 1924–27, finding special charm in that small coastal community.[115]

Likewise, the majority of California Impressionists gave short shrift to scenes of industry and manual toil, though Charles Reiffel not infrequently depicted working ranches and even distant mines in his landscapes, but he appears exceptional in this regard. Otherwise, perhaps understandably given the pictorial attraction of the Pacific Coast, paintings of shipyards, fishing boats, and canneries were occasionally undertaken by local artists, though they were never a specialty.[116] Serious commercial activity was depicted by Charles Reiffel at San Diego Harbor, while San Pedro Bay, the harbor for Los Angeles, was explored by Thomas Hunt and Sam Hyde Harris, but even here the human figure rarely intrudes. People do appear in some such works by Bischoff, painted around 1914, and in later pictures by Donna Schuster. The Canadian-born Thomas Lorraine Hunt was in the Los Angeles area in 1924, living in Hollywood and San Bernardino; in 1927 he established himself in Laguna

Beach. Hunt displays no sense of toil in his untitled painting (plate 27) that probably depicts the old cannery on Newport Harbor, across the channel from downtown Newport, a subject also painted by George Brandriff.[117] The fishing boats, Hunt's favorite subject, are docked next to the sheds and commercial buildings of the single old cannery in Newport, but any implication of labor is counteracted by the sparkling Impressionist color and brilliant California light. Hunt exhibited boat pictures regularly during the early 1930s.

Sam Hyde Harris's picture of the *Todd Shipyards, San Pedro,* of about 1925 (plate 28), is more gritty in its neutral tonalities, barren and dreary in the almost empty waters of the fore- and middle grounds backed by smoke-belching factories; the artist was captivated with effects of color-reducing atmosphere, influenced by the art of the great English landscapist Joseph Turner. Nevertheless, the

PLATE 27

Thomas Hunt (1882–1938)

Untitled (Los Angeles Harbor)

Oil on canvas, 28 x 31 inches

The Irvine Museum

PLATE 28

Sam Hyde Harris (1889–1977)

Todd Shipyards, San Pedro, c. 1925

Oil on canvas, 20 x 23 inches

The Irvine Museum

artist's vision here is one of pollution and desolation, rare among the California Impressionists; other paintings by Harris depict such industrial subjects as gas tanks, mills, and cargo boats, while titles such as *Flotsam and Jetsam* and *Shackville* suggest an underlying pessimism. The English-born Harris was primarily a commercial artist who came to Los Angeles in 1904. As a fine artist, he studied with Hanson Puthuff, and painted with Mannheim and Payne, preferring the rural environs of Pasadena and San Gabriel; he painted his harbor scenes in the 1930s, and later in his career he specialized in desert landscapes.[118]

The painter who probably provided the most abundant imagery of coastal labor was the relatively short-lived George Kennedy Brandriff. He painted lively scenes of the single cannery at Newport Beach, such as his *Cannery Row, Newport Beach* of about 1928 (plate 29); this subject was also depicted by Hunt and Arthur Rider. Brandriff's fishing boats and wharf buildings are rendered with slashing brushstrokes reminiscent of some of the work of New York's Ashcan school, but again, the scene is devoid of figures, and the prismatic coloration, especially in the foreground waters, is pure Impressionism. Brandriff had come to California from the East in 1913 and become a dentist; he studied art under Anna Hills and began to paint in the mid-1910s, only devoting himself to art full time in 1927.[119] In the early 1930s, Brandriff also painted a unique group of still lifes, not floral effusions but rather allegorical reflections of contemporary social and political events.[120]

The one group of man-made structures that attracted almost all the California Impressionists was the missions; the first of these was founded in San Diego by the Franciscan missionary Father Junípero Serra in 1769. These were the most notable structures remaining from California's early colonial period and, as such, their depictions may be considered historical imagery as well as the romantic equivalents of paintings of the European monuments so revered by earlier American artists and patrons. But of course, these pictures contained more specific and relevant currency also, for it was under the leadership of Charles Lummis, who founded the Association for the Preservation of the Missions and became President of The Landmarks Club in 1895, that their historical significance was undergoing re-evaluation and they were being preserved and restored from the decrepitude into which they had fallen.[121] Nor was the concern for the plight of the missions confined to California; a good many articles appeared in eastern journals, contemporaneous with Lummis's efforts.[122] Today the missions stand again, some restored and many replaced by replications.

The missions had earlier been painted in their ruinous state by many artists, and whole series of the twenty-one structures had been created by San Francisco's Edwin Deakin in 1878–98 and at much the same time by Santa Barbara's Henry Chapman Ford, in etching and in watercolor, as well as by others.[123] In the Impressionist era, Guy Rose and Alson Clark had painted the Mission San Gabriel; Benjamin Brown the Mission San Luis Rey and the branch mission at Pala, north of San Diego; and both Arthur Hill Gilbert and E. Charlton Fortune painted the Santa Barbara Mission (Gilbert's eponymous painting of 1924, created before he moved to Monterey, is in the Terry and Paula Trotter collection; Fortune's of 1928 is a promised gift to the Monterey Peninsula Museum of Art). Fortune also exhibited a painting of the Carmel Mission at the Panama-Pacific International Exposition.

It was the Mission San Juan Capistrano, founded in 1776, that drew the greatest attention, its restoration having become a personal project of Charles Lummis. Guy Rose appears to have been almost alone in ignoring this subject. We have already noted the activity of Joseph Kleitsch and Colin Campbell Cooper at the Mission. Alson Clark not only painted the Mission as soon as he arrived in Southern California in 1919, he exhibited one of his pictures of it at the Art Institute of Chicago that year, and another in 1923. Clark's *Ruins of the Chapel, San Juan Capistrano*, 1919 (plate 30), carries the gold and blue tints of the wild flower fields into the realm of massive architecture. Here, the poignancy of the seemingly abandoned and roofless structure is alleviated by the rich coloration and brilliant California light, offering the redemption that was, indeed, occurring under the guidance of Father St. John O'Sullivan.[124] In his *San Juan Capistrano Mission Yard* of about 1922 (plate 31), Franz Bischoff offers not only a restored building but, as expected of a painter of flowers, a colorful garden of geraniums and hollyhocks, complete with lily pad pool. The peeling plaster affirms the building's venerable state, but the *campanario*, the wall of bells in their niches along with the cross at top, silhouetted against the cloud-filled heavens, suggests a functioning religious structure. In his *Mission Garden, San Juan Capistrano*, painted about 1929 (plate 43), Arthur Rider presents an upright, asymmetric version of this scene, concentrating as much on the garden as on the structure itself. Earlier than any of these, Channel Pickering Townsley, in his 1916 *Mission San Juan Capistrano* (plate 44), further restores the Mission by centering his scene upon a Franciscan friar walking along a flower-bordered path. Otherwise, figures appear only very occasionally in Impressionist paintings of the missions, though they are included more often in earlier, nineteenth-century renderings.

PLATE 30
Alson S. Clark (1876–1949)
Ruins of the Chapel, San Juan Capistrano, 1919
Oil on board, 31 x 25 inches
Joan Irvine Smith Fine Arts, Inc.

Early in 1915, Townsley acknowledged the Impressionist bent his art assumed in California by referring to the unique qualities he found in the landscape: the luminous atmospheric veil, the purple hills, and the subtle, rich, and tender light.[125] Townsley had studied with William Merritt Chase in New York, and subsequently in Paris, and had gone on to manage Chase's New York School of Art. After Chase abandoned his summer art school at Shinnecock, Long Island, and began to teach summer classes abroad, Townsley continued as his manager, directing the summer program for several years, beginning in 1903 in Holland. He repeated this role when Chase taught a class in Belgium in 1912 and again in the summer of 1914 in Carmel; he then remained in California, continuing to teach summers in Carmel in 1915 and 1916. Joining Jean Mannheim, Townsley reorganized the Stickney Memorial School in Pasadena.[126] He remained as director until taking over at the Otis Art Institute in Los Angeles in 1918; he died three years later.

PLATE 31
Franz A. Bischoff (1864–1929)
San Juan Capistrano Mission Yard, c. 1922
Oil on canvas, 24 x 30 inches
The Joan Irvine Smith Collection

Southern California Impressionists did not completely ignore the figure, but it was not a primary concern for most of the painters associated with the movement, especially during the first decade and a half of this century. Even when they chose to paint long sandy beaches, these scenes are almost always devoid of the bathers who would normally be enjoying the warm sunshine and sparkling surf; only Joseph Kleitsch, in the late 1920s, developed a significant body of paintings of bathers at Laguna Beach, while a few others, Alfred Mitchell and Alson Clark at La Jolla, and Jean Mannheim, occasionally populated their scenes with beachgoers. A review, for instance, of the Second Annual Exhibition of the California Art Club, held in Los Angeles in December 1911 (no catalogue of the first exhibition has been located), suggests that, in addition to one sculpture by Julia Bracken Wendt, among the forty-four works, thirty-seven pictures were landscapes, two were interiors, one was a still life (*Roses,* by Franz Bischoff), and only three were figures—and these were portraits of Native Americans by Joseph Sharp, the Taos, New Mexico, painter. In contrast, at the Seventh Annual Exhibition five years later in October 1916, judging by the titles of the seventy-two works shown, forty were landscapes and garden scenes, three were urban views, seven were sculptures or studies for sculptures, one was a still life and one an interior, and twenty were portraits and figure pieces. At the same time, the illustrations of California paintings that appeared in *California's Magazine,* the sumptuous two-volume publication that appeared in 1916 commemorating the Panama-Pacific International Exposition, were divided just about equally between figure and landscape work.[127]

Not surprisingly, landscape still dominated the artistic production in the region, but figure painting was finding new adherents and respect. Nancy Moure has pinpointed the change to the year 1915, attributing it not only to the plethora of landscapes that

had appeared up to then but also to the appearance of new painters on the scene, such as Donna Schuster and Meta Cressey. She also notes that historians have attributed the increased impact of Impressionism, generally, to its predominance in the Fine Arts Gallery at the Panama-Pacific International Exposition, held from February 20 to December 4, 1915, in San Francisco, where so many major eastern Impressionists, such as Frederick Frieseke, William Merritt Chase, Childe Hassam, Edmund Tarbell, and others were honored with large displays of their work. Indeed, for his contribution, Frieseke won the ultimate award, the Grand Prize.[128] Figure paintings were more numerous than among the California painters. This, too, may have led local artists to emulation.

Still, as Arthur Millier reminisced in 1972, when they arrived in Southern California, "the figure painters and portraitists soon switched to landscape. Who in their right mind wanted pictures of people as souvenirs of Paradise in Sunshine Land?"[129] Among the artists so far discussed, Joseph Kleitsch was the only one who was as involved with the figure as with landscape, though he was, of course, only in California in the 1920s. *The Oriental Shop (Jade Shop)* of 1925 (plate 32) is one of Kleitsch's best-known paintings, a marvelously colorful depiction of a lovely, contemplative young woman in a commercial, though seemingly domestic, interior. Kleitsch had painted an earlier *Oriental Shop* in 1922, which was exhibited in Los Angeles two years later and portrayed a more obviously commercial establishment, identified as G. T. Marsh and Company, a shop in the Ambassador Hotel in Los Angeles;[130] whether the 1925 picture is also situated there is undetermined. Its format suggests, above all, the work of the Boston Impressionists such as Tarbell, but such eastern paintings tended toward the austere, and to abjure color in favor of the refined and subtle play of light and atmosphere. In contrast, Kleitsch's chromaticism is variegated and dramatic, favoring

PLATE 32

Joseph Kleitsch (1882–1931)

The Oriental Shop, 1925

Oil on canvas, 32 x 26 inches

Joan Irvine Smith Fine Arts, Inc.

intense tones applied in sometimes broad, slashing brushwork that borders on Expressionism. Indeed, the work owes its effectiveness to just this pictorial dialogue between the reflective mood of the painting and its passionate execution.

As already noted, Donna Norine Schuster was one of the new arrivals in California in the wake of the Panama-Pacific International Exposition. Schuster was yet another painter who had studied at the Art Institute of Chicago, beginning in 1900; then, from 1906 to 1909, she worked under Tarbell and Frank Benson at the school of the Museum of Fine Arts, Boston, before studying with William Merritt Chase, first in Belgium in the summer of 1912 and then two years later when Chase taught at Carmel. This may have been Schuster's introduction to California, but she first achieved acclaim there for her depictions of the Panama-Pacific International Exposition, which was under construction in late 1914. This series of eighteen brilliantly colored watercolors was exhibited that December at the Los Angeles Museum of History, Science, and Art, and aroused considerable admiration.[131] Schuster's place of residence at this time is confusing; in exhibition catalogues, she gave Los Angeles as her address in 1914, but the following year she was also listed as still a resident of St. Paul, Minnesota; by the end of 1915 she definitely had settled in Los Angeles.[132]

Schuster varied her formal approach in depictions of her favored subject matter, generally outdoor scenes including prominent figures of genteel young women, though she also painted vigorous figurative works along the San Pedro harbor. Some of her

pictures are conceived in a manner utilizing orthodox Impressionist strategies: small brushstrokes of bright, contrasting colors and scintillating light, applied to domestic subjects—women seated, in gardens, on verandas, in front of their homes—not unlike some of the work of Tarbell, her teacher. Others, however, such as *On the Beach* (plate 33), employ much more dramatic color contrasts, somewhat akin to Kleitsch's aforementioned approach, and, like him, she was inclined to portray such subjects more immediately and up close. These tendencies are more modern than those that appear in Schuster's purely Impressionist pictures, and would suggest that they were painted later, but this does not appear to be the case; she seems to have painted in both modes simultaneously. Be that as it may, Schuster was, in fact, allied with more liberal circles in the Southern California art world, a member of the relatively long-lived Group of Eight, "conservatively" progressive artists who began having yearly shows in the region in 1921.

Meta Gehring Cressey arrived in California in 1914 with her husband, the painter Bert Cressey; both had studied with Robert Henri in a summer class held in Spain in 1912. She and her husband were among the somewhat conservative progressives in Los Angeles, and as such were two of the painters who formed the Los Angeles Modern Art Society in 1916, a group that held several exhibitions in the later teens, in 1916 and 1918.[133] As Susan Anderson has defined

Donna Schuster in her studio, Los Angeles, c. 1925.
Courtesy of The Redfern Gallery, Laguna Beach.

the artistic approach of Cressey and her associates, "California Progressive painters of the 1910s created a personal art without asserting any visible ideology, arriving at a distinctive blend of Modernism and the regional *plein-air* tradition, rather than forging a daring confrontation with that tradition."[134] Also a landscape and still-life painter, Cressey drew some of her figural subject matter from the Cressey family ranch at Compton and from her garden in the Hollywood Hills, where she probably painted *Under the Pepper Tree* around 1926–27 (plate 34); this may be the same picture as the one Cressey exhibited with that title in the Eighth Annual Exhibition of Painters and Sculptors held at the Los Angeles Museum of History, Science, and Art in April 1927. Cressey replaced the impact of Henri's dramatic tonal approach with the brilliant colors and glowing light of Impressionism, but, like Schuster's and Kleitsch's work, Cressey's is both more vivid and more decorative than orthodox Impressionism, with both foreground and background rendered with equal intensity, while her paint handling is more frenzied. Reviewing a show of Cressey's paintings at the Hollywood Woman's Club in March of 1927, one critic noted, "They sail gaily into the most complicated garden pattern of sunlit flowers and leaves…."[135] Meta Cressey, like Schuster, often painted, as here, domestic images of women, though the nominally passive scene gains in animation from Cressey's somewhat Modernist formal strategies. Cressey gloried in her pepper trees, which were featured not only in pictures that she and her husband painted, but were also depicted by both still-life specialists and other landscape painters, including Guy Rose. The pepper tree was celebrated in poetry, too; see the poem "The Pepper Tree," by Mabel Balch, published in 1924.[136] With the loss of her garden owing to the impact of the Depression in 1929, the despondent Cressey abandoned painting.

Above:

PLATE 34

Meta Cressey (1882–1964)

Under the Pepper Tree, c. 1927

Oil on canvas, 36¾ x 40½ inches

Joan Irvine Smith Fine Arts, Inc.

Left: Meta Cressey aboard the SS *Carpathia,* en route to Spain with Robert Henri's class, July 1912. Courtesy of David and Donna Cressey.

Even more associated with the Modernist camp in Southern California and much more of a figure painter was Edouard Vysekal, who, like Bischoff, was born in Bohemia.[137] He came to the United States in 1907, studying in St. Paul, Minnesota, and then at the Art Institute of Chicago. He subsequently taught there from 1912 to 1914, after which he and his artist-wife, Luvena Buchanan Vysekal, arrived in California to paint a series of murals in the Hotel Barbara Worth in El Centro. They settled in Los Angeles for the rest of their careers. They became associated with the more progressive art circles in the city, joining with Donna Schuster and others in the Group of Eight in 1916; showing with other painters as the California Progressive Group in 1919 and with the Group of Independent Artists of Los Angeles, which held its first exhibition in 1923; and forming in 1925, with other painters including Karl Yens, the Modern Art Workers. Edouard Vysekal's *Joy* (plate 35), depicting a smiling, golden-haired child on a garden swing with two companions, is typical of the wedding of Modernism and Impressionism in Los Angeles in the late 1910s and 1920s. There is a nod here to Cézanne in the simplified structure of the figures, and to Post-Impressionism in the decoratively patterned background, though the bright light and color is very Impressionist. Overall, however, it is the joyous, pleasure driven subject matter that communicates most assertively—the carefree world of childhood, the lush garden setting—just as it does in Cressey's *Under the Pepper Tree* and Schuster's *On the Beach*. The California dream is invested as much in the figure paintings as in the landscapes, and in quasi-Modernist as well as purely Impressionist art.

Above:

PLATE 35
Edouard Vysekal (1890–1939)
Joy, 1917
Oil on canvas, 46 x 35 inches
The Irvine Museum

Left: Edouard Vysekal, c. 1925. Courtesy of George Stern Fine Arts, Los Angeles.

Though San Diego falls within the perimeter of Southern California and, as a city, was and is smaller than Los Angeles, an art colony fairly distinct from the one located in Los Angeles and Pasadena developed there. Once rail traffic made the area accessible, artists, particularly from the Northeast, had begun to flock to San Diego in the late nineteenth century for reasons of health and for the general restorative powers of the climate. Art organizations were slower to develop, surely owing to the smaller community of professional painters, sculptors, and graphic artists, but several artists worked within the broader strategies of Impressionism, and one, Maurice Braun, became one of the state's most celebrated painters.[138]

After immigrating with his family to the United States in 1881, the Hungarian-born Braun had worked in New York, where he studied at the National Academy of Design from 1897 to 1900 and with William Merritt Chase, establishing himself as a figure and portrait painter before arriving in San Diego in 1910. Turning to landscape, undoubtedly inspired by the glorious California scenery around him, Braun immediately became recognized as an important and distinctive figure in the community. In 1910 he organized the San Diego Academy of Art, the city's first art school, and became involved with the San Diego Art Guild, which was founded in 1915. Even more significantly, Braun joined the Theosophical Society colony established in 1897 by Katherine Tingley at Point Loma, known as "Lomaland," on the northern edge of San Diego. Braun was a true believer, and writers have debated the impact of Theosophical spiritual beliefs on the landscapes that became Braun's

Maurice Braun in his studio, San Diego, c. 1916. Courtesy of Charlotte Braun and the estate of Maurice Braun.

artistic preoccupation once he had settled in California. This author is pretty well convinced that they did, in fact, affect the nature of Braun's art, much as George Inness's later paintings reflect his deep beliefs in Swedenborgianism. This seems obvious in such a rare figurative landscape as Braun's 1914 *A Morning Idyll* (Theosophical Society, Pasadena), in which small figures of dancing maidens in classical dress echo the softly swaying trees reaching to the golden heavens behind them: woman, or humanity, and Nature in complete accord. But spiritual resonances also appear in Braun's many pure landscapes, such as *San Diego Countryside with River* (plate 36). Detractors have denigrated such works for their "taffy-colored palette,"[139] but the intentionally unreal hues, the softened shapes of natural forms, the evocation of blissful harmony, the suggestion of vibratory sensations, and the great expansiveness of Braun's scenes suggest rather an unreal, or perhaps a surreal, purified landscape, uncontaminated by the depredations of either time or human activity.[140] Joachim Smith succinctly and perceptively defined the religious and philosophical intent of Braun's art: "Braun's painting tended to distill the material world toward an emptiness for which his melting, evaporating fields of light and fading, dissolving space stood as metaphor."[141]

Of all the California Impressionists, Braun was the one who most departed from the reality of direct observation. Critics noted that "Braun has never been conquered by facts, but he has used them as aids and allies."[142] Braun himself confirmed the unreality for which he was striving when he noted, "landscape should not be taken too literally. It is what we visualize and the interpretation we give the phantasy of our minds that counts."[143] Apropos Braun's utilization of the light of California to convey the spiritual essence of the landscape, he himself wrote that "the art student finds in Theosophy a clear, bright light with which, with true vision…his

PLATE 36
Maurice Braun (1877–1941)

San Diego Countryside with River, c. 1925

Oil on canvas, 30 x 40 inches

Joan Irvine Smith Fine Arts, Inc.

best efforts may come to their proper maturity."[144] It is noteworthy that, except for subjects in his immediate area—San Diego, Point Loma, and La Jolla—Braun's titles invoke specific locations far less often than his Southern California contemporaries; his landscapes are, in a sense, generic, embodying the general "truths" of Nature rather than her precise identification.

Braun was not only recognized as San Diego's preeminent landscape painter, his reputation extended both within and outside of California. He exhibited regularly with the California Art Club in Los Angeles and was represented by the Kanst Art Gallery there; he was a member of the Los Angeles–based Ten Painters Club, almost all prominent California Impressionists, which showed at Kanst. In New York, Braun's paintings were exhibited by William Macbeth and at the Babcock Gallery. An artist of national reputation, Braun showed throughout the Midwest and the East, including the National Academy annuals; he even painted for a time with the Old Lyme art colony in Connecticut, in 1922–23.

The vibratory component of Braun's painting was rejected by his pupil Alfred R. Mitchell in his mature landscapes. Orthodox Impressionist techniques appeared only in Mitchell's early examples. After a peripatetic youth, Mitchell had settled in San Diego in 1908 and become one of Braun's early students at the San Diego Academy of Art, in which he enrolled in 1913; he went on to study at the Pennsylvania Academy of the Fine Arts in Philadelphia in 1916. A Cresson Fellowship enabled him to go abroad in 1921. Mitchell returned to San Diego in 1922 and subsequently established himself as both rival and successor to his teacher as the city's leading landscapist. He was also extremely active with the La Jolla Art Association in that community just north of San Diego; the Association had been formed in 1918, and Mitchell exhibited annually with them from 1923 until 1966.[145]

Mitchell remained in the San Diego area throughout his career, and his art was even more devoted to the landscape in and about the city than Braun's. His scenes are rendered in broad color planes, such as the flat, beige-colored beach, the unbroken shadows, and the soaring orange and blue-purple cliff depicted in *In Morning Light* of 1931 (plate 37). Indeed, vast cliffs and mountain forms are signature elements in Mitchell's painting; the solidity of his forms are the converse of Braun's ephemeral dematerialization. Here, the great flat planes accentuate the emptiness of the view, but the glaring light and bright colors mitigate any sense of loneliness or despair. The present work may depict a stretch along La Jolla Shores, a favorite painting ground for the artist.

Of the artists included in this exhibition, Charles Reiffel was one of the latest to settle in Southern California, and one of several San Diego painters who had begun their careers in Buffalo, New York, where Reiffel first worked as a lithographer. He then began to establish a reputation there for strong tonal paintings, but by the time he became a mainstay in the art colony that developed in Silvermine, Connecticut, in 1912, he had turned to more Impressionist concerns for color and light, and to more personally expressive interpretations of the local landscape. Reiffel joined in the annual exhibitions held at Silvermine in 1913, and became the first president of the Silvermine Guild of Artists when it was founded in 1922. Reiffel may have met Maurice Braun, who was painting on the Connecticut coast in 1922–23; he moved to San Diego in 1925.[146] By then he had adopted the rich colorism, long, sinuous brushwork, and rhythmic compositions that became hallmarks of his later approach to landscape painting, a manner that he easily adapted to the landscape of Southern California, as in his *Summer* (plate 38).

Reiffel often deliberately sought out scenes abounding in irregular surfaces and contrasting natural forms, as in *Summer*'s almost impassable boulders in the foreground and the abrupt rise of the sun-covered hillside. His subject matter was usually drawn from the richly colored mountains that guard San Diego on the north and east. Critics noted the impact of European Modernism on his art, especially the planar concerns of Paul Cézanne and the nervous flow of Vincent van Gogh.[147] There is often a degree of inaccessibility to Reiffel's paintings, which can be antithetical to the

Right:

PLATE 37

Alfred Mitchell (1888–1972)

In Morning Light, 1931

Oil on Masonite, 44 x 56 inches

The Irvine Museum

Below:

PLATE 38

Charles Reiffel (1862–1942)

Summer

Oil on canvas, 34 x 37 inches

Joan Irvine Smith Fine Arts, Inc.

pantheistic loveliness radiating from Braun's landscapes. One critic praised a not-dissimilar picture by Reiffel, *In the San Felipe Valley,* dating from the late 1920s, saying that "its deep purple shadows are gloriously animated by the late afternoon sunshine which comes drifting in across the rolling mesas of the foreground."[148] Although the Impressionist Braun, the Realist Mitchell, and the Modernist Reiffel each approached nature with disparate strategies, they were the most renowned painters in the San Diego art community, and together, in 1929, they joined with seven colleagues to form the Contemporary Artists of San Diego, the first serious professional artists' group in that city.[149] In the following decade, Reiffel turned to urban and waterfront scenes while continuing to paint landscapes in an increasingly expressive mode. He was one of the relatively few artists considered here who welcomed rather than denigrated Modernism.[150]

The artistic situation was very different in Northern California, and in San Francisco at least, Impressionism found relatively meager encouragement, despite its early appearance there in exhibitions held during the 1890s. This was probably caused by a number of factors. For one, San Francisco had an artistic tradition going back to the days of the Gold Rush. Landscape specialists such as Thomas Hill, William Keith, and even the celebrated Albert Bierstadt had appeared to celebrate with seemingly topographical accuracy the spectacular glories of California's unique natural wonders. San Francisco, too, was an urban center, which established a home ground for the artistic community in a manner that Los Angeles was never to provide—panoramic celebrations of the vast California landscape found eager patronage among the wealthy railroad, mining, and land barons. And the climate in the South that is delightful year round allowed the scenic painter a range of pictorial opportunities unavailable in the North, as well as the sparkling, golden light that radiates from Southern California canvases.

When northern artists began to abandon their extolling of the distinct features of their landscape, they retreated into the private preserves of their personal sensibilities vis-à-vis nature, as William Keith began to do in the 1880s. This took on a more astringent form in the Tonalist work of younger painters, above all Arthur Mathews, who dominated the artistic community in the Bay Area from the late nineteenth well into the early twentieth century, as it did also the teaching at the California School of Design, which he directed beginning in 1890 and where his principles found numerous adherents. The distinction between the art of the north and the south was not lost on contemporary California critics; one of the most perceptive assessments of this difference was by Arthur Millier in 1927. He noted that the art circles of Los Angeles and San Francisco were poles apart, and that the people had different traditions, lived differently, and that their artists viewed life from different angles, looking for different things in nature. Millier based his observations primarily on the long-standing urban notions of civic tradition in San Francisco, with its distinct ethnic neighborhoods, while Los Angeles was decentralized and had drawn her population from agrarian states. He concluded that country people were not so concerned either with art or with cultural tradition, but were "necessarily face to face with nature." Millier noted, too, that San Franciscans had respect for and were interested in world artistic achievements, both of the past and present, while the concerns of Los Angelenos "reflected nothing but Southern California."[151]

The multitalented Theodore Wores was one of San Francisco's leading painters and teachers; he first studied at the California School of Design. Wores's art developed from dark and dramatic paintings inspired by his subsequent study in Munich, beginning in the late 1870s, to the heightened colorism of Impressionism. Following his return to San Francisco in 1881, he began to devote himself to Chinatown subjects, and then became one of the first American painters to reside in Japan, first from 1885 to 1887, and again in 1892 to 1894. He also painted in Hawaii and later in the American West, creating a series of fifty images of Native Americans (Los Angeles County Museum of Natural History). In 1907, Wores succeeded Mathews as director of the School of Design.[152]

In California itself, Wores was occupied especially with colorful floral imagery. He painted numerous banks of the familiar wild flowers, poppies and lupines, along the cliffs near San Francisco as well as more formal garden scenes at his house in Saratoga, which he occupied in the spring and summer. Around Saratoga, Los Gatos, Los Altos, and the Santa Clara Valley, he was drawn during the 1920s to flowering trees that line the hillsides and roadways, as seen in the pair, *A Hillside in Saratoga* and *A Saratoga Road* (plates 45, 39).

Theodore Wores. Courtesy of Drs. Ben and A. Jess Shenson and Ruth Westphal.

PLATE 39

Theodore Wores (1859–1939)

A Saratoga Road

Oil on canvas, 44 x 24 inches

Joan Irvine Smith Fine Arts, Inc.

In these Wores recalls his earlier depictions of flowering trees in Japan, and projects the spontaneity associated with Impressionism, though the two pictures vary carefully with the artist's conceptual program. In the first, the pink blossoms of almond or fruit—apple, cherry, plum, peach, or pear—trees play harmoniously against the blue of the sky, while the tree shadows fall upon the soft green hillside. In *A Saratoga Road,* the umbrellalike shapes of the trees rhythmically repeat the arc of the road and the distant hills. Wores wrote of arriving "one beautiful day in the little town of Saratoga, where thousands of acres of fruit trees were in bloom. We were quite overpowered by the beauty of this magnificent spectacle.... Those square miles of tapestry of blooms were a wonderful revelation to me, and the hillsides covered with varicolored orchards, with the distant mountain vistas and blue hills for background, suggest endless possibilities for picture making." [153] Wores began to concentrate on this theme by 1920, when a show at the Bohemian Club in San Francisco was designated "California's Spring Blossoms." One reviewer wrote of the "limitless rows of trees, each with their special blossoms," [154] and another noted that "Wores catches the romance and poetry of the Santa Clara orchards as few painters do. His blossoms are not simply white paint. They are blossoms which melt into the landscape in green or gray whites, or delicate pinks." [155] Wores opened his Saratoga Art Gallery in March of 1926, coinciding with the annual Blossom Day Festival; it became an instant success and a long-time tourist attraction. [156] In his later San Francisco years, Wores concentrated on the landscape.

A younger artist, and one of the city's leading figure painters at this time, was Matteo Sandona, who was extremely active at the Bohemian Club and with numerous art organizations; but he is almost totally forgotten today. Italian born, Sandona settled in San Francisco in 1901 and was best known as a portraitist, but he also painted more decorative figural works, such as *In Her Kimono* (plate 48), which call to mind the pictures of the eastern Impressionist Robert Reid. Here, Sandona, like Reid, presents an attractive young woman in a colorful gown paired with a floral still life; both artists show women as passive and reflective, solely as images of loveliness, and offered up for the viewer's delectation. Reid often, as Sandona here, clothed his figures in kimonos, not only referring to the popularity of Japanese accessories but also employing a loose-fitting garment that caresses the flesh and at the same time functions as an informal, domestic garment, intimate and easily removed. The wicker furniture further accentuates the casual nature of the setting, while the figure, crouched down within the arms and back of the chair, seems confined, oblivious to the thin strip of outdoor landscape seen through the window above her. [157] Sandona's painting is more vivid in its coloration and more vibrant in its scintillating brushwork than many of Reid's, suggesting awareness of more contemporary artistic concerns. Sandona's restrained Modernism accounts for his role as one of the founders of the California Society of Artists, which began holding annual exhibitions in San Francisco in 1902. *In Her Kimono* may, in fact, be the picture that Sandona exhibited under the title *The Kimono* at the California Liberty Fair held in Los Angeles in 1918 to raise funds in support of American participation in World War I, and which offered a panorama of the achievements of the region's Impressionist school, with fourteen of the present artists included.

Joseph Raphael, one of the greatest, and certainly the most original of those who might be called Bay Area Impressionists, was neither an Impressionist in the conventional sense nor active in and around San Francisco. Like Guy Rose, Raphael was one of the few artists of the movement who was actually born in California, and his maturation too took place abroad. Furthermore, Raphael studied at the California School of Design—designated the Mark Hopkins Institute during the years 1893–97 that he was there under the tutelage of Arthur Mathews and the sculptor Douglas Tilden—and then went to Paris for further study. But until World War II, Raphael spent his career abroad, first dividing his time between Paris and the artists' colony in Laren in the Netherlands, then in 1912 moving to Uccle, a suburb of Brussels; he remained there until 1929 when he returned to the Netherlands and lived in Oegstgeest.[158] Raphael's earlier Netherlandish paintings are dark, dramatic figural works, sometimes with Symbolist overtones; the best-known of these are *The Town Crier and His Family* (Fine Arts Museums of San Francisco) and *La Fête du Bourgmestre* (San Francisco Art Institute), which depict Captain N. W. van den Broek, a Laren burgomaster; both were exhibited at the Paris Salon, in 1905 and 1906 respectively.

But just before his move to Belgium, Raphael's methodology changed radically and he began to paint colorful outdoor scenes, sometimes including figures, and often set in fields of flowers and vivid gardens—typical Impressionist themes. Raphael applied paint in large dabs, creating a decorative tapestry of colors more closely Post-Impressionist, while flattening space and simplifying forms. Curiously, some of the best-known of these pictures were painted on visits back to the Netherlands, especially in Noordwijk, in part because he was directing his concerns to rural areas. But he painted the urban scene also, and Brussels offered the artist appropriate subject matter for his avant-garde strategies, as is attested by his *Market of St. Catherine, Bruxelles* (plate 47). Even in it, however, nature takes "first place," with the great church, reminiscent of Monet's earlier renderings of Rouen Cathedral, seen through a row of trees along the avenue. As his art developed during the second decade of the century, Raphael utilized paint ever more expressively, to the point where he may be said to have "jumped" the Impressionist canon to Expressionism.

Still, Raphael deserves consideration among the California Impressionists since he was acknowledged as such in his own time; his paintings were much admired in San Francisco, where they were frequently exhibited, particularly at the Helgesen Gallery, beginning in 1912. In his spring show there in 1916, the critic for the *Oakland Tribune* praised Raphael's Dutch and Belgian scenes for their "vividness that makes the picture bring before the beholder the beauties of the original gardens. Raphael revels in color, and his themes are chosen largely for their radiant qualities which he paints with splendid force and conviction."[159] Raphael's greatest champion was Albert Bender, a major mover and shaker in the contemporary San Francisco art world and the foremost San Francisco patron of the work of some of the more Modernist painters there. It was to Bender in January of 1912 that Raphael first wrote from Uccle of his new interests: "With my work I have experimented and really studied and progressed not in the way of doing big things (it's not in me) but in the outdoor work"; and subsequently: "I work every day—landscape. I'm painting the 4 points of the compass the hottest sunny days preferred…."[160]

In Northern California, Impressionism flourished not in San Francisco itself but in the artists' colonies at Monterey, nearby Carmel, Pacific Grove, and Pebble Beach. In some ways, Monterey was to Northern California what Laguna Beach was to the South, but its genesis was quite different. Monterey had begun to attract professional artists far earlier, just as the cultural establishment had developed in San Francisco before it had in Southern California. Monterey, in fact, can be said to have known two periods of artistic fame. The first began when Jules Tavernier settled in Monterey in 1875 and attracted colleagues and students from San Francisco; later, Evelyn McCormick, one of the earliest San Francisco painters to have joined the artists' colony in Giverny, began painting there as soon as she returned to San Francisco from France, probably late in 1891.

But Monterey developed as a leading art center in Northern California as a direct result of the 1906 earthquake and fire, when so many San Francisco painters found temporary refuge there, and some remained permanently. Their activities were fostered and supported by the Del Monte Hotel, which had been built by the Pacific Improvement Company as the main destination of the Southern Pacific Railroad when it reached Monterey in 1880. In 1907, regular art exhibitions were instituted at the Hotel, and in 1914 a Society of Monterey Artists was established.[161]

In 1905, a year before the fire, the Arts and Crafts Club had been established in Carmel, hitherto distinguished primarily by the ruins of its mission; their clubhouse opened two years later with a First Annual Art Exhibition only three months after the Del Monte's. In 1913, the Club began a three-month-long summer school; it was here that William Merritt Chase taught his final summer term in 1914, when Donna Schuster and E. Charlton Fortune were two of his students; Channel Townsley offered instruction during the following summers, and Matteo Sandona came from San Francisco to teach there.[162]

But of prime importance to the development of the art colony were: the combination of the relative proximity of Monterey to San Francisco; the illustrious history of the region, which went back to the days of Spanish rule and included the residence of Robert Louis Stevenson; and the area's natural and distinct beauty—the wild and rugged coastline, the dense pine forest nearby, the stands of cypress trees, and the empty, scrub grass–filled sand dunes—which attracted so many artists there for four decades after the earthquake.[163]

Immediately after the 1906 exodus the artistic presence was understandably dominated by the low-keyed, more poetic, Tonalist landscape work that prevailed in San Francisco, where artists such as Arthur Mathews, Charles Rollo Peters, Xavier Martinez, Gottardo Piazzoni, Francis McComas, and others had taught or trained.[164] This aesthetic was prevalent in the early exhibitions held at the Del Monte Hotel, though a number of Southern California Impressionists—such as Benjamin Brown, Hanson Puthuff, and John Gamble, himself a refugee in Santa Barbara from the San Francisco earthquake—did exhibit in those shows. The appearance in the Monterey-Carmel region of a greater Impressionist presence may have been expedited by the triumph of the movement at the 1915 Panama-Pacific Exposition, which brought out Childe Hassam, the country's most esteemed Impressionist painter, who had been in San Francisco the year before in connection with his mural work for the Exposition and had painted both there and in Carmel (*Point Lobos, Carmel,* Los Angeles County Museum of Art). But Impressionism had begun making headway in the region several years earlier, when increasing numbers of Impressionist painters such as Benjamin Brown and Donna Schuster began to visit and paint there; others such as William Wendt (who had painted in Monterey as early as 1896), Jean Mannheim, and Maurice Braun sent work to the Del Monte shows; and a few painters settled, at least temporarily, in the area, including Granville Redmond, who was in Monterey in 1908–10, and Detlef Sammann, who moved more or less permanently from Los Angeles to Pebble Beach in 1912.

A distinguishing feature of the Monterey-Carmel art colony was the quantity of professional women artists, proportionally more, certainly, than at Laguna Beach as well as at some of the other major Impressionist centers back East. In fact, Evelyn McCormick and Mary Brady, the first California woman to have worked in Giverny, were identified in 1908 as "the pioneers of the present settlement of Monterey as a mecca of art." [165]

Mary DeNeale Morgan, who studied at the California School of Design beginning in 1884 and subsequently opened a studio in Oakland, was one of the earliest professionals there to be associated with Impressionism. Morgan first appeared in Carmel in 1903, buying a cottage there and returning the following year, though she did not make it her permanent home until 1910;[166] she became one of the instructors and the director at the Carmel Summer School from 1917 to 1925.[167] Morgan's landscapes, painted primarily in the watercolor medium for which she was known, underscore the arbitrariness of stylistic characterization. *Cypress at Monterey* (plate 51) shows a favorite motif, not only of Morgan but of many of her colleagues, especially some of the Tonalists such as Mathews and McComas; the latter was the other major watercolor specialist there. To a certain degree, Morgan shares with those artists a preference for simplified, somewhat stylized compositions, a predilection associated with California Tonalism, but she introduces into that formula the sunlight and bright colors of Impressionism, in this work even adopting the Impressionist broken brushstroke, not easily achieved in watercolor. After she had settled in Carmel, Morgan became well known for her rendering of groves of cypress trees, not only in San Francisco but also in Los Angeles, where her work was shown at the Kanst Art Gallery in October of 1911.[168] Morgan had turned to this theme immediately on visiting Carmel in 1903, for she exhibited a work titled *Point Lobos Cypresses* at the San Francisco Art Association that November.[169]

Euphemia Charlton Fortune was a more powerful exponent of Impressionism in Monterey. Some of her finest and most colorful paintings depict the town and surrounding landscape; *Study of Monterey Bay* (plate 1) is preparatory for one of her best-known views, *Monterey Bay* (also known as *Above the Town*) (private collection), painted in 1918, a work that received an award at the San Francisco Institute of Art. The Sausalito-born Fortune had first studied art in Edinburgh, Scotland, and in London before enrolling at the Mark Hopkins Institute in San Francisco in 1905. After the earthquake she continued her studies in New York, and then in 1910 went abroad; she returned to San Francisco in 1912 and established a studio in Monterey the following year. Fortune's work up to then appears to have consisted primarily of portraits and figure studies. In 1914 she was a student in William Merritt Chase's summer class held in Carmel, and it was from this time that she began to work in the colorful, high-key manner that distinguishes her art. That same summer she was numbered, along with Joseph Raphael, among the exhibitors at the Del Monte Gallery whom Josephine Blanch described as having "widely departed from the older and more academic methods." [170] Fortune's painterly, Impressionist propensities were only reinforced by the art exhibition of the Panama-Pacific International Exposition the next year, where she not only showed a group of landscapes, one of which won her a Silver Medal, but which she herself recorded in paint. Her teacher, Chase, purchased her *Interior of San Carlos Mission at Carmel* from the exhibition. [171]

Fortune devoted much of her art not only to the land and the sea, but, unlike most of her contemporaries in both Northern and Southern California, also to the town of Monterey itself, picturing it as the comfortable community that she and the other painters so enjoyed. Still, this portrayal of society reflects more contemporary concerns than those of the majority of her fellow California Impressionists; Fortune was an influential painter in Northern California, and had impact on some of the Modernist members of the Oakland-based Society of Six. [172] Not only are buildings of every sort introduced into her pictures, but figures and farm animals are also often included; in fact, one of the major distinctions between *Study of Monterey Bay* and the finished work is that three figures, absent in the study, appear in the foreground of the latter. But Fortune was also aware of and, unlike many of her colleagues, sympathetic to aspects of Post-Impressionism, especially the paintings of Paul Cézanne, and in both paintings under discussion, the blocky, proto-Cubist treatment of the buildings, rendered to some degree as blots of color, suggests a measure of affiliation with the work of Cézanne. This was, in fact, recognized at the time, though couched in typically chauvinist terms; in 1927, Anna Cora Winchell wrote in regard to a show of Fortune's work at Helgesen's Gallery in San Francisco: "A masculine forcefulness announces itself in much of her work, and her style is such that a stranger rather inclines to the opinion that the painter is a man. She is by far the strongest woman artist of this Coast…." [173]

In 1921, Fortune left for a six-year stay in Europe. In the works she painted in the artists' colony of St. Ives in England and at St. Tropez in France—equally as colorful and as Impressionist as her Monterey scenes—figures are even more prominent, and she emphasized the activities of the fishing fleets in both communities. On her return to California in 1927, Fortune re-established her studio in Monterey and, the next year, as a devout Roman Catholic, founded the Monterey Guild, an organization committed to the revival of ecclesiastical art. Fortune turned increasingly to interior church decoration and liturgical work, and gradually relinquished easel painting. [174]

It was during the early and middle years of the 1910s that Impressionism took a strong hold in Monterey, often with painters who concentrated on coastal themes. One of the finest of these, but also one of the least documented, is Ernest Bruce Nelson, another of the relatively few California Impressionists born in the state, in Santa Clara County. He enrolled in and studied art at Stanford University, with which he maintained connections even after he went on to New York for further training. He returned to San Francisco in 1912 and the following year established a studio at Pacific Grove on the Monterey Peninsula. The year of his return to California, Nelson held two shows of his work at Stanford and another successful exhibition at Helgesen & Marshall Gallery in San Francisco; during the following four years Nelson continued to have major one-artist shows in the region, in Palo Alto and San Jose, as well as continuing representation at Helgesen's and also at the Merick Reynolds Gallery in Los Angeles. He was also exhibiting at the Del Monte Gallery in Monterey by 1914, while at the inauguration of the Oakland Art Gallery in 1916, an entire room was devoted to thirty of his pictures. Nelson won a Silver Medal at the Panama-Pacific International Exposition for *The Summer Sea,* one of four works shown. The artist had thus become a force to be reckoned with in Northern California art circles, but in 1917 he began service with the Army Camouflage Corps. Though his work continued to be exhibited in both San Francisco and Los Angeles in the late teens and early twenties, after his Army discharge in 1918 Nelson went to Cooperstown, New York, where his close friend Dr. Henry S. F. Cooper, a great-grandson of James Fennimore Cooper, was living. Nelson painted murals in the breakfast room at Fynmere, the Cooper family homestead, and remained in that upstate New York town, painting the local scenery and severing his California ties.[175]

When Nelson had begun to exhibit his paintings in 1912, he was concentrating on landscapes, often with seasonal emphases. Some were painted in the Catskills or around the village of Mayfield, further north in New York State, some on trips to Oregon, and many in and around Stanford University; titles suggest traditional themes of groves of eucalyptus, oaks, poplars, sycamores, hickory, and maple trees, as well as poppy paintings and blossoming trees. Then, in his Helgesen Gallery show held in November 1914, Nelson appeared with a large group of pictures of the Monterey coast, shore and sea, as well as depictions of the fishing fleet, and of the pines and meadows there, suggesting that it was during the previous summer that he had begun to produce the pictures now admired most, brilliantly colored coastal scenes in full sunlight, such as his 1915 *The Summer Sea* (plate 52). Some of Nelson's work, as here, suggests an affinity with the contemporaneous work of William Wendt, in the artist's concentration upon more blocky, geometric forms, especially in the representation of the coastal rocks, though the technique is pervasive throughout the water and foreground grass as well. Also somewhat related to the preferred strategies of Southern California artists is the panoramic sweep of the scene, whereas many of the paintings by his Monterey Peninsula colleagues were concentrated on a more restricted tract of rocks and sea.

Bruce Nelson in Cooperstown, New York, 1918.
Courtesy of Ruth Westphal.

One of the leading marine painters in the region, and one of the most distinguished and influential of all the artists in the Monterey colony, was Armin Hansen. He was born in San Francisco and studied at the Mark Hopkins Institute, but after the earthquake he went abroad, training in Stuttgart, Germany. In 1908 he settled for four years in the artists' colony of Nieuwpoort, on the Belgian coast, working as both painter and printmaker and specializing in scenes of the lives of North Sea fishermen along the Yser River and in neighboring Oostend. (Any possible connection with his fellow San Franciscan, Joseph Raphael, who moved to Uccle, outside of Brussels, during this time, has yet to be established.) Hansen returned to his native city in 1912, and the following year took the coast packet *Eureka* down to Monterey and painted there; he exhibited in 1914 at the Del Monte Gallery. Hansen moved his studio to Monterey in 1916 and settled there permanently in 1918. He was soon recognized as one of the leading and most distinctive artists of the colony, was active with the Carmel Art Association, and helped to found the Monterey History and Art Association, as well as teaching summer classes at Monterey for the California School of Fine Arts, beginning in 1918.[176]

Though he also created extremely beautiful studio interior still lifes, Hansen devoted himself—in both his oil paintings and his etchings—primarily to depictions of the maritime activities of the region.[177] These are not coastal landscapes but records of the sardine and salmon fishing boats and other vessels, along with the Portuguese and Sicilian fishermen who manned them, often almost engulfed by the swirling sea. *Making Port* (plate 50) is typical of these, though here the artist offers added interest in the contrast between the gleaming, white, full-rigged schooner and the dark, smoke-belching tug, much smaller but heroically attempting to reach the larger ship.[178] Hansen's tremendous facility with broad swaths of paint that represent the fury of the sea activates the scene, while the asymmetrical composition—both vessels pressed into the upper right corner—is a Modernist device ultimately harking back to Japanese aesthetic conventions. In general, California Impressionists avoided depicting labor activities, though when they did they usually concentrated on harbor scenes; but Hansen is unique in making this his foremost concern.

In these paintings, Hansen abandons some of the rich chromaticism of Impressionism either for deeper and more contrasting hues or, as here, for a more neutral palette, which in either case increases the sense of dramatic tension. But more orthodox chromatics can be found in his still lifes and in some of his land-based scenes, such as *The Farmhouse* of about 1915–16 (plate 40). Traditionally Impressionist also is the softer, broken brushwork and the tremendous interest in patterns of light, with the trees casting purple shadows on both the white cottage and the light-colored roadway. Here, even though the canvas is without figures, Hansen emphasizes human habitation and activity by featuring the horse-drawn cart that appears to await its occupants.

Hansen acknowledged that he received a major career boost when he was introduced in 1918 to William Ritschel, who immediately arranged for Hansen to show in a New York gallery.[179] German-born and -trained, Ritschel was, at the time, one of Northern California's and, indeed, one of the nation's most acclaimed painters of the sea. Ritschel had several years' experience as a sailor in Europe before he immigrated to New York in 1895; in 1911 he began working in Carmel, and the following year he started to exhibit paintings of the coast at Monterey and Carmel in New York and Chicago while also showing his work in Monterey at the Del Monte Gallery. In 1918, Ritschel built a great castlelike house overlooking the ocean in Carmel Highlands, his "Castel à Mare," though he maintained his New York connections and gave that city as his permanent address until 1929. In later years, Ritschel traveled the world over, painting marine subjects in the South Seas, Asia, and at Majorca and Capri.[180] Fittingly, Armin Hansen wrote a moving tribute to Ritschel for his Memorial Exhibition, held at the Carmel Art Association Galleries in October 1949.[181]

Ritschel's paintings, such as *Purple Tide* (plate 41), are much more in the tradition of Winslow Homer than are Hansen's, and are reminiscent of Homer's great Prouts Neck, Maine, pictures of the sea rolling up against the craggy coastline; indeed, when Ritschel had a one-artist show at Knoedler's in New York in March 1911, he was ranked alongside Homer, only half a year after the latter's death.[182] But Ritschel is a later artist than Homer, and one working with Impressionist strategies, so that colors are brighter and more diffused, the rocks glow with myriad touches of color, and light glints throughout the surface of the water. Even Ritschel's title conjures up the hue most associated with Impressionism. Indeed, Ritschel's house and its surrounding gardens were said to reflect the Impressionist palette of his coastal paintings: John Frederick Harley, Jr., noted in 1946 that "the inexorable sea, piling stone upon stone, might well have inspired the Carmel Highlands home of the William Ritschels—the green, pinks, mauves, blues and purples of a capricious ocean have come to rest in a garden which might well have been fashioned of foam and spray."[183] Such paintings as *Purple Tide* reflect a common theme among painters working in and around Monterey—the rugged, solid cliffs counterpoised to the elemental force of the ocean. These may be seen as parallels of the many coastal views painted by Southern California artists at Laguna Beach, but the latter tend toward more panoramic vistas while the Monterey paintings tend to zero in on a small segment of Nature.

Hansen and Ritschel were among the best-known artists of the Monterey colony in the 1910s; Fortune, who socialized very little with her colleagues there, maintained a friendly relationship with both painters and respected their work. In any case, by the second half of the decade, Impressionism was firmly entrenched on the Peninsula, especially in the delineation of the dramatic coastal scenery there. In 1918, the year after Bruce Nelson departed from

Monterey, Guy Rose spent the first of three consecutive summers in Carmel, producing during a two-month vacation there some of his finest California paintings and among the most sought-after of his works today. He was back by late July 1919, and in 1920 stayed until early autumn, returning to Pasadena in early October.[184] Rose himself had the intention of producing works that differed from his previous California work painted in the south, though exactly what his objectives here were beyond the change of scenery is difficult to determine.[185] The majority of these pictures concentrated on the rugged coastal cliffs, sometimes, as in his *Incoming Tide* of about 1917 (plate 49), emulating the tradition of Winslow Homer and, closer to home, William Ritschel, in depicting the meeting of the flowing Pacific waters and the sloping rocky shore line.

In other canvases, Rose chose more specific and identifiable locales, such as his view of *Point Lobos,* painted around 1918–19 (plate 56), an even more circumscribed view that focuses on the distinctive rock formations off the Monterey shore. This was a particularly rugged, unusual section of the coast, and its special attraction for Rose, both for its natural configuration and its historic evocations, were detailed in 1919 by his wife, Ethel. She wrote of Point Lobos as

> even more impressive a place that inevitably affects people and even animals in a creepy, uncanny way. This crowded chaos of cliffs rises abruptly from the water, crowned by extraordinary trees, carpeted with wild flowers, slashed by gorges at the bottom of which gleams water of translucent sapphire and emerald; threaded by narrow, slippery paths twisting among the tree trunks and over the torturous rocks, some of them old Indian trails along the face of the cliff where in shallow smoke-blackened caves lie piles of shining particles that once were clam and mussel shells, detritus of Indian feasts of happy memory.[186]

The coast at Point Lobos was a subject that had attracted artists since Albert Bierstadt visited there in the early 1870s, and Rose painted the scene a number of times in changing atmospheric conditions, somewhat reminiscent, though only in paired examples, of Claude Monet's serial imagery of grain stacks, poppy fields, poplars, and the like, which Rose would have known from his distant days

PLATE 41
William Ritschel (1864–1949)
Purple Tide, c. 1915
Oil on canvas, 36 x 40 inches
The Joan Irvine Smith Collection

in Giverny. The affiliation with Monet did not go unnoticed by California critics, but Rose's distinction was also asserted: "Are these pictures the California of an impressionist nurtured on Monet traditions? Perhaps. But they are also, you will presently discover, your California and mine. Don't forget that Guy Rose is native to this soil."[187]

Point Lobos attracted extended attention when it was reproduced in an article that Rose V. S. Berry published in January of 1925. Berry noted that it was

> one of the pictures painted on a clear day in California, when the ocean in color rivals the blue of an Italian sea, and when something of the vastness of the Pacific may be apprehended from the distance of the horizon line. The large rocks in the foreground lose none of their massive quality nor their adamantine character by the detailed handling of their formation. And they have been made none the less impressive by the painter having used them in a high key as light surfaces, adjuncts of his brilliant sunshine. The fluid mass of the calm sea loses none of its weight or impenetrable depth by Rose's technique, while the low hills to the right give a variety and a different appeal to the horizon line. Rose has painted the famous Point Lobos in rather minute detail at the left of the canvas. Many fail to grasp the beauty of these rocks, as Rose has given them. The low, clinging cypress trees, scarcely more than bushes, with roots reaching deeply in the crevices of the rocks, please the painter's love for design, and obtain the observer's sympathetic admiration as living things which have clung to life in spite of tempestuous battles with infuriated ocean winds.[188]

During the Impressionist years, Point Lobos, at the southern end of Carmel Bay, attracted resident artists such as William Ritschel and Arthur Hill Gilbert; other visiting Californians, such as John Gamble; and visiting painters from the East and Midwest such as Lillian Genth from New York, William J. Edmondson from Cleveland, and perhaps most notably, Childe Hassam, whose 1914 *Point Lobos, Carmel* is his one located picture created on the Peninsula.

In his masterly paintings, Rose allows full expression of his command of form, detailing the unique rock formations with amazing geological precision. This would seem, on the face of it, the antithesis of Impressionism, and yet the artist's freedom in the rendering of the water, and his brilliant light and color, while vividly true to the subject matter, reflect the strategies of that artistic movement. We need only consider the seascapes of painters of an earlier generation such as Homer to realize the degree of Modernism introduced here. Rose exhibited his work in Carmel itself, at least in September 1920, but he was, of course, based in Pasadena at the time, and it was there that these pictures of the Monterey coast were soon shown in venues such as the California Art Club, the Friday Morning Club, the Los Angeles Museum of History, Science, and Art, and various commercial galleries such as Kanst, Cannell and Chaffin, Battey, and Stendahl. These works especially continued to represent Rose's artistic proficiency after his debilitating stroke in February of 1921, appearing not only at some of the above-named venues but also in the first shows held at the newly formed Laguna Beach Art Association in the summer of 1922, at the National Academy of Design in New York the following year, as well as at the Pasadena Art Institute and the Biltmore Salon in Los Angeles. They were also the subject of the important above-cited article by Rose V. S. Berry, which appeared in *International Studio* in January of 1925. One of Rose's major achievements was to bring the Northern

California landscape not only to the south but to the general American public.

Rose, of course, painted other themes on the Monterey Peninsula, including the ever-popular cypress trees and groves of oaks. Even more distinctive than his coastal scenes, which bear a generic similarity to his Laguna and La Jolla pictures, were the many paintings of the empty dunes that Rose often made in Carmel, a solitude-invoking subject that appears to have fascinated him almost as much as the rocky shores. Naturally, it was a subject that was not limited to Rose alone; Arthur Hill Gilbert's *Land of Gray Dunes, Monterey* (plate 42) is a masterly evocation of the austere beauty of this deserted landscape, projecting fully the poetic melancholy of the scene with, perhaps, even more dramatic intensity than Rose's similar paintings. Gilbert, still another California Impressionist originally from the Chicago area, was a much later arrival on the Monterey Peninsula. He had studied at the Art Institute of Chicago before going to Los Angeles in 1920 to continue his training at the Otis Art Institute. During the 1920s, Gilbert was a regular exhibitor with the California Art Club and at the annual shows of the Painters and Sculptors held at the Los Angeles Museum as well as at the Ebell Club and the Biltmore Salon, and with such commercial galleries as Kanst, Cannell and Chaffin, and Stendahl. Hill appears to have visited Giverny probably the year after Claude Monet's death in 1926; he held a show of his French paintings at Stendahl's in December of 1927 and exhibited *The Church of Claude Monet, Giverney* (*sic*; this would have been the church of Ste. Radegonde) at the Ninth Annual Exhibition of the Painters and Sculptors, in April of 1928, as well as a landscape of the neighboring town of Vernon in 1929 at the California Art Club.

By that time, Gilbert had settled on the Monterey Peninsula, first in Pebble Beach, then in Carmel, and still later in Monterey, where he became well known for his paintings of the familiar local themes—in addition to the dunes, coastal views, and especially groves of oak trees—and was active with the Carmel Art Association.[189] *Land of Gray Dunes, Monterey* must have been one of his first pictures painted there, for it was exhibited under the title of *Monterey Dunes* in the spring of 1929 at the Annual Exhibition of the National Academy of Design in New York, where in the previous winter he had exhibited another, presumably similar picture, *Duneland: Monterey.* Gilbert gave his address as Pebble Beach, and the subject here abuts what is now the golf course and resort area along the famous 17-Mile Drive. Gilbert settled in Northern California only during the final years of the predominance of the Impressionist movement in California, but he enjoyed a successful, mostly regional career, even when many younger painters had begun to investigate other aesthetic approaches that appeared more relevant to contemporary concerns.[190]

An even later artist to reside on the Monterey Peninsula was Paul Dougherty, though he had already painted there earlier, exhibiting paintings of the Monterey coast as early as 1919. By the time he established his home and studio in the Carmel Highlands in 1931, near that of his colleague William Ritschel, Dougherty was nationally recognized as one of the country's leading marine painters, and, even more than Ritschel, was designated and honored as the heir to Winslow Homer; Ameen Rihani wrote in 1921 in *International Studio* that "there is no doubt that the mantle of Winslow Homer has fallen upon Paul Dougherty."[191] Born in Brooklyn, Dougherty is said to have studied in New York with Henry Ward Ranger in the late 1890s before going abroad. He had returned to New York by 1904, and it was then that he began to specialize in marine subjects, generally just dramatic depictions of surf crashing upon rocks. In 1905 Dougherty honed his interests by spending three months sketching on Monhegan Island, off the coast of Maine. This became his favorite painting ground, and the results were on view annually at the Macbeth Gallery in New York, with which he became associated in 1907. His friend and colleague Leon Kroll recalled that by then "he was supposed to be almost as good as Homer."[192] Dougherty also worked in a number of other coastal areas favored by painters, such as Brittany in France, and St. Ives in Cornwall, and traveled to Asia, where he painted in Japan and the Philippines. Arthritis sent him to Arizona and New Mexico in 1928, and then to California; he divided his time between Palm Springs, where he spent the winters, and Carmel, where he was active with the Art Association.[193]

Given the length of Dougherty's established career before he settled in Northern California and the nature of his sea and rock paintings, and since the artist did not always date his pictures, it is difficult to determine which paintings were created on the Monterey Peninsula. However, when he exhibited in New York at the Macbeth Gallery in 1931, one critic noted that his recent works were "brilliantly executed in a much looser technique and higher key than formerly.... Several of the earlier seascapes are here, but they are hardly to be mentioned in the same breath with the new western canvases."[194] Apparently this is a vast oversimplification; although *The Twisted Ledge* (plate 54) certainly incorporates the looser technique and higher key the critic discerned in Dougherty's western pictures, as well as the brilliant sunlight that had become a hallmark of California Impressionism, the painting is actually an early one, which had been exhibited in the winter 1907 exhibition of the National Academy of Design and illustrated and mentioned in an article on Dougherty published in 1908.[195] A reviewer of the Academy show, in fact, compared Dougherty's painting to the work of the French Impressionist Maxime Maufra, also known for his pictures of waves crashing upon the rocks.[196]

By the early 1930s, when Dougherty joined the art world of California, a new climate had settled over the state and indeed the entire nation. Landscape, though still practiced of course, was no longer the dominant theme; as Arthur Millier noted in 1934: "Until a decade ago, painting in Southern California produced innumerable landscapes, seventy per cent of which were bought by tourists as souvenirs."[197] The Great Depression blew an ill wind upon the cultural scene generally, and many artists responded by reflecting the banalities, and occasionally the grim realities, of urban life as well as the nature, both positive and negative, of agrarian existence. Few of the California Impressionists changed their modus operandi, and while many certainly experienced a decline in both critical favor as well as in available patronage, most continued to offer up their impressions of the paradisiacal landscape; after all, the land itself had changed little, though even here, residential, commercial, and industrial sprawl were taking their toll upon the artists' beloved scenery. But the sunshine may have, by then, seemed somewhat shallow, when filtering down upon what may have seemed the mundane bleakness of a new era. Yet, for three decades, that sun had shone brightly in California as it had nowhere else, and answered affirmatively the question, posed in 1921 by Mabel Seares, "Has California a school of painting peculiar to herself?"[198]

PLATE 42
Arthur Hill Gilbert (1894–1970)
Land of Gray Dunes, Monterey
Oil on canvas, 32 x 40 inches
The Irvine Museum

Impressionism in Southern California, 1890–1930

Jean Stern

In the early nineteenth century, California was a distant and largely unknown land. The discovery of the New World in 1492 and subsequent explorations by Spain in the early 1500s revealed a diverse population living in villages along the coast in California. Finding little gold or precious stones, the Spanish explorers lost interest and California became a quiet colonial backwater, with only occasional subsequent contact. For over two hundred years, California remained essentially unexplored, until the latter part of the eighteenth century.

Wary of the Russian Empire, which had expanded its presence in Alaska by building forts and trading posts in the Pacific Northwest, Spain decided to make its presence known in California. Over a span of half a century, a series of twenty-one missions were built throughout California, the first of these in San Diego in 1763. By the early 1820s, Spanish power in North America had been supplanted by the emerging nation of Mexico, and following upon the tumultuous events of the Mexican War of 1846–48 and the Gold Rush of 1849, California became a part of the United States, with formal statehood coming in 1850.

The Mission Era marked the height of Spanish presence in California, and even though the period lasted only about fifty years, it ingrained a deep-rooted myth of a Golden Age, replete with haciendas of red-tiled roofs and adobe walls, courtyards and fountains, bougainvillea and swallows. Since the late nineteenth century this iconographic assemblage has been embraced by popular culture, and today it remains an integral part of the state's image, playing a role in not only how the world visualizes California but also how Californians see themselves.

In the 1860s and 1870s, California entered a period of great economic growth, thanks to the benefits of improved transportation. The initial transcontinental railroad, the Union Pacific, was completed in 1869 with its western terminus at San Francisco. Prior to the completion of the Union Pacific, the only approaches to California were overland by horse and wagon, a perilous and often hostile journey, or by ship from Panama or around South America. The route through Panama before the canal was built necessitated docking on the Atlantic side, crossing the isthmus to the Pacific, and boarding a ship to continue on to California.

PLATE 43
Arthur G. Rider (1886–1975)
Mission Garden, San Juan Capistrano, c. 1929
Oil on canvas, 22 x 20 inches
Joan Irvine Smith Fine Arts, Inc.

The state's tremendous agricultural potential lay untapped until economically expedient ways were established to move produce to eastern markets. In 1876, a railroad route was opened between Los Angeles and San Francisco, and in 1885 the Santa Fe Railway, an all-weather route from Los Angeles to Chicago via the Southwest, was completed. This new route eliminated the risk of costly delays owing to snowfall and avalanche over the Union Pacific tracks where they traversed the Rocky Mountains. In due course, the railroads exploited the prospect of passenger transport going the other way, from east to west, and as a result, Southern California experienced an enormous increase in population during the late 1880s.

San Francisco's greatest era of growth and prosperity came as a direct outcome of the Gold Rush. This economic expansion led to the development of a thriving social and artistic environment, and with it, a nascent artistic community as early as the 1850s. The direction and quality of artistic and cultural matters are, in large part, determined by the patrons who support those activities. Art patrons in mid-nineteenth-century San Francisco demanded works that mirrored European canons, especially current French modes.

The fashionable art styles in France, and indeed in upper-class America, were derivatives of the French Beaux-Arts or "Salon" style and an aspect of the Romantic-Realist style practiced by the Barbizon school. Other European styles, notably the Munich and Düsseldorf schools, were indeed popular with artists and patrons, but the French modes were clearly more influential.

The Salon style is named for the popular art exhibitions sponsored by the French Academy and held annually in Paris. Entries to the Salon were juried, and inclusion was an important step toward artistic and professional success. Paintings for the Salon were frequently large, pretentious historical and figural compositions, which were immensely popular with the French art public. Superbly painted, carefully crafted, and nearly photographic in appearance (figure 1), these works reflected the highest standards of French academic art at the time.

William A. Bouguereau (1825–1905) was one of France's foremost artists and teachers. His paintings were exhibited in the Salon for fifty years. By the 1870s, he had become the director of the Salon. Since entries were juried, Bouguereau, as director, had considerable control over what was presented in the venerable exhibitions. Because of his stature as the leader of the academic style and his effective role as director of the Salon, Bouguereau would come to be condemned by the generation of young artists who identified with Impressionism.

An alternative to the dominant academic style began to be formed in the 1830s by the Barbizon school, a group of French landscape painters, notably Theodore Rousseau (1812–1867) and Narcisse Diaz de la Peña (1807–1876), who lived and painted in the village of Barbizon. They imbued their works with dark tones, an active brushstroke, and a dramatic sense of light, most often energizing their compositions with vivid end-of-the-day sky effects. The Barbizon style found a quick and willing group of followers in mid-nineteenth-century Europe and America, particularly among America's landscape painters.

Landscape painting is a time-honored tradition that is inseparable from the spirit of American art. Indeed, from Colonial times, American art had been governed by circumstances unique to our country. American art, unlike Europe's, was initially nurtured in the absence of empowered patronage, such as that of the monarchy or the church, both of which were important determinants in the progress of European art. In contrast, American artists displayed a penchant for showing the everyday character of American life. Such "democratic" tendencies encouraged the development of landscape painting as the ideal vehicle for expressing the American spirit and created a metaphor of the American landscape as the fountainhead from which sprang the bounty and opportunity of rustic American life. Moreover, landscape painting afforded an avenue to express God and Nature as one, an understanding of spirituality that disavowed official religious patronage. The art traditions that emerged in America in the nineteenth century reflected what was paramount to American society: its people and its land—the art was, for the most part, genre and landscape.

The tradition of American landscape painting matured in upstate New York. The Hudson River school, a group of early nineteenth-century artists led by Thomas Cole (1801–1848) and Asher B. Durand (1796–1886), ventured into what was then the "wilderness" of the Hudson River Valley. They were in awe of the beauty and grandeur of nature and developed a popular and long-lived style that centered on the landscape. At the same time, America produced a vigorous school of genre painters, most notably Winslow Homer (1836–1910), who specialized in directly painted scenes of everyday life in a country that, at the time, was characterized by farms and small towns.

In keeping with this factual and honest approach to art, the artist resolved to paint as realistically as possible. The desire for realistic portrayal of forms has been a crucial characteristic of American art. In this country, the search for truth in art expressed itself in a carefully observed and highly detailed manner associated with the artistic style called Realism.

Realism was a philosophical, literary, and artistic movement with the express goal of giving a truthful, objective, and impartial representation of the real world, based on meticulous observation of contemporary life. In painting, it is best illustrated by the French artists Gustave Courbet (1819–1877) and Jean François Millet (1814–1875) and later with the American master Thomas Eakins (1844–1916).

In France, Realism had a markedly social and political agenda. Its concern with nature was not so much as artistic subject matter, but rather the belief that people found salvation by re-establishing their connection to nature, specifically by returning to life on the farm. Coming in the mid-1800s, at the height of the Industrial Revolution, with its attendant mass urbanization, environmental pollution, and social transformations, Realism harked back to the idyllic life of the immediate past, to a time, real or imagined, when people were in harmony with nature and its bounty. It was a movement to democratize art, closely aligned with other midcentury demands for social and political democracy. Declaring that art must have relevance to contemporary society, the Realists refused to paint moralistic or heroic models from the past and instead directed their thoughts to portraying people and events in more commonplace circumstances and in their own time.

In America, artists of the mid-nineteenth century were keeping alive the tradition of realistic representation while, at the same time, scrutinizing all the influences from contemporary European art. In California, ever more artists were arriving to examine the aesthetic potential of this newly admitted state.

The Gold Rush attracted large numbers of people to San Francisco, including many artists. They came for a variety of reasons: to profit from the economic boom, to make a new start, or simply to paint the scenic beauty of California. Artists like Virgil Williams (1830–1886), William Keith (1839–1911), and Thomas Hill (1829–1908) were working in San Francisco as early as 1858. All three of these pivotal artists were trained in academic European styles and achieved maturity prior to the advent of Impressionism. They, and several other notable artists who painted landscapes in a Romantic-Realist style closely associated with the French Barbizon school, shaped the art of Northern California, and their students and followers continued in their style for many years. As such, they represented an entrenched artistic tradition that effectively inhibited the establishment of an Impressionist aesthetic in San Francisco until well after the turn of the twentieth century. In consequence, young artists looking to settle in California in the late nineteenth century turned south.

Thomas Hill. Courtesy of Jean Stern.

Much has been said about the desirability of the Southern California climate, with its generous number of sunny days, as being a factor in the advent of Impressionism in the south. Likewise, the southward migration caused by the San Francisco earthquake of April 1906 was significant. While both factors exerted considerable influence, the chief motivation was surely economic opportunity. Los Angeles, which at the time did not have a substantial artistic community, became the alternative metropolitan center that absorbed the infusion of young artists.

With the growth of its population during the early 1880s, Los Angeles began to attract professional artists. By the late 1880s, several artists were already permanent residents. Among the most prominent were John Gutzon Borglum (1867–1941) and his wife Elizabeth Putnam Borglum (1848–1922), Elmer Wachtel (1864–1929), and John Bond Francisco (1863–1931).

Gutzon Borglum trained in Los Angeles and San Francisco and painted large narrative works in the popular Tonalist-Barbizon style, which combined the visual poetry of Tonalism with the rustic statements of the Barbizon style. Borglum achieved a significant reputation depicting scenes of the history of California in the accepted western conventions of the day. One such series of his paintings dealt with stagecoaches. Borglum would later turn to sculpture and become best known for the monumental presidential portraits carved on Mount Rushmore.

His wife, Elizabeth Borglum, first came to Los Angeles in 1881. She was known as Elizabeth Jaynes Putnam or Mrs. J. W. Putnam before she married Borglum. Almost twenty years his senior, she was first his teacher and later married him, in 1889. She had studied art in San Francisco, in 1885 with William Keith and in 1887 with J. Foxcraft Cole (1837–1892), both of whom were practitioners of the Tonalist-Barbizon style, which she also adopted. She and Gutzon sketched throughout Southern California, painting landscapes, pastoral scenes, and views of the local missions before their separation in 1902.

Elmer Wachtel came to Southern California in 1882 to live with his older brother John, who was married to a sister of Guy Rose (1867–1925) and worked as manager of the Rose family ranch in San Gabriel, just east of Los Angeles. An aspiring violinist, Elmer Wachtel became first violin of the Philharmonic Orchestra in Los Angeles in 1888. In 1904, Elmer married Marion Kavanaugh, a young artist who had been referred to him by William Keith. Elmer Wachtel and Marion Kavanagh Wachtel (1876–1954) spent the next twenty-five years as inseparable painting companions, he working in oils and she in watercolor. They traveled throughout California, the deserts of Arizona and New Mexico, and in Mexico. It was during a painting trip to Guadalajara in 1929 that Elmer died. Both Elmer and Marion Wachtel shunned the many art organizations that developed in Los Angeles in the early 1900s. They were among the very few who declined to join the California Art Club, a stand that in no way affected the considerable esteem in which they were held by fellow artists.

Something of an artistic maverick, Elmer Wachtel's early paintings showed his strong affiliation with the Tonalist-Barbizon aesthetic of the San Francisco painters. These works were soft, poetic landscapes imbued with moody and dark tones. *Golden Autumn, Cajon Pass* (plate 9) is one of these elegant tonal works, in which the palette is dominated by the earth tones, with emphasis on shades of brown, green, and olive. As he progressed, Wachtel brightened his palette and made use of complementary pairs. Many of his mature works show a more decorative and lyrical style, very reminiscent of Arthur Mathews (1860–1945), the San Francisco landscape and figure painter who influenced a generation of Northern

Gutzon Borglum and Elizabeth Borglum sketching at the Old Mill, San Marino, c. 1895. This item is reproduced by permission of the Huntington Library, San Marino, California.

California painters (see following essay by Harvey L. Jones), although Wachtel rarely included figures in his compositions.

J. Bond Francisco arrived in Los Angeles in 1887. The son of a noted journalist who encouraged his children in the arts, Francisco's immediate love, as a child, was the violin. While a young man, he was sent to Berlin to study music and painting. He continued his studies in Paris and Munich. In 1880, the family came to Los Angeles, where his father took a position with the newly founded *Los Angeles Times*. J. Bond Francisco was in Los Angeles by 1892 as a professional artist in two fields: music and painting.

At first, Francisco earned his livelihood from music, as the young Los Angeles art community was devoid of sufficient patronage for his paintings. In 1897, he was one of the founders of the Los Angeles Symphony Orchestra, for which he was concertmaster. In 1899, he opened a music school and an art school. By 1900, he was the preeminent artist in Los Angeles. He found patronage with wealthy businessmen, and his works were purchased by local museums, business clubs, and private collectors. Francisco died in Los Angeles on January 8, 1931, at the age of 68. At the time of his death, many considered him the greatest artist who ever lived in Los Angeles.

By the early 1890s, Impressionism was no longer uniquely French. Artists who had been art students in Paris in the 1880s, who had seen firsthand what the style promised and had accepted the methods of Impressionism, were returning to their home countries. Originally the product of a small group of alienated French artists beginning in the late 1860s, Impressionism was proclaimed in Paris in a momentous exhibition in 1874. This exhibition included works by Paul Cézanne (1839–1906), Edgar Degas (1834–1917), Edouard Manet (1832–1883), Claude Monet (1840–1926), Camille Pissarro (1830–1903), Pierre Auguste Renoir (1841–1919), and the Englishman Alfred Sisley (1839–1899). These young artists pursued a perceptual, nonacademic, nonreligious, essentially naturalistic approach to art. Their art was founded on nature and on people.

Reacting strongly against the artistic tenets of the French Academy, the Impressionists lamented the lack of natural light and color that usually characterized an academic canvas, a consequence of finished paintings being produced exclusively in the studio and from posed models and based on sketches and underdrawings. They preferred instead to paint directly on primed canvas and to set the easel out-of-doors. Uniformly, they focused on light and atmospheric effects. They sought more relevance in subject matter, turning to everyday life for artistic motivation and aspiring to reflect people, usually the middle classes, as they were. Reluctant to pose a composition, Impressionists explored the fleeting moment or the "temporal fragment" of ordinary life.

The selection and placement of color is one of the profound contrasts between an Impressionist painting and an academic one. Impressionism produced paintings of bold color, and with it, more convincing effects of natural light. The revolution in color use was the outcome of several factors, notably the exploitation of newly published treatises on scientific investigations of color and light as well as the development of more vivid, chemically stable pigments.

The most popular color theorist of the day was Eugene Chevreul (1786–1889), a consulting chemist in a tapestry factory. Charged with the responsibility of developing more vivid dyes, he deduced that the role of the chemist was not as consequential as the role of the artist, and that more brilliance could be attained by proper color placement than by stronger dyes. He published these findings and others in France in 1839 as *Laws of Simultaneous Contrast of Colors*. His most significant conclusions were adopted by the young Impressionist painters, including many of his findings on the role of complementary colors, that is to say, colors that are opposite each other on the color wheel. Chevreul noted that the greater the difference between two colors, the more they will enhance each other when placed side by side, and inversely, the less the difference, the more they will tend to dull each another. He stated that apparent intensity of a particular color does not depend so much on the inherent pigmentation as it does on the hue of the adjacent color.

The advent of Impressionism in France was greeted with scorn and belligerent criticism. It was regarded by most art writers as an insult to the exhibition-viewing public. The Impressionists' penchant for breaking forms into small bits of color was particularly irritating to viewers who were accustomed to very tightly drawn, highly naturalistic forms and figures. The paintings did not appeal to popular taste. Because the artist worked quickly to capture the fleeting light effect, the completed work had a rude and unfinished appearance, especially when compared to the highly polished surface of an academic painting (see figure 1). The strong and often intense color scheme offended those accustomed to subtle tones. Moreover, Impressionism's preference for contemporary urban genre endowed it with references to social activism and political radicalism. Many of the subjects, such as ordinary people eating lunch or walking about the boulevards, were considered base and unworthy of attention as fine art.

By contrast, the introduction of Impressionism in the United States, in the mid-1880s, was received with much less hostility. The decade intervening between its introduction in Paris and in America had allowed much of the hostility to dissipate. Many of America's leading artists had been students in Paris in the early 1870s. As students, they sought out the innovative and avant-garde fashion and were captivated by what they saw. When they returned home as professional artists, they promoted and championed Impressionism. Moreover, given America's artistic traditions of genre and landscape that developed during the nineteenth century, what was intimidating and unfamiliar to the French audience was looked upon with interest and curiosity by Americans.

The first exhibition of French Impressionist paintings in America was held in Boston in 1883, a display sent by the Paris art dealer and great champion of Impressionism, Paul Durand-Ruel. The show consisted of works by Monet, Pissarro, Sisley, and others. A second, significantly larger exhibition organized by Durand-Ruel was staged in New York in 1886. It served to confirm the movement's great popularity in America. That show displayed not only recent works by the French Impressionists, but also a good number of Impressionist paintings owned by important American collectors. The World's Columbian Exposition in Chicago in 1893 signaled the almost total critical acceptance of Impressionism in America, with a number of exhibition halls and a large selection of Impressionist paintings, by American artists as well as painters from France and other European countries.

In the United States, Impressionism was readily adopted by an entire generation of painters in the late 1890s. However, unlike their French counterparts, American artists generally avoided the sociopolitical aspects of the style. The French Impressionists' penchant for urban settings was championed by only a few Americans. The American preference for rustic genre or landscape subjects was continued with vigor by the American Impressionists. French Impressionism is often characterized by dissolved forms, in which visual elements of the painting seem to soften away into the background in a maze of lively brushstrokes and color daubs. By contrast, American Impressionism retains a solid sense of form, in keeping with its tradition of directness.

Mary Cassatt (1844–1926) was one of the first American painters to be associated with Impressionism. In fact, she was a fully accepted member of the French group and participated in their later exhibitions. Her paintings of mothers and children were very popular and went a long way in promoting the new style. Theodore Robinson (1852–1896) lived a great part of his short life in France, and he was one of the first American artists to return to the United States espousing Impressionism. In 1898, the Ten American Painters was formed in New York City. The Ten was a group of professional Impressionist artists who organized to exhibit and sell their paintings. Among the better-known members of The Ten were Frank W. Benson (1862-–1951), William Merritt Chase (1849–1916), Childe Hassam (1859–1935), Edmund Tarbell (1862–1938), and J. Alden Weir (1852–1919), all of whom were influential among artists and tastemakers.

By 1900, Impressionism was the style of choice among American painters. Clearly, it was a modified and toned-down rendering of the prototype French movement. The significant contributions of French Impressionism to American art were in the use of color and adoption of the distinct brushwork. The scientific theories of color, as advanced by Chevreul, were well received by Americans, and the outcome showed in paintings with brilliant and convincing effects of natural light. The loose, choppy brushstroke characteristic of an Impressionist work was the consequence both of the quick manner of paint application and the desire to produce a brilliant surface covered with a multitude of small daubs of bright color. When one considers the resolute sense of Realism that prevailed in American art, then perhaps the American experience with Impressionism would best be described as "Impressionistic Realism."

The Panama-Pacific International Exposition of 1915, in San Francisco, was both the last great Impressionist show in America and the first major Impressionist exhibition in California. The exposition brought to California the major figures of American Impressionism. William Merritt Chase, Childe Hassam, Edmund Tarbell, and Edward Redfield (1869–1965), among others, were given individual galleries to hang their works. The Grand Prize of the Exposition went to Frederick Frieseke, a friend and neighbor of Californian Guy Rose in Giverny, and the Medal of Honor to Willard Metcalf (1858–1925), a consummate Impressionist. The Panama-Pacific Exposition was a tremendous success with California's Impressionist artists.

Nineteen-fifteen also marks the beginning of San Diego's professional artist community. In competition with San Francisco, San Diego, too, also marked the opening of the Panama Canal with an exposition, the Panama-California Exposition, held in the newly constructed Balboa Park. Only one exposition in any given year could use the designation "International," however, and San Francisco's bid for the title was successful in 1915. Both expositions were extended for the following year, which created a rich source of confusion for scholars and trivia aficionados: in 1916, the "International" designation was awarded to San Diego and the 1916 appellations were "Panama-Pacific Exposition" for San Francisco, and "Panama-California International Exposition" for San Diego.

Among California's myriad painters landscape was by far the most popular subject. Where the French Impressionists yearned to capture the immediate moment, or the temporal fragment of social activity, California's Impressionists sought to catch a fleeting moment of specific natural light, as it bathed the landscape. The clear and intense light of California, which appears so often in these paintings, defined the landscape. The biblical analogy of light as the creative instrument is appropriate to the California landscape and the way artists addressed it, for without that unique light, and the divine energy it represented, the land would not exist. Thus, the goal was to capture this striking visual sensation on canvas quickly, before the light changed. The key to achieving this goal was to get out of the studio and to paint outdoors, or *en plein air,* and to accentuate the role of color to produce brilliant light effects.

One of the first Impressionist painters in California, Benjamin C. Brown (1865–1942) came to Los Angeles to visit and sketch as early as 1886, and he settled as a permanent resident in 1896. After finding few patrons for his portraits, Brown turned to painting landscapes in a daring, vigorously Impressionistic style. Brown was active with many of the developing art societies in Southern California, and as an etcher, along with his brother Howell, founded the Print Makers Society of California, which sponsored annual international print exhibitions for many years.

Brown's *The Joyous Garden* (plate 24) reveals one of the attractions to the host of painters who came to Southern California: the lavish, flower-filled gardens. To more than a few eastern artists, the discovery of California's luxuriant flora was noted with great interest and anticipation. *The Joyous Garden* is set in front of a house in Pasadena, where Brown lived. Far from being a still-life of cut flowers, the painting shows a "rabbit's-eye" view of living, growing mounds of red and white stock in the afternoon sun.

An avid Impressionist, Brown was outspoken in his criticism of other styles of art. He had patrons in California as well as in the East. Hoping to encourage more sales, one New York dealer suggested that Brown open a studio there and, to spur interest in his paintings, conceal the fact that he was from California. Brown angrily refused and thereafter defiantly added the word "California" beneath his signature.

The Los Angeles art community prior to the turn of the century could be characterized as an informal circle of artists who were also friends. They frequently socialized at one another's studios and on occasion painted together. With the coming of the new century, and the significant increase in the number of artists who chose to live in Southern California, a number of clubs and associations were formed. The most important and longest-lived of these is the California Art Club. Formed in late 1909, it held its first exhibition in January of 1911. The California Art Club brought together the leading artists of Southern California and afforded them a venue for

Benjamin Brown painting *en plein air* near Pasadena, c. 1925. Courtesy of The Redfern Gallery, Laguna Beach.

A group of artists in Laguna Beach, c. 1918. Included are Guy Rose (center), Maurice Braun (standing, second from right), and Donna Schuster (seated in front, second from right). Courtesy of Charlotte Braun and the estate of Maurice Braun.

public exhibition and sales as well as a forum for discussion and the exchange of ideas. The founding president of the Club was Frank R. Liddell, a businessman who painted in his spare time. After a year of administrative start-up, the Club rapidly became active when William Wendt (1865–1946) was elected its second president in 1911. Wendt's tremendous prestige among his fellow artists and his great organizational skills allowed him to carry out important programs. Wendt astutely sent several of the Club's annual exhibitions to San Francisco, thus making the club's presence known to a larger audience and garnering wider prestige. Within a few years, the Club's membership included nearly every professional artist in Southern California and even boasted many out-of-state artists as members. The California Art Club is still active today. Its president is Peter Adams, and its large membership includes many of the best-known of today's plein-air painters.

With the turn of the century, Los Angeles experienced a sudden influx of Impressionist painters, among them several of the important artists who later would define the California plein-air style: Granville Redmond (1871–1935), Hanson Puthuff (1875–1972), Marion Kavanagh Wachtel (1876–1954), William Wendt, Franz A. Bischoff (1864–1929), Jack Wilkinson Smith (1873–1949), Jean Mannheim (1863–1945), and Maurice Braun (1877–1941). In addition, Edgar Payne (1883–1947) and his wife Elsie Palmer Payne (1884–1971) were making frequent visits to Los Angeles and Laguna Beach, and, with the arrival of Donna Schuster (1883–1953) in 1913 and the return of Guy Rose the following year, the stage was set for one of the most remarkable and distinctive schools of regional American art.

Granville Redmond contracted scarlet fever at the age of two and a half, an illness that left him permanently deaf. He never learned to speak and communicated by writing notes or using sign language. In 1874, his family left Philadelphia and came to Northern California, and in 1879 Redmond enrolled in the Institution for the Deaf, Dumb, and Blind at Berkeley (now the California School for the Deaf, in Fremont.) An excellent student, Redmond received a stipend from the school and in 1893 went to Paris, where he enrolled in the Académie Julian. After five years in France, he returned to California and opened a studio in Los Angeles. In 1908, he relocated to Northern California and soon earned the reputation of one of San Francisco's leading painters. In 1917, Redmond returned to Los Angeles, this time with the intent of auditioning for the movies. He felt that his natural skills as a pantomimist would make him an ideal actor, as all movies at the time were silent. Charlie Chaplin gave him an audition, and the two became good friends. Chaplin cast Redmond in several small roles in his productions, but more intuitively, he gave Redmond space on his movie lot to set up a painting studio.

Granville Redmond with Charlie Chaplin, c. 1918. Redmond was deaf and mute, and this photograph shows Chaplin communicating by finger-spelling words to Redmond. Courtesy of Mildred Albronda.

Redmond's patrons loved his cheerful paintings of rolling hills covered with golden poppies and other wild flowers, such as *California Landscape with Flowers* (plate 12) Yet Redmond, who suffered from long periods of recurring depression, preferred to paint in a moody, introspective style, using the dark tonalities of the Northern California aesthetic of his early art training. *Nocturne* (plate 11) is a night scene painted in tones of blue. The title of the painting recalls James McNeill Whistler (1834–1903), who used the term for many of his night scenes. Furthermore, the extensive use of blue to represent moonlight may be in reference to the work of Redmond's contemporary, Frank Tenney Johnson (1874–1939). Johnson, a painter of the American West, earned widespread fame with his blue-moonlight painting technique for night scenes of the Navajos in Arizona and New Mexico.

The practice of moonlight painting in America is a long and rich one. Washington Allston (1779–1843), Albert Pinkham Ryder (1847–1917), and Ralph A. Blakelock (1847–1919) were fond of setting their subjects at night. In the early nineteenth century, a moonlight scene was painted according to the same canons as a daylight landscape, either as a dimly lit day scene or a very dark landscape illuminated by a spectacular moon. As in a day scene, where shadow signifies the absence of light, a night scene was shrouded in shadow, often so dark that detail was barely perceptible. It is an interesting irony that the art of painting, in essence the representation of light and its effect on various objects and surfaces, would, in a night scene, be faced with the task of depicting the absence of light.

Just as painting the sunlit landscape was revolutionized in the 1860s by the Impressionist method, so was painting the moonlit scene. The realization that a convincing effect of dim light could be depicted without sacrificing clarity changed the initial appearance of the night scene from a dark, obscure painting to that of a clear, "bright" night painting, usually bathed in blue moonlight. The use of blue to represent night illumination found widespread acceptance. Claude Monet, who was severely criticized for his liberal use of blue in his shadows, painted many completely blue night scenes. Other Impressionists followed suit, and Vincent van Gogh's *Starry Night,* with its vivid blue sky, may well be the most-popular and best-known Impressionistic night scene.

In 1903, Hanson Puthuff came to Los Angeles from Denver, where he had attended the University of Denver Art School. He found employment designing posters and painting billboards for an advertising firm. He also began to paint easel works, which he first exhibited in 1905. *Los Angeles Times* art critic Antony Anderson reviewed the show favorably, and the two men became friends. Together they founded the Art Students League in Los Angeles. As

The William Merritt Chase School, New York, 1897. Chase is standing in the center, front row, wearing a boutonniere. Alson S. Clark is standing in the back row, second from left, wearing a bow tie. Courtesy of Carol Clark and the estate of Alson S. Clark.

was all too common with artists in Los Angeles in the early 1900s, Puthuff could not earn a living solely from the sale of his paintings and he relied on commercial work to make ends meet. Over the years, his growing success as an artist allowed him more and more time to paint easel works, and by 1926 he finally gave up his commercial career in order to concentrate all his time on fine art.

Many of Puthuff's works depict the environs near his home in La Crescenta and the San Gabriel Valley. A congenial companion, he would often go with fellow artists on paintings trips to the Owens Valley and into the Sierra Nevada Mountains, or on extended trips to Mexico. *Monarch of the Malibu* (plate 6) is set in what was then the small coastal community of Malibu, about twenty miles north of Los Angeles. Originally an ancient Chumash Indian village, Malibu became, in the early 1800s, part of a large Spanish land grant, and in the first part of the twentieth century, a small fishing village that catered to weekenders from Los Angeles.

Marion Kavanagh Wachtel came to Los Angeles in 1903. She had studied at the Art Institute of Chicago and in New York with William Merritt Chase. After a few years of teaching at the Art Institute of Chicago, she traveled to San Francisco to study with William Keith, who encouraged her to go to Los Angeles to meet Elmer Wachtel. They were married in 1904, in Chicago, and became inseparable painting companions, traveling throughout Southern California, the Southwest, and Mexico.

Marion Wachtel worked primarily in watercolor. She received high praise for her works, which are delicate, lyrical interpretations of the landscape, in a manner that shows her masterly control of tone and color. In many of her paintings, like *Landscape with Oak Trees* (plate 10), pastel is used to highlight her compositions. She was admitted to the New York Water Color Club in 1911, was elected an associate of the American Water Color Society in 1912, and was a founding member of the California Water Color Society in 1921.

William Wendt (1865–1946)

FIGURE 2
I Lifted Mine Eyes Unto the Hills
Oil on canvas, 36 x 50 inches
The Fleischer Museum, Scottsdale, Arizona

FIGURE 3
Serenity, 1934
Oil on canvas, 30 x 36 inches
Collection of Paul and Kathleen Bagley

William Wendt was born in Germany and came to the United States in 1880. From his base in Chicago, Wendt visited California on several occasions, between 1896 and 1904, with his friend Gardner Symons. In 1906, Wendt and his wife, the sculptor Julia Bracken Wendt, settled in Los Angeles. A well-respected and successful painter, he became a leading member in the young Los Angeles art community and was a founding member of the California Art Club in 1909. He moved his home and studio to the art colony at Laguna Beach in 1912, the same year that he was elected to the National Academy of Design. Wendt was Laguna's most important resident artist-teacher.

Many of Wendt's works bear elegant titles drawn from epic poetry or biblical passages. One majestic view of Laguna Canyon is entitled *There Is No Solitude, Even in Nature* (plate 55) His 1922 Spalding Prize–winner (offered by the Art Institute of Chicago) is called *I Lifted Mine Eyes Unto the Hills* (figure 2), a title drawn from Psalm 121.

Wendt worked out-of-doors, often painting large, finished works there. Only rarely did he include people or animals in his landscapes. In his mature works, after about 1912, such as *The Silent Summer Sea,* dated 1915 (plate 2), he employed a distinctive block-like brushwork, giving solidity to his renditions of natural forms. A prolific painter, he was known as the dean of Southern California's landscape painters. To Wendt, nature was a manifestation of God, and he viewed himself as nature's faithful interpreter, yet his works never show any outward sign of religious zeal (figure 3). Wendt's spirituality was universal and visible to all who viewed his paintings.

William Wendt painting outdoors. Courtesy of De Rus Fine Arts, Laguna Beach.

Franz A. Bischoff (1864–1929)

FIGURE 4
Roses
Painted porcelain vase, 17¾ inches high
The Irvine Museum

FIGURE 5
Cambria, A Peaceful California Village, 1927
Oil on canvas, 24 x 30 inches
Collection of Mr. and Mrs. Thomas B. Stiles II

Franz Bischoff was born in Austria and trained as an artist in Vienna. He specialized in porcelain decoration (figure 4). In 1885 he immigrated to the United States and lived in Dearborn, Michigan, eventually becoming one of the foremost porcelain painters of his day. He formulated and manufactured many of his own porcelain colors, participated in exhibitions, and won many awards. Flowers were his favorite subject, and he was called the "king of the rose painters."

He first visited California in 1900 and hoped to live in San Francisco, but after the earthquake there in 1906, he settled in Los Angeles instead. In 1908 Bischoff built a studio-home along the Arroyo Seco in South Pasadena, with a gallery, ceramic workshop, and painting studio. After moving to California, Bischoff turned to landscape painting in addition to continuing his flower paintings and his porcelain work. Through the 1920s, he painted the coastal areas of Monterey and Laguna Beach, the Sierra Nevada Mountains, and the desert near Palm Springs. In that period, he visited the charming central coast community of Cambria, where he painted many views of the village. *Cambria, A Peaceful California Village* (figure 5), painted in 1927, draws the viewer into the idyllic lifestyle of this little farming and dairy hamlet.

Bischoff often featured flowers in his paintings. *San Juan Capistrano Mission Yard* (plate 31) is enlivened by the masses of hollyhocks and water lilies that graced the historic old Mission in the spring. Although the subject here is the Mission, the painting is nonetheless a flower study.

Jack Wilkinson Smith began his art career working as a "paint boy" in a Chicago outdoor advertising company painting shop, where he met Gardner Symons. In his spare time, Smith took classes at the Art Institute of Chicago, and he was influenced by the work of his friend and painting companion William Wendt. In 1906 Smith visited California, which he called "nature's own paradise of scenic splendor and variety." He established a studio-home in Alhambra, a suburb of Los Angeles.

Smith was best known for his seascapes and Sierra Nevada Mountains views. He was adept at creating the effect of moving water, and his scenes of crashing surf were particularly popular. *Crystal Cove State Park* (plate 18) depicts the coast at Laguna Beach. The majestic space is dominated by the brilliance of the rhythmic water. Smith captures the shimmering of the ocean, in the cool foreground shade as well as the bright middle ground and background.

The German-born Jean Mannheim studied in Paris at the Académie Delecluse, the Académie Colarossi, and the Académie Julian. In 1881 he came to the United States and resided with his sister in Chicago, where he earned a living as a portrait painter. Around

Franz A. Bischoff in his studio, Dearborn, Michigan, c. 1900.
Courtesy of Ed and Jacqueline Peabody.

1903, Mannheim went to London to teach at the Brangwyn School of Art, operated by Frank Brangwyn (1867–1956). He returned to the United States two years later and moved to Los Angeles in 1908, where he opened his own school.

Mannheim's work comprises exceptional portraits and figural paintings, some of which reflect his rigorous academic training. He also painted landscapes in a rich, painterly style, chronicling his many trips throughout California. One of the founders of the Laguna Beach Art Association, in 1918, Mannheim often painted in that scenic coastal community. *Arch Beach, Laguna Beach* (plate 22) represents one of the picturesque coves just south of Laguna. The painting shows Mannheim's bold brushstroke and his use of gentle, almost tonal color.

Maurice Braun was born in Hungary and immigrated to the United States with his family when he was four years of age. His artistic training included classes at the School of the National Academy of Design and a year with William Merritt Chase. He earned

a reputation as a figure and portrait painter in New York. However, Braun's interest in landscape painting led him to move to California. In 1910 he opened a studio on Point Loma, the peninsula that juts out to form San Diego Bay. In 1912, he founded the San Diego Academy of Art and became that city's most important art teacher. Braun re-established his studio in New York City in 1921. He also opened studios in Silvermine and Old Lyme, Connecticut. After a few years he returned to San Diego, but continued from 1924 to 1929 to spend part of each year in the East. In 1929 he joined nine other artists in forming the Contemporary Artists of San Diego.

Braun was affiliated with the Theosophical Society, and Theosophy had a profound influence on his art. His paintings were expressions of nature's moods, rather than purely descriptions of the landscape. Perhaps the best explanation of Maurice Braun's art can be found in a review of a memorial exhibition in 1954. The art critic John Fabian Kienitz wrote: "Maurice Braun was an artist of deep philosophical conviction for whom all expressions of life were divine. So it is natural that in the look and feel of his work you should find pastoral peace. This peace is born of his sense of wholeness. Through an interplay of religious respect and aesthetic resolve he found equilibrium and this was for him, as it can be for us, the secret of life itself."

Edgar Payne was essentially a self-taught artist. He traveled for a number of years throughout the South, the Midwest, and in Mexico, taking various jobs as a house painter, sign painter, scenic painter, and portrait and mural artist. He settled in 1907 in Chicago, where he enrolled in a portraiture class at the Art Institute but left after only two weeks. Payne visited California in 1909 and was captivated by the beauty of Laguna Beach. Later that year, he visited San Francisco, where he met his future wife, the artist Elsie Palmer. He returned to California in 1911, painting again in Laguna Beach. For several years afterward, the couple made annual trips to California. *Sycamore in Autumn, Orange County Park* (plate 8) was painted on a visit to Laguna Beach in 1916. Orange County Park is

Edgar Payne in his Paris studio, c. 1922. Courtesy of Evelyn Payne Hatcher and the estates of Edgar A. Payne and Elsie Palmer Payne.

now called Irvine Park; originally part of the sprawling Irvine Ranch, this beautifully forested 160-acre park was given by James Irvine to the people of Orange County in 1897.

In the summer of 1917 Payne rented an abandoned factory in Glendale, California, to execute a major mural commission for the Congress Hotel in Chicago. After he completed the project, he and his wife settled in Laguna Beach. Payne became active in the art colony there and was a founding member and first president of the Laguna Beach Art Association in 1918. The Paynes traveled throughout California, Arizona, and New Mexico, as well as in Canada. However, Edgar Payne's favorite painting locales were in the Sierra Nevada Mountains. *The Sierra Divide* (plate 7) is one of his best-known scenes of that region. Painted in 1921, just before his momentous trip to Europe, *The Sierra Divide* reveals the distinctive penchant of California Impressionists for the instantaneous moment of light. One looks at this painting and knows precisely the time of day and atmospheric conditions. An alpine lake high in these mountains, Payne Lake, is named in his honor.

In the summer of 1922, the Paynes went to Europe for two years, painting in France, Switzerland, and Italy. Edgar Payne's paintings of the Alps, particularly Mont Blanc, were well received in the United States. One of these, *The Great White Peak* (Newport Harbor High School collection), received an Honorable Mention at the Paris Salon in the spring of 1923.

Donna Schuster was an honor student at the Art Institute of Chicago, and later studied with Edmund C. Tarbell and Frank W. Benson at the Boston Museum of Fine Arts school. She was in Belgium in 1912 with William Merritt Chase and won the William Merritt Chase Prize. Schuster moved to Los Angeles in 1913. In 1923 she built a studio-home in the hills of Griffith Park, above Hollywood, and spent her summers at a second studio-home in Laguna Beach. In 1928 she began a friendship and course of study with Stanton MacDonald-Wright (1890–1973) who, along with Morgan Russell (1886–1953), devised Synchromism, a disciplined approach to painting that created rhythmic movement and emotional content solely through the use of color (see figure 6). Schuster's contact with MacDonald-Wright greatly influenced her work. A restless artist, she also explored Cubism and Expressionism.

FIGURE 6
Stanton MacDonald-Wright (1890–1973)
Untitled (still life), c. 1924
Oil on canvas, 23 x 17 inches
George Stern Fine Arts, Los Angeles

Guy Rose was the only one of the early plein-air artists to be born in Southern California. In 1861, his father, L. J. Rose, had led a wagon train to California and established Sunny Slope, a large and successful ranch in the San Gabriel Valley, where Guy was born in 1867. As a child, he was a prodigious artist. In 1886 and 1887, he attended the California School of Design in San Francisco, studying under Virgil Williams and Emil Carlsen (1853–1932). In 1888 Rose went to Paris and enrolled in the Académie Julian. He was an accomplished student who soon had his paintings accepted for the Paris Salon.

In 1894 Rose underwent a serious episode of lead poisoning, which forced him to avoid oil painting for about eight years. He returned to the United States in the winter of 1895 and concentrated on a career as an illustrator, which enabled him to work instead with pen and ink and watercolor. At the same time, he taught drawing and portraiture at Pratt Institute in Brooklyn. In 1899 he returned to Paris, where he continued to do illustration work for *Harper's Bazaar* and other American magazines.

Rose was greatly influenced by Claude Monet, and in 1904 he and his wife Ethel bought a cottage in Giverny, where other artists had gathered around Monet (see figure 7). He practiced a serial style of painting like that of Monet, depicting the same scene in different seasons or at different times of day. In Giverny, he associated with American artists Richard Miller (1875–1943), Lawton Parker (1868–1939), and Frederick Frieseke (1874–1939), and the four of them exhibited in New York in 1910 as "the Giverny group."

Rose returned permanently to the United States in 1912 and stayed for a time in New York. He arrived in Pasadena at the end of 1914 and became active in local art circles, serving for several years on the board of trustees of the Los Angeles Museum of History, Science, and Art. He became the director of the Stickney Memorial School of Fine Arts in Pasadena and invited Richard Miller to teach there in 1916.

From his home in Pasadena, Rose began exploring California as an Impressionist subject. In 1916 and 1917, he concentrated on the southern part, with trips to Laguna Beach, La Jolla, and the desert near Palm Springs. One of his first trips was to the seaside village of La Jolla, just north of San Diego. *Indian Tobacco Trees, La Jolla* (plate 58) was painted at the cliffs overlooking La Jolla Cove. On the same trip, Rose painted in Laguna Beach. *Laguna Eucalyptus* (plate 17) is his tour-de-force rendition of those graceful trees. An Australian import, the fast-growing and elegant trees have come to be associated with California plein-air painting. *Laguna Eucalyptus* is an homage to Emil Carlsen, Rose's teacher in San Francisco, whose landscapes manifest an almost surrealistic sense of space. When one compares the plein-air study (*Windswept Trees, Laguna;* frontispiece in *Guy Rose, American Impressionist*) with this version, the differences are striking. The larger, final canvas was painted in the studio, and is a moody, introspective work of great authority. By contrast, the study is a vivid evocation of light, a purely Impressionist painting, owing much to Claude Monet, the leading influence in Rose's style.

Incoming Tide (plate 49) was painted at Rockledge, a cove in Laguna Beach. It is one of at least five versions of this specific scene that Rose painted on his visit (see *Guy Rose, American Impressionist,* p. 130, for another version.) Each one shows the cove in slightly different light and from barely differing vantage points. In the summer of 1918, Rose made the first of many trips to Carmel and

Monterey. *Point Lobos* (plate 56) is the companion piece to *Mist over Point Lobos* (figure 8). Rose painted the latter before the morning mist dissipated, then moved his easel to a slightly different site and painted the former, a sun-filled painting.

Rose is generally regarded as California's foremost Impressionist, and was held in the highest esteem by his peers and patrons. He was disabled by a stroke in 1921, which left him unable to paint during the four years prior to his death in 1925.

Alson S. Clark (1876–1949) studied at the Art Institute of Chicago for one term in 1895. Dissatisfied, he left for New York and he enrolled in the newly formed school of William Merritt Chase. In 1898, Clark went to Paris to continue his studies at the Académie Carmen, the atelier of James McNeill Whistler, and later at the Académie Delecluse. In 1901 his painting *The Violinist* was accepted at the Paris Salon.

Clark returned to the United States and early in 1902 opened a studio in Watertown, New York. In the fall of 1902 he was back in Paris with his new bride, Medora. For several years Clark and his wife divided their time between France and the United States. In October and November of 1910, they visited Giverny, where they stayed with Lawton Parker, an old classmate. In Giverny, Clark met Frederick Frieseke and Guy Rose, who were living there at the time.

A seasoned wayfarer, Clark traveled throughout Europe and the United States. In 1913 he visited Panama to undertake the project of recording on canvas the construction of the Panama Canal. Eighteen of those paintings were later exhibited at the Panama-Pacific International Exposition in 1915, earning him a Bronze Medal. The Clarks were in France until the outbreak of World War I, at which time they returned to Chicago. In April 1917, Clark enlisted in the Navy and was sent to France as an aerial photographer. For most of the war, he flew in an open cockpit, and when the time

Alson S. Clark in his studio, Watertown, New York, c. 1902.

Alson S. Clark on a painting trip near Lone Pine, California, 1921. Photographs courtesy of Carol Clark and the estate of Alson S. Clark.

came to take his photographs, he would lean over the side of the airplane and snap pictures of the battlefield far below. After the war, health problems caused by the numbing cold and dampness of his duty obliged him to recuperate in California, where he went in 1919. While in Los Angeles, Clark inquired about interesting places to paint and was told of the California missions. He painted several small sketches of Mission San Gabriel, near Los Angeles, and then proceeded south to Mission San Juan Capistrano, the most picturesque of them all.

The Mission San Juan Capistrano was founded in 1776, by Father Junípero Serra. It was originally part of the chain of twenty-one settlements that marked El Camino Real, the King's Highway. It is the most romantic and the most tragic of the California missions. In December 1812, a violent earthquake destroyed the newly built stone church, killing forty people who were attending Mass. The church was never rebuilt and the ruins became part of California's heroic past. When Alson Clark visited the mission in 1919, he was moved by the appearance of the stone remains and painted *Ruins of the Chapel, San Juan Capistrano* (plate 30), showing the intense, crisp California light reflecting off the austere mission walls.

The Clarks decided to live in California, and in January of 1920 they built a house and studio along the Arroyo Seco in Pasadena. Alson Clark renewed his acquaintance with Guy Rose, who had returned to California in 1914. Attracted to the southwest landscape, Clark made numerous painting trips throughout California and in Mexico. In 1924, Clark spent the summer in La Jolla, outside of San Diego. *The Weekend, Mission Beach* (plate 16) is from a series he painted along the coast between San Diego and La Jolla. It is compositionally reminiscent of works by William Merritt Chase, one of his teachers; the low horizon compels the viewer to contemplate the vastness of the blue San Diego sky. Clark remained active in Pasadena's dynamic artistic community, painting murals, designing programs for the Tournament of Roses, and decorating the Pasadena Playhouse. He suffered a stroke in his studio in 1949 and died a week later.

Sam Hyde Harris (1889–1977) was born in England and came to the United States with his family in 1904, settling in Los Angeles. A full-time commercial artist, Harris studied in the evenings at the Art Students League and at the Cannon Art School with F. Tolles Chamberlin (1873–1961), Stanton MacDonald-Wright, and Hanson Puthuff. In 1913 he returned to England, where he assimilated the works of the great English masters of light and atmosphere, John Constable and Joseph Turner.

Back in Los Angeles, Harris returned to his commercial art career. He worked at Union Station, in downtown Los Angeles, designing advertisements and posters for the Southern Pacific, Union Pacific, and Santa Fe railroads. All the while, on weekends, he continued to paint elegant, light-filled studies of farms and vistas in the San Gabriel Valley. During the 1920s he studied privately with Puthuff, taking painting trips with him to the deserts of California and Arizona. Whereas most of his contemporaries only painted the elegant landscape of Southern California, Harris often turned to the urban settings of Los Angeles and its suburbs. He was fascinated by the passage of time, as evidenced by dilapidated and abandoned buildings, which he painted as heroic figures that had served their purpose and were then left to decay. In the 1930s he lived in Sunset Beach, a coastal village about thirty miles south of Los Angeles. In the mornings, he would take the Pacific Electric railcar from his home in Sunset Beach to the Los Angeles train station and arrive in less than an hour, a feat that would be hard to duplicate on today's freeways. Harris painted the beach community in Sunset Beach as well as harbor scenes in San Pedro and Newport Beach.

Todd Shipyards, San Pedro (plate 28) shows Harris's love of the relics of urban growth. From the battered remains of an old dock, we look across the tainted waters of Los Angeles Harbor toward an impressive, modern ship-building plant. The painting demonstrates the conflict between old and new: the decaying wooden dock that once received countless sailing ships of the past against the dynamic plant, turning out steamships and freighters. Between the two stands the lifeless, polluted water of the modern harbor.

The Philadelphia-born Colin Campbell Cooper (1856–1937) attended the Pennsylvania Academy of the Fine Arts and continued his studies in Europe, first painting in Holland and Belgium before moving on to Paris. In Paris he studied at the Académie Julian, the Académie Delecluse, and the Académie Viti. In 1895, Cooper returned to the United States and taught watercolor painting at the Drexel Institute in Philadelphia for three years. An inveterate traveler, he returned to Europe in 1898, painting in Holland, Italy, and Spain, and developing a reputation as a painter of the architectural treasures of Europe. Back in the United States in 1902, he painted impressionist cityscapes of New York, Philadelphia, and Chicago.

In 1915, Cooper was in San Francisco to attend the Panama-Pacific International Exposition. Unable to resist depicting the architectural marvels of the Exposition, Cooper painted several views (figure 9). He spent the winter in Los Angeles, and in the spring of 1916 visited San Diego to paint and tour the Panama-California International Exposition. In January of 1921 he moved to Santa Barbara. Cooper explored his new surroundings and painted freely around the little village. *Pergola at Samarkand Hotel, Santa Barbara* (plate 25) is rich with light and color, in keeping with the sunny atmosphere of its locale. The Samarkand was a popular tourist hotel that was converted to a hospital during World War II and is now a retirement home. Cooper was elected an Associate of the National Academy of Design in 1902 and gained Academician status in 1912. He was also a member of numerous artists' associations and clubs in New York and Southern California.

Frank Cuprien (1871–1946) is the best known of a large number of seascape artists in Laguna Beach. He was among the first of that art colony to focus on the sea, having taken the noted marine painter William Trost Richards (1833–1905) as his guiding spirit. Before coming to Laguna Beach in 1914, Cuprien had trained for several years in Europe, studying both painting and music, and then settled in Florida and painted along the Gulf of Mexico. Around 1912 he moved to California, living first in Santa Monica and then on Catalina Island. He was one of the leading artists of the Laguna community and helped to found the Laguna Beach Art Association in 1918, serving as president 1921–22. His paintings of the sea, in all its various moods, consistently earned the popular prize in the Laguna Beach Art Association exhibitions during the 1920s and 1930s.

Frank Cuprien. Courtesy of The Irvine Museum.

FIGURE 9

Colin Campbell Cooper (1856–1937)

Panama-Pacific International Exposition, 1915

Oil on canvas, 20 x 26 inches

Collection of Paul and Kathleen Bagley

John Frost (1890–1937) was born into a family of artists; his father was Arthur B. Frost, Sr. (1851–1928), a well-known American illustrator. When John was still a child, the family moved to Paris, and John and his older brother, Arthur B. Frost, Jr., took classes at the Académie Julian. John also studied with Richard Miller in Paris from 1906 to 1908. The two artists remained friends and Frost often visited Miller's home in Giverny. During their time in Europe, both John and Arthur Jr. contracted tuberculosis, a disease that eventually proved fatal to both. Because he spent several years in sanitariums for the treatment of his tuberculosis, Frost's paintings are scarce. After the family moved to Pasadena in 1919, he spent much time in the desert, near Palm Springs.

Guy Rose was a lifelong painting and fishing companion of Arthur Frost, Sr., and Rose, who must have seemed like an uncle to the Frost children, exerted a strong influence on John. There are great similarities between their styles. *The Flowering Desert* (plate 15) of 1922 is one of Frost's Palm Springs paintings. The snow on the distant mountains and the flowering verbena place this painting in March or April, just after the winter rains. *The Pool at Sundown* (plate 57) is set along the Owens River, the valley of which marks the upper reaches of the Mojave Desert, along the eastern side of the Sierra Nevada Mountains. The Owens Valley is characterized by occasional areas of cottonwood trees, which line the river and offer cool oases in the usually hot and dry valley.

John Gamble (1863–1957) came to San Francisco from Morristown, New Jersey. He enrolled at the San Francisco School of Design in 1886 and continued his studies in Paris, in 1890, at the Académie Julian and the Académie Colarossi. He returned to San Francisco in 1893 and began to paint landscapes with colorful fields of wild flowers. The San Francisco earthquake and fire of 1906 destroyed his studio, and he resolved to move to Los Angeles, to be with his friend Elmer Wachtel. On the way, he stayed in Santa Barbara and decided to remain there, where he lived the rest of his life. Gamble's paintings of California wild flowers earned him a national reputation. Although *Santa Barbara Landscape* (plate 53) is harmonized to the cooler blues and greens, some of his views of the vivid orange California poppies strewn across the landscape led some critics to refer to them as "Gamble's prairie fires." When asked how he came to specialize in that subject, he said that he saw the flowers simply as brilliant patches of color splashed over the hills: "I liked the way they designed themselves across the field."

Alfred Mitchell (1888–1972) was the most successful student of Maurice Braun. Born in York, Pennsylvania, he came to California in 1908 and settled in San Diego where, in 1913, he began to study at Braun's San Diego Academy of Art. While a student, he won a Silver Medal at the Panama-California Exposition in San Diego, in 1915. Encouraged by Braun, Mitchell enrolled in the Pennsylvania Academy of the Fine Arts and studied with Daniel Garber (1880–1958) and Edward Redfield. An outstanding student, in 1920 Mitchell won the coveted Cresson European Traveling Scholarship, which enabled him to visit England, France, Italy, and Spain.

Mitchell's early works are impressionistic, owing much to the Bucks County painters, particularly Redfield, who was his lifelong friend. His 1924 painting *Sunset Glow, California* (figure 10), is an atmospheric piece painted in soft, gently harmonized colors. The composition is set in a series of receding planes, each of a dominant color tone, leading to the luminous background where the last

Alfred Mitchell, Balboa Park, San Diego, 1949. Courtesy of Jean Stern.

glow of sunlight warms the mountainsides. His later works, however, are more strongly realistic and often have an emotional presence frequently seen in American Realism of the twentieth century. *In Morning Light* (plate 37) dates to 1931 and displays Mitchell's sense of dramatic realism. Imbuing the light of a fresh new day with majesty and mystery, the painting shows the cliffs of La Jolla, as the warming light of the morning sun slowly unveils the mist. The sense of drama and solitude that permeates this painting arises from the way Mitchell presents the essential forms. The oblique shadow line in the foreground sand traces the crest of the cliffs, announcing the approaching sunlight. The dark ledge in the foreground yields to the coming day and unfolds into the richly glowing, cathedral-like cliffs of the background. The three rowboats wait patiently, proclaiming the presence of yet-unseen people.

Arthur Hill Gilbert (1894–1970) graduated from the United States Naval Academy and served in the Navy prior to coming to California in 1920. He turned to art, and in hopes of becoming a professional painter enrolled at the Otis Art Institute, in Los Angeles, and then continued his training with classes in Paris and London. In 1928 Gilbert moved to Monterey. He drew public and critical acclaim for his paintings of the picturesque trees, dunes, and rugged coastline. *Land of Gray Dunes, Monterey* (plate 42) is handled with a limited palette, giving it the cold and gloomy feel of a stormy day in Northern California. In 1929, his painting *Monterey Oaks* (location unknown) won the coveted Hallgarten Prize at the National Academy. In 1930, he won two more significant awards, the Academy's Murphy and Ranger Prizes, and was elected an Associate Member of the organization.

The Hungarian-born Joseph Kleitsch (1882–1931) was a portrait painter whose first visit to California was in 1914, after he left Mexico City, where he had painted portraits of President Francisco Madero and his wife. Later, he lived in Chicago, and in 1920 he settled in Southern California. He established himself in Laguna Beach, earning a substantial living with his portraits. He quickly joined the Laguna Beach Art Association and started to paint landscapes, still lifes, and views of his new residence. He was a bold colorist and employed a bravura brushstroke, and many of his paintings are strongly Impressionist, with high-keyed colors and dissolved forms. Among his favorite subjects were the houses and streets of Laguna Beach. These are presented as scenes of a peaceful little village, the quaint charms of which would soon succumb to real estate development (figure 11). In the early 1920s, he befriended Father John O'Sullivan, pastor of the Mission San Juan Capistrano. *Bougainvillea, Mission San Juan Capistrano* (plate 23) shows Kleitsch's full acceptance of Impressionism as an artistic approach. The forms are almost completely dissolved, seeming to melt into a background of brilliant and vivid strokes of color. *The Oriental Shop* dates to 1925 (plate 32). It shows Kleitsch's wife in a store she managed in the Biltmore Hotel in Los Angeles. In this painting too the forms are reduced to elements of light, color, and texture, swept over the surface of the painting in a rhythmic pattern of large, painterly brushstrokes.

In 1925 Kleitsch and his wife traveled to Europe, staying in Giverny and Spain, where he painted portraits and landscapes. After returning to California in November 1927, he continued to paint in Laguna until his death at the age of forty-nine.

George K. Brandriff (1890–1936) came to California to be a dentist. In 1914, he enrolled in the College of Dentistry at the University of Southern California, and four years later, he opened a dentistry practice in Hemet, a small desert community near Palm Springs. Brandriff enjoyed painting in his spare time. In the 1920s, he began visiting Laguna Beach, where he painted and made friends with many of the artists there, including Edgar and Elsie Payne, Hanson Puthuff, William Wendt, Arthur Hill Gilbert, Clarence Hinkle (1880–1960), and William Griffith (1866–1940). In 1923, he took art lessons with Anna Hills (1882–1930) and Carl Oscar Borg (1879–1947). In 1927 Brandriff built a studio in Laguna Beach, which he used on a part-time basis. A year later he closed his dentistry practice and moved to Laguna with the aim of becoming a full-time, professional painter. His subjects included landscapes, seascapes, still lifes, figure studies, and harbor scenes. *Cannery Row, Newport Beach* (plate 29) is a small sketch handled in broad, painterly strokes. The fully developed work, *A Colorful Port* (figure 12), painted in Brittany in 1929, shows Brandriff's masterly control of light and brush. While the subject matter owes much to his close friend Edgar Payne, the technique is Brandriff's own elegant Post-Impressionism.

Brandriff was active in Southern California's art groups, exhibiting often with the California Art Club and serving as president of the Laguna Beach Art Association from 1934 until his death. A fine painter who started late, he died young, committing suicide in 1936 in desperation over having cancer. He garnered a number of awards, including a Silver Medal from the Painters of the West in 1929 and Second Prize from the California State Fair in 1930.

Arthur G. Rider (1886–1975) was an art student at the Chicago Academy of Fine Arts when he attended a lecture, in 1911, by the noted Spanish artist Joaquín Sorolla (1863–1923). The exhilarating experience of seeing Sorolla's paintings would stay with him for the rest of his life. He continued his studies in Paris, at the Académie Colarossi and the Académie de la Grande Chaumière, and then in Spain, where he met and befriended Sorolla. He spent several summers in Spain, painting magnificent Sorollalike scenes on the beach in Valencia. Like his mentor, Rider was a superb colorist. *The Spanish Boat* (plate 14), a scene of a returning fisherman beaching his boat in the hot afternoon sun, is a subject Sorolla painted repeatedly. Through his command of color, Rider conveys the potent quality of Spanish light and the unmitigated heat of the afternoon sun.

Rider left Chicago in 1928 and moved to Laguna Beach. The light of Southern California beguiled him, and he painted landscapes and beach scenes near his house, using oil paints as well as watercolor. As was the case with many painters of Laguna Beach, Rider visited the Mission San Juan Capistrano on several occasions, painting views of the gardens and fountains. In 1931, he moved to Los Angeles and remained there for the rest of his life, taking occasional painting trips to Mexico and Hawaii. He worked as a scenic painter for Twentieth-Century Fox and MGM studios. Employment with the movie studios was a circumstance common to a number of noted artists, including Emil Kosa, Jr. (1903–1968) and George Gibson (born 1904), who frequently painted with Rider in their spare time. In his movie studio role, Rider prepared sets for a large number of important films, including *The Wizard of Oz, The Robe,* and *Ben-Hur.* Unfortunately, in his day movies did not give screen credit to scenic artists, and few people know of his tremendous contributions to the golden age of Hollywood.

The seeds of change, though slow to germinate, were gradually sprouting in the warm, fertile soil of California art. By 1915, a large and diverse group of artists had settled in Southern California.

Left: Arthur G. Rider painting on the beach in Valencia, Spain, c. 1920.
Right: Rider painting in the Mission San Juan Capistrano, c. 1928.
Photographs courtesy of Robert M. Bethea and the estate of Arthur G. Rider.

The plein-air painters were in their heyday. As the "establishment," with their coterie of dealers, patrons, and writers, they functioned as an effective impediment to the generation of Modernist artists after World War I.

Whereas it took nearly ten years for Impressionism to arrive in the United States after its birth in France, the impact on American artists of early twentieth-century Modernism was notably quicker. Moreover, the tidal wave of new ideas emanating from the Armory Show in New York in 1913 broke in California concurrently, and by 1917, there were enough young artists interested in Modernist styles to form the Los Angeles Modern Art Society. The more notable members of this circle included Bert Cressey (1883–1944), Meta Cressey (1882–1964), Helena Dunlap (1876–1955), Edgar Keller (1868–1932), Henrietta Shore (1880–1963), Edouard Vysekal (1890–1939), and Karl Yens (1868–1945). The society held non-juried invitational shows, featuring Modern works by local as well as foreign artists.

Meta Cressey had come to California in 1913 after marrying Bert Cressey, a native of the Los Angeles basin. The two had met in Robert Henri's class at the National Academy School. The young couple settled on a five-acre portion of the Cressey Ranch, in Compton, just south of Los Angeles, and built a studio-home. *Under the Pepper Tree* (plate 34) is a powerfully Post-Impressionist painting, with strong inclinations toward Fauvism. Indeed, the treatment of color and the tilted perspective are precisely the artistic elements that earned this work the label of "modern" in mid-twenties Los Angeles. Cressey showed *Under the Pepper Tree* at the 1927 Painters and Sculptors Annual Exhibition at the Los Angeles Museum of History, Science, and Art.

Edouard Vysekal came to the United States from Prague in 1907. In Chicago, he studied with Stanton MacDonald-Wright and Morgan Russell, the avant-garde American artists who created Synchromism. By 1914, Vysekal and his wife, the painter Luvena Buchanan Vysekal (1873–1954), were living in Los Angeles and he was teaching at the Art Students League. There, he rekindled his friendship with MacDonald-Wright, who had become the school's director. Already a progressive artist, known for his vivid and bold use of color and his daring and dynamic approach to form, Vysekal became even more progressive and was regarded as one of California's eminent Modernists. *Joy* (plate 35) shows three little girls in the intense light of a sunny afternoon. While the image of the first girl, sitting on a swing, is somewhat solid, those of the other two girls are softer and more dissolved, as each is progressively hidden in the shade of the bushes. The background shrubbery is a marvelous, rippling pattern of painterly brushstrokes, handled in large daubs of pure color. Light defines the colors and the colors define the forms. The Vysekals were childless, yet many of Edouard's paintings deal with children, often in playful, unaffected poses.

Robert Henri's art class, New York, 1912. Henri is seated in the front row, at left, holding a cane. Meta Gehring Cressey is standing to his left, wearing a large bow. Bert Cressey is standing in the back row, far right. The Cresseys met in this class and were married the next year. Courtesy of David and Donna Cressey.

Karl Yens was a fully trained artist before he came to the United States in 1901. After periods in New York and Washington, D. C., where he painted several murals, Yens came to Los Angeles in 1910. In 1918 he moved to Laguna Beach, where he was a founding member of the Laguna Beach Art Association. *America the Beautiful* (plate 20) was painted in 1918. The work is thoroughly in keeping with the patriotic fervor that swept our country during World War I. The foreground is anchored by the brilliantly lit rock that points toward the American flag, proudly streaming in the wind. Indeed, all perspective lines point to the flag: the crest of the wave, the rocks in the distance, the slope of the cliffs. Yens loved to imbue his paintings with arcane meaning, and his work was regularly the subject of much attention. His titles were often cryptic, among them *Sun and Soul, Birds of the Holy Grail,* and *Rin Tin Tin, A Friend of Mankind. America the Beautiful* is by contrast sympathetic, and leads one to visualize the last line of the patriotic hymn, "from sea to shining sea."

Thomas L. Hunt (1882–1938) was a Canadian who came to California in 1924. He was trained by his father, the artist John Powell Hunt, and also studied with Hugh Breckenridge (1870–1937) at the Pennsylvania Academy. Hunt lived and painted in Gloucester, Massachusetts, and Cleveland, Ohio, before coming to Los Angeles. In 1927, he moved to Laguna Beach to stay. Hunt's style gradually evolved from Impressionism to a distinctive form of Post-Impressionism. His paintings celebrate color at the expense of objective exactitude. Untitled (Los Angeles Harbor) (plate 27) demonstrates how progressive artists modified color and form in order to create a more subjective painting. The scene, which represents one of the canneries in Los Angeles Harbor, exhibits simplified forms and a markedly altered sense of space. The structure of the cannery and the tuna boats have been reduced to a few areas of pure color, with one or two massive brushstrokes indicating a boat, a dock, or the side of a building. While there is some consideration of three-dimensional form in the handling of those elements, there is scarcely any in the representation of the foreground shoreline and water, which appear as extensive masses of pure color painted in large, robust strokes. Likewise, the space in the painting is diminished, with a tilted foreground leading to a flat background. Overall, the forms are simple, colorful, unadorned, and intense.

At the end of the 1920s, the Southern California art community experienced a series of dramatic transformations. Many changes occur at generational intervals in the history of art. The plein-air painters had been students of academic artists and later turned to the "new" and different style of Impressionism. Now, a generation later, their students turned to the "new" styles, characterized by a move away from the perceptual toward more conceptual approaches to painting. Furthermore, in 1929, America suffered a terrible blow with the onset of the Great Depression. Almost overnight, the dynamic relationship between artists, dealers, and patrons ground to a halt as much of America's disposable income vanished. The Depression was an indiscriminate misfortune to all artists. Modernists as well as plein-air artists joined in the Works Progress Administration programs, such as the Federal Arts Project, which allotted mural commissions in public buildings. Additionally, the American character turned inward and began a prolonged, restless period of self-examination. The arts followed suit, and artists applied themselves to exploring the American experience in this time of solemnity. The bright, buoyant landscape paintings of the plein-air style were replaced with somber, comfortless views of the cities and the farms.

With economic recovery in the late 1930s, Modernism made its inroads, and by the outbreak of World War II, most of the prominent names of California Impressionism had died or withdrawn from the public eye, and the style itself became a nostalgic souvenir of a bygone era.

NORTHERN CALIFORNIA
IMPRESSIONISM

Harvey L. Jones

California was first imagined as a Terrestrial Paradise by a sixteenth-century Spanish writer named Garci Rodriguez de Montalvo, who described the exotic beauty and fabulous treasure of the legendary Queen Califia's fabled island located near the Indies. The earliest paintings of the real California landscape were made by artists and draftsmen who accompanied various expeditions sent out from Spain, England, France, and Russia during the late eighteenth century. Before the expeditionary artists visited California, the native peoples had left evidence of their own pictorial tradition in the form of painted designs on cave walls or rock formations that constitute mysterious representations of animals or figures with ceremonial significance. However, depictions of external observations of nature were not found in their cultures. Under Hispanic rule the painting tradition was largely limited to the mural decorations with religious subjects and geometric designs, of Spanish or Mexican origin, that adorned the chain of California missions along the Pacific Coast. A few early images of the landscape are found in the documentation of the California missions made by visiting amateur artists and naturalists in the first half of the nineteenth century.

The establishment of California landscape painting, as an art form, dates from the Gold Rush of 1849 and the arrival of the first group of artists trained in the European tradition of easel painting. Among the shiploads of gold seekers from many parts of the world who arrived almost daily in San Francisco Harbor were a few professionally trained artists whose intent was to strike it rich in the gold fields. Many of the unsuccessful prospectors soon turned to the professions for which they were trained.

San Francisco and, inland, Sacramento soon became the centers of artistic activity where painters established studios and began to offer a wide range of services that included portraiture, scenic panoramas, illustration, commercial design, and architectural decoration. In most Gold Rush paintings, a depiction of the California landscape was relegated to secondary importance as background for genre scenes and portraits. Gold Rush painter Thomas A. Ayres (1816–1858), the first artist to depict the spectacular Yosemite Valley in 1854, was soon followed by William Smith Jewett (1812–1873), George Henry Burgess (1831–1905), and others whose Yosemite paintings from the late 1850s brought attention to what has become California's best-known scenic wonder.

PLATE 44
Channel P. Townsley (1867–1921)
Mission San Juan Capistrano, 1916
Oil on canvas, 32 x 40 inches
Joan Irvine Smith Fine Arts, Inc.

125

It was nearly a decade after the Gold Rush, with the arrival of such painters as Frederick Butman (1820–1871), Alburtus del Orient Browere, Thomas Hill (1829–1908), William Keith (1838–1911), and Albert Bierstadt (1830–1902), that depictions of the landscape began to dominate the art of California.

During the first decade that followed completion of the transcontinental railroad in 1869, California's scenic wonders—particularly the rugged Sierra Nevada, with its giant redwoods and its rivers and lakes, and especially Yosemite—became more accessible to visiting artists from Europe or eastern America. Among the prominent landscape painters who visited the state or established studios in San Francisco during the 1870s were Thomas Moran (1837–1926), Martin Johnson Heade (1819–1904), James Hamilton (1819–1878), and Enoch Wood Perry (1813–1915). Earlier arrivals Thomas Hill, William Keith, and Virgil Williams (1830–1886) were to become permanent residents with lasting reputations. Most of these artists traveled far on foot or on horseback during extended sketching trips in the Sierra to gather images that were later used in developing "finished" landscapes painted in their San Francisco studios. They all drew upon European influences for their own development of the classic American landscape in the West. The great panoramic landscapes of California's mountain scenery were often idealized, and sometimes dramatized, in the manner of the German academic style taught in Düsseldorf and reinforced by the conventions of the American Hudson River school. The Hudson River painters had remained faithful to the physical reality of the landscape in paintings that also expressed a spirit of expanding national pride and a sense of the sublime in allegories of God in nature, paintings that transcended mere visual representation. The compositional features of a classical American landscape as applied to western scenery usually included an expansive luminous sky framed by detailed depictions of mountain topography and vegetation.

Albert Bierstadt, whose several visits to California began in 1863 with sketching in Yosemite, set up his studio in San Francisco in 1872. His worldwide reputation conferred celebrity status that was as notable as his grandiose landscape paintings. This exerted a positive influence upon the local artists and greatly stimulated art patronage among wealthy San Franciscans.

Albert Bierstadt's contemporaries in San Francisco Thomas Hill and William Keith shared his enthusiasm for painting the grandeur of panoramic mountain scenery. Their works were much sought after, both in California and in the East. A stylistic shift of European academic influences from Düsseldorf toward Munich, and more importantly to the French Barbizon school so admired by many California landscape painters, led artists such as Hill and Keith to modify their painting styles as early as the mid-1870s. They adopted a looser, more spontaneous brushwork in the Munich style and were also attracted to the broader naturalistic vision of landscapes in the French manner. Although both Keith and Hill produced many large paintings of mountain subjects on the epic scale of Bierstadt's impressive road-show attractions, they were also drawn toward the simpler, more intimate motifs in nature that became a popular feature in paintings by the next generation, a change in popular taste that eventually eroded Bierstadt's reputation.

William Keith, California's other resident master of landscape during the late nineteenth century, modified his painting style three times over the several decades of a long career. The carefully detailed realism of his early work of the mid-1860s, reminiscent of that of the Hudson River school, may have been an extension of his involvement with descriptive detail as an engraver/illustrator. In the 1870s he indulged his enthusiasm for describing the picturesque mountain wilderness with its high mountain peaks, wild rivers, and placid lakes in the Romantic-Realist style that combined the spectacle of a Bierstadt with the paint surfaces of the Munich school. In the 1890s, Keith, inspired by the French Barbizon painters, abandoned the Realist approach in favor of an even freer application of paint in his evocation of modestly scaled "intimate" landscapes—in which nature's episodes were measured by mere moments instead of hours, and by a few acres rather than miles.

In the early 1870s San Francisco's growing enthusiasm for art was centered on the newly founded San Francisco Art Association. Membership grew rapidly, from the already established community of resident artists and with the recent influx of prominent painters from the East, which provided sufficient funds to implement the organization's intent to create its own art school to provide sound technical training by accomplished artists.

Virgil Macy Williams (1830–1886), who was born in Maine and had studied in Rome with renowned painter William Page, was hired in 1874 as the first director of San Francisco Art Association's School of Design. He was highly regarded as a teacher and beloved by his students, some of whom are among the nation's most respected painters. Most of Williams's own paintings were figurative subjects that reflected on his experiences in Italy, but he also produced a few fine California landscapes.

Under Williams's leadership, the California School of Design provided its students with basic academic art training by a faculty that included some of the best painters in the West. Originally located in spaces on the second floor of a building on Pine Street, in 1893 it moved to the Nob Hill mansion donated by the widow of Mark Hopkins and became known as the Mark Hopkins Institute of Art. The school's curriculum, modeled on that of the French Ecole des Beaux-Arts in Paris, placed emphasis on the mastery of basic drawing skills and included sketching from plaster casts of Greek Antique or Italian Renaissance sculptures from the Louvre. A number of the state's first generation of native-born artists, including John A. Stanton (1857–1929), Lorenzo P. Latimer (1857–1941), and Theodore Wores (1859–1939), were among the early graduates of the School of Design. Enrollment of women often outnumbered that of men. Among those who achieved prominence were Clara McChesney (1860–1928), Mary Curtis Richardson (1848–1931), and Grace Carpenter Hudson (1865–1937).

Theodore Wores, a San Francisco–born artist whose talent was recognized early and encouraged by his first teacher, Joseph Harrington, was at age fifteen among the first students to enroll at the Art Association's School of Design under Virgil Williams. In 1875, the Californian Toby Rosenthal, who later became a prominent expatriate painter/teacher but was then a student at the Royal Academy in Munich, urged Wores to study painting there. For six years Wores received instruction from the Munich Academy faculty and from the Americans Rosenthal, William Merritt Chase, and Frank Duveneck. Wores's travels in Europe took him to Venice and Paris, where he met James McNeill Whistler, whose Japanese-inspired works and personal encouragement prompted Wores to visit the Far East at a later date. Wores returned to San Francisco in 1881 to paint local scenes and portraits, and he had a particular interest in and success with Chinatown subjects before he embarked in 1885 on what was to be the first of two extended visits to Japan. Theodore Wores was among the first artists of the West to live and work among the Japanese, adopting their dress, customs, and language, in order to record sensitively the scenes and atmosphere of that country. Although Wores's low-key color palette, adopted from the Munich school, was modified to a brighter range of hues with

Right:

PLATE 45

Theodore Wores (1859–1939)

A Hillside in Saratoga

Oil on canvas, 44 x 24 inches

Joan Irvine Smith Fine Arts, Inc.

Opposite:

PLATE 46

William F. Jackson (1850/51–1936)

Radiant Valley

Oil on canvas, 20 x 30 inches

Joan Irvine Smith Fine Arts, Inc.

broader brushstrokes for his Japanese subjects, the artist had not become an Impressionist.

After the great earthquake and fire of 1906 destroyed the Mark Hopkins Institute of Art building, Wores was appointed to succeed Arthur Mathews as director when the school reopened in 1907, and he held this teaching position for six years.

Sometime during the 1920s Wores purchased a vacant Methodist church in Saratoga, which he converted to a studio-home and art gallery. The artist expressed his reasons for acquiring the studio thusly: "Of all the countries I have visited in search of material for my brush, California ranks first as a land of sunshine and flowers, both wild and cultivated. I have found endless possibilities in colorful orchards in spring blossom time in various portions of the state and especially in Saratoga—in the Santa Clara Valley." The artist's canvases of wild flowers and blossoming orchards in the Santa Clara Valley painted during the 1920s are among the most

persuasive reasons to identify Theodore Wores as taking an Impressionist approach to plein-air painting.

Another student of Virgil Williams during the early years of the San Francisco Art Association's School of Design was William F. Jackson (1850–1936), who was born in Iowa and traveled to Sacramento in a covered wagon in 1862. Following his training in San Francisco, Jackson opened a studio in Sacramento and traveled around California painting landscapes. In 1885 he accepted a position as the first curator of the Crocker Art Gallery after it was presented to the city of Sacramento. He was allowed to set up his studio at the Gallery, which would later lead to the establishment of The Sacramento School of Design in 1886, with Jackson as headmaster. Jackson's major contribution was the introduction of plein-air painting to his students at a time when, traditionally, landscape paintings were finished in the studio. William F. Jackson is best remembered for his paintings of fields of California poppies and

other wild flowers painted directly from nature, outdoors. Jackson employed freely applied dabs of bright pigment to suggest an atmospheric landscape illuminated by diffused midday sunlight. A prolific painter, he continued his duties at the Crocker Art Gallery until his death at age eighty-five.

Upon the death of Virgil Williams in 1886, the esteemed still-life painter Emil Carlsen (1853–1932) came from New York to take over as director of the School of Design, in 1887. Carlsen had received his early training at the Royal Academy in his native Denmark, and further study in Europe brought him under the influence of works by the Old Masters, particularly the still-life paintings of Jean-Siméon Chardin. Although during a long, productive career Carlsen was well regarded for his landscape and figurative subjects, his brief four-year period in San Francisco is remembered for sophisticated still-life compositions, typically of dead game and copper pots, rendered in muted tonalities reminiscent of Chardin. Carlsen was a respected teacher, and his pupils at the School of Design who developed successful art careers included Guy Rose (1867–1925), John Gamble (1863–1957), Percy Gray (1869–1952), and Anne Bremer (1868–1923). Emil Carlsen's early departure from San Francisco, owing to the paucity of support and recognition for its best artists, was a poor reflection on the city's artistic sensibilities of the time.

By the 1890s, when the first of the California-schooled artists began to receive recognition as well as gain confidence in their own work, the prevailing style of American painting was changing. Painters were turning away from the crisply defined, descriptive realism of an Albert Bierstadt toward more subjective interpretations realized through an aesthetic style that has been termed "Tonalism." George Inness was America's most respected landscape painter at the time of his influential visit to California in 1891. California's own old-master painter of landscapes, William Keith, was a great admirer of Inness, with whom he shared the philosophical ideal that the painter should strive to synthesize the poetry of nature with objective fact.

The Tonalists explored quiet contemplative moods of nature experienced in the diminished light of early morning, late afternoon, or evening. Often, mysterious or romantic lighting effects were achieved through representations of atmospheric fog, mist, or haze rendered in carefully controlled, low-key color harmonies that seem to envelop the subject, soften or blur the imagery, and leave details to the poetic imagination of the observer. Northern California provided two important underpinnings for a regional basis for the style. In addition to the fog and haze characteristic of coastal California, the artistic influences of the two major American painters, Inness and Whistler, were conveyed through the art and teachings of two of California's leading artists of the time: William Keith and Arthur Mathews. The lessons of Whistler's carefully organized compositions, arranged in a subdued palette of grayed tones, were embraced by San Francisco's dominant artistic influence of the period, Arthur F. Mathews (1860–1945). His own form of decorative Tonalism, now referred to as the "California Decorative Style," merged his academic figurative training with a Whistlerian-influenced color harmony.

In 1890 Arthur Mathews was appointed director of the School of Design, where he implemented reforms in the curriculum that included de-emphasizing Antique classes in favor of life drawing from nude or draped models in segregated men's and women's classes. Mathews, who had trained at Académie Julian in Paris, encouraged his best pupils to study further in Europe. As both a teacher and an accomplished painter, Mathews would be a major influence on the artistic life of Northern California in the early years of the twentieth century.

Above left: Arthur Mathews with life class of women art students at the California School of Design, San Francisco, c. 1893. Courtesy of the Oakland Museum of California.

Above right: Arthur Mathews in his studio, c. 1893. Collection of the Oakland Museum of California, Paul C. Mills Archive of California Art.

Below: Granville Redmond, photograph by Arnold Genthe, 1907. Courtesy of Mildred Albronda.

A prominent muralist, easel painter, designer, architect, teacher, art jurist, writer, and civic arts advocate, Mathews embodied the concept of a Renaissance man of arts more than any other artist in California. It is arguable that Mathews's personal rejection of the tenets of French Impressionism influenced a generation of California artists and resulted in the delayed impact that the once-vanguard style had on the plein-air painters of California. Most of his successful students—who included his wife Lucia Kleinhans Mathews (1870–1955), Gottardo Piazzoni (1872–1945), Xavier Martinez (1869–1943), Giuseppe Cadenasso (1858–1918), Francis McComas (1875–1938), and Granville Redmond (1871–1935)—were instead influenced by Arthur Mathews's Tonalism. However, it must also be stated that several of Mathews's students eventually embraced the Impressionist approach to landscape painting *en plein air*. Exposure to Impressionist painting while studying in Europe brought Armin Hansen (1886–1957), Joseph Raphael (1869–1950), E. Charlton Fortune (1885–1969), and Granville Redmond under its influence. By the early teens, many Northern California painters had been exposed to Impressionism in France or through the numerous examples of what by then was an international style of Impressionism exhibited, for example, in the Palace of Fine Arts at the 1915 Panama-Pacific International Exposition in San Francisco

Joseph Raphael (1869–1950), born in California's gold mining country, received his early formal art training under Arthur Mathews at the California School of Design. After nearly a decade working as a newspaper illustrator, by 1903 Raphael had saved enough money to pursue further study in Paris at the Ecole des Beaux-Arts and the Académie Julian. For several years he divided his time between Paris and a Dutch artists' colony near Amsterdam, where he painted the scenes of peasant life and dark cottage interiors that were popular among young Paris art students of the day. Raphael exhibited his Dutch works at the San Francisco Art Association in 1910 before returning to Europe and settling in Uccle, near Brussels. Regular visits to Paris, and artistic influences from the Impressionism he encountered there, soon resulted in Raphael lightening his palette and developing broader brushstrokes in his out-of-doors paintings. Through the years, his paintings were shown regularly in San Francisco galleries. He was awarded a Silver Medal for one of six works he exhibited at the Panama-Pacific International Exposition in 1915.

Joseph Raphael's paintings were an important influence on a number of young San Francisco artists who idolized him in the years before the advent of Modernism. His landscapes, and landscapes with figures, are filled with brilliant effects of light and atmosphere rendered in bold strokes that, at close viewing range, almost obscure the subject. Although virtually all of Raphael's Impressionist-inspired plein-air works were painted in Belgium in the years before he resettled in San Francisco at the onset of World War II, he remains one of California's most admired painters in the Impressionist style.

PLATE 47
Joseph Raphael (1869–1950)
Market of St. Catherine, Bruxelles,
c. 1911
Oil on panel, 7 x 7 inches
The Irvine Museum

PLATE 48
Matteo Sandona (1881–1964)
In Her Kimono
Oil on canvas, 35 ¼ x 28 ½ inches
Joan Irvine Smith Fine Arts, Inc.

The Italian-born Matteo Sandona (1881–1964), who demonstrated his interest in art at an early age, immigrated to the United States with his family in 1894. He returned to Europe to study art for four years at Verona and Paris before settling in San Francisco in 1901. Leaving no evidence of any interest in landscape painting, Sandona's reputation as an artist rested primarily with portraiture. He sometimes employed the techniques of Impressionist brushwork, with broken color effects, for his figure and still-life subjects as well as for the portraits commissioned by many socially prominent or famous personalities of his day.

PLATE 49
Guy Rose (1867–1925)
Incoming Tide, c. 1917
Oil on canvas, 24 x 29 inches
The Joan Irvine Smith Collection

PLATE 50
Armin Hansen (1886–1957)
Making Port
Oil on canvas, 30 x 32 inches
The Joan Irvine Smith Collection

In the earthquake and resulting fire of 1906, San Francisco's visual arts heritage from the nineteenth century suffered a devastating loss. Important private collections of precious Northern California paintings perished in the flames that also took much of the life's work of several artists whose houses and studios were burned. For several years during the rebuilding of the city, the center of artistic life shifted to the Monterey Peninsula, where many painters opened studios in Carmel-by-the-Sea, Pacific Grove, or Monterey. Other San Francisco artists moved to the East Bay cities of Oakland, Alameda, or Berkeley, where some remained permanently.

The Monterey area, with its historic missions and adobe ruins, offered breathtaking beauty in natural surroundings that also included a deep blue crescent bay, sandy beaches, and windswept rocky promontories on which grew gnarled cypress trees, tall graceful Monterey pines, and ice plants with intensely magenta blossoms. The Carmel Valley provided sunny vistas of rolling hills robed in the greens or golds of its seasons.

The center of activity became the Hotel Del Monte Art Gallery in Monterey, which opened in 1907 with the cooperation of San Francisco's leading artists. The gallery provided a much-needed place for artists to exhibit and sell their work. A virtual who's who of California painters from the first half of the twentieth century regularly worked and exhibited in Monterey.

Armin Hansen, a San Franciscan who was the son of the well-known western painter Herman Wendelborg Hansen (1854–1924), began his art studies at the Mark Hopkins Institute under Arthur Mathews. He became a permanent resident of Monterey in 1913, after several years in Europe that included study under German Impressionist Carlos Grethe at the Akademie Stuttgart. Hansen's experiences as a deckhand aboard a Norwegian fishing trawler, and a period of time spent at the seaside artists' colony of Nieuport,

Belgium, seem to have informed his later choice of marine subject matter for paintings and etchings. His coastal landscapes and marine paintings, depicting the men and boats of Monterey's fishing industry, are rendered in bravura brushstrokes that express the powerful forces of nature within his carefully considered composition.

Hansen also produced a body of work that included landscapes of the Monterey Peninsula and scenes of the American Southwest rendered in painting techniques that were more conventionally Impressionistic, in their color and brushwork, than were most of his marine subjects. Armin Hansen exhibited widely and was the recipient of numerous prestigious awards during his long career, for which he is acknowledged to be among California's finest twentieth-century artists.

Another artist with strong ties to the Monterey Peninsula is E. Charlton Fortune, one of California's most important exponents of the French Impressionist style of plein-air painting. Born in Sausalito, across the Golden Gate from San Francisco, to Scottish parents, Euphemia Charlton Fortune began her studies at the Edinburgh College of Art while still in her teens. After further training in London, she returned to San Francisco, where she enrolled in the Mark Hopkins Institute as a student of Arthur Mathews. She then went on to New York to study with William Merritt Chase and Frank Vincent Dumond, among others, which gave her perhaps the most impressive credentials among California's painters at that time. Fortune again visited Europe, traveling and painting in the British Isles and France, before settling first in Carmel in 1912 and, soon after, in another studio in San Francisco. She was active in both art communities and was a frequent exhibitor whose paintings received Silver Medals at both the San Francisco Panama-Pacific International Exposition and the San Diego Panama-California Exposition. Another extended visit to Europe in the 1920s yielded twenty-eight impressionistic paintings of quaint fishing villages in St. Ives and St. Tropez, which were exhibited at the Oakland Art Gallery (now the Oakland Museum) in 1927. An unsigned foreword to the exhibition's catalogue stated: "Miss Fortune's work has the comprehensibility of the academicians, the color and light of the impressionists, and some of the organization of the 'Moderns.'" After 1928, Fortune, who was devoutly religious, devoted her efforts to painting liturgical subjects for church interiors.

PLATE 51

Mary DeNeale Morgan (1868–1948)

Cypress at Monterey

Watercolor and gouache,

18½ x 24½ inches

Joan Irvine Smith Fine Arts, Inc.

Mary DeNeale Morgan (1868–1948), of San Francisco, was a pupil of both Virgil Williams and Emil Carlsen at the School of Design. She also received instruction from two Bay Area old masters of landscape painting, Amadée Joullin (1862–1917) and William Keith, before she opened her first studio in Oakland in 1896. Morgan is best remembered for her paintings from a long period of residence in Carmel, where she became an active member of the arts community after 1907. Scenes of the coastal cypress trees and the rolling dunes of white sand along the Monterey beaches, rendered in watercolors or oils, were among her most popular subjects. On the suggestion of E. Charlton Fortune, Morgan invited the renowned American Impressionist William Merritt Chase to teach classes at the Carmel Summer School of Art in 1914, an important event for the Monterey/Carmel art community.

A Northern California painter active on the Monterey Peninsula whose works most resemble the bold, impasto brushstrokes and luminous color effects of Joseph Raphael was Bruce Nelson

(1888–1952). Little is known about his art training before 1905, when he met Robert Harshe, head of Stanford University's Art Department, who offered encouragement to Nelson's artistic pursuits while he was studying civil engineering and architecture. He furthered his art studies with Birge Harrison and John F. Carlson at the Art Students League in New York. After Nelson's return to California in 1912, he exhibited twenty paintings at a San Francisco art gallery, for which the artist received generous praise for his handling of color and atmospheric effects. In 1913 Nelson established a studio in Pacific Grove, where he also offered classes in plein-air painting. In 1915 Nelson exhibited four paintings of Pacific Grove seascapes at the Panama-Pacific International Exposition, where he was awarded a Silver Medal for *The Summer Sea* (plate 52). Nelson settled in Cooperstown, New York, after serving in the U.S. Army during World War I, and he never returned to California. His few surviving paintings remain among the most radiant evocations of coastal seascapes painted along the Monterey Peninsula.

In 1911, the painter William F. Ritschel (1864–1949) became a permanent resident of the Carmel Highlands, where he was regarded as the dean of American marine painters. The Bavarian-born Ritschel was a sailor prior to entering the Royal Academy in Munich for his formal art training. For six years he traveled and painted throughout Europe before immigrating to the United States in 1895. Ritschel enjoyed his first artistic success in New York, where he was elected an Associate of the National Academy of Design in 1910 and made a full National Academician in 1914. The lure of the sea attracted him to California's Carmel coast sometime after 1909. On a high promontory overlooking the Pacific Ocean at Carmel Highlands, Ritschel built a stone "castle" that was to be his studio and residence until his death in 1949. From this spectacular vantage point Ritschel painted the many moods of the ocean—from storm-tossed waves crashing on the rocks to a placid bay at sunset—the subjects that define his contribution to California painting.

Paul Dougherty (1877–1947), despite his protestations to the contrary, is, like Ritschel, probably best remembered as a marine painter. First trained for a profession in law, Dougherty was essentially self-taught as an artist. During the 1890s he studied briefly with Robert Henri in New York before going to Europe, where he studied independently in a number of the cultural centers on the continent. He settled in New Jersey, where he garnered a reputation for his seascapes, which typically featured waves crashing on the coastal rocks. A late arrival among plein-air painters in California, Dougherty was attracted to the favorable climate and new pictorial opportunities along the Pacific Coast. After 1928 Dougherty began to divide his time between Carmel and Tucson, Arizona, while continuing to show in the East. One New York critic noted a change in the artist's style toward a looser technique and a brighter palette in the execution of his California seascapes.

Throughout the 1920s and 1930s the Monterey Peninsula's picturesque landscape continued to appeal to plein-air painters, including a number of Southern California–based artists such as Guy Rose, Granville Redmond, Arthur Hill Gilbert (1894–1970), John Gamble (1863–1957), and Franz Bischoff (1864–1929), among many others.

During the 1920s a group of Oakland-based painters who called themselves the Society of Six, William Clapp (1879–1954), August Gay (1890–1949), Seldon Gile (1877–1947), Maurice Logan (1886–1977), Louis Siegriest (1899–1989), and Bernard Von Eichman (1899–1970), carried the tradition of plein-air painting forward to the beginnings of Modernism in Northern California painting.

Their experiments with landscape painting were inspired by French Post-Impressionism, along with other European Modernist styles such as Fauvism and even Cubism, examples of which these artists had seen in the exhibitions at the Palace of Fine Arts during the 1915 Panama-Pacific International Exposition in San Francisco. The Six adopted their own manifesto that began, "All great art is founded upon the use of visual abstractions to express beauty." They frequently painted together, and they exhibited and socialized as a group, which stimulated their work as well as that of a generation of Bay Area painters who came to prominence a decade or two later.

The plein-air painters of Northern California remained active and popular until the onset of the Great Depression in the early 1930s, when the art market collapsed along with everything else. The most progressive artists of the 1930s and 1940s abandoned the "pure landscape" as the principal subject for painting at a time that coincided with pronounced changes in California's land use—brought about by expanding urbanization and the rapid growth of large-scale agriculture. Many Northern California artists showed greater interest in Social Realist painting, to better reflect the times, and there was also a younger generation of artists who chose to experiment with various vanguard approaches to abstract painting that drew little inspiration from the landscape.

PLATE 52
Bruce Nelson (1888–1952)
The Summer Sea, 1915
Oil on canvas, 30 x 40 inches
The Irvine Museum

THE NATIONAL ACADEMY:
A CALIFORNIA PERSPECTIVE

David Dearinger

From its inception, the National Academy promoted itself as a truly national organization. Samuel Morse, the Academy's first president, told his fellow artists that the word *national* was an integral part of the title as it helped to express "the entire character of our institution."[1] The catalogue for the Academy's first exhibition, held in 1826, reiterated the point and stated it more specifically by declaring that the Academicians wished to benefit "all Artists throughout the United States." During the first half-century or so of its history, though, that intended geographic scope remained more or less theoretical. It was not until 1870 that the Academy made an effort, through constitutional changes, to broaden its own horizons. This is not to criticize the Academy's founders. After all, they lived in a nation whose great westward expansion had yet to begin. If these individuals returned today, they might be surprised to hear that California had become part of the Union, much less that it had produced art of high quality. Having heard this, though, they almost certainly would applaud the display of these works in the Academy's galleries. Thus, it is appropriate that the Academy present *All Things Bright and Beautiful: California Impressionist Paintings from The Irvine Museum.*

The history of the National Academy begins in November 1825, when thirty professional and amateur artists met in New York City to form "a Society for the Improvement in Drawing," which they called the New-York Drawing Association. Their initial intent was to provide artists with a congenial place to congregate, draw from plaster casts of antique sculptures, compare the results, and discuss the purpose and meaning of art.[2]

The leader of this group was the portrait and history painter Samuel F. B. Morse. Morse's ideas about the mission of the new organization quickly evolved to something of a more sophisticated theoretical and aesthetic nature. He felt that, on the brink of its fiftieth birthday, the United States desperately needed to improve its cultural profile.[3] The only previous serious effort to do this, at least in New York City, was with the establishment in 1802 of the American Academy of Fine Arts. For Morse and his friends, however, the American Academy had serious flaws, most of which resulted from the fact that nonartists dominated its administration. Artists, Morse believed, know what is best for artists. "Every profession in society," he wrote, "knows best what measures are necessary

Notes for this essay begin on page 167.

PLATE 53
John Gamble (1863–1957)
Santa Barbara Landscape
Oil on canvas, 24 x 36 inches
Joan Irvine Smith Fine Arts, Inc.

for its own improvement."[4] The conclusion: artists should run their own show. In January 1826, he made such thoughts known to the members of the drawing society. Agreeing with him, they quickly redefined the organization's purpose, transforming it into what they hoped would be a bona fide academy of art. Accordingly, they named their reconstituted society "The National Academy of the Arts of Design." By 1827, when the catalogue for the Academy's second annual exhibition was published, the title had been simplified to "The National Academy of Design."[5]

The first official meeting of the Academy took place on January 19, 1826, at Morse's residence in New York City. There, the fifteen founding members (including Morse, Henry Inman, Asher Durand, John Frazee, and William Dunlap) admitted, by ballot, an additional fifteen members (including Thomas Cole and Rembrandt Peale). Morse was elected president, a position he held until 1845 and, again, in 1861–62. The other original officers were Henry Inman, vice president; John L. Morton, secretary; and Charles C. Wright, treasurer. (Thomas S. Cummings replaced Wright the following year as treasurer, a post he held until 1850 and again from 1859 to 1864.)

Samuel F. B. Morse (1791–1872), *Self-Portrait,* watercolor on ivory, National Academy, New York. Courtesy of the National Academy.

The purpose of the new National Academy of Design was threefold. First, it was to be an honorary organization with a limited and exclusive membership. Members were to be professional artists working in one of the four categories of the "arts of design," defined as painting, sculpture, architecture, and engraving. Two levels of membership were established: Associate National Academician (ANA) and National Academician (NA). No known restrictions as to gender or race existed: the first woman elected to membership, Anne Hall, joined in the Associate category in 1827. The Academy's constitution required that newly elected Associates present the Academy with a portrait of themselves (not necessarily a self-portrait, as is so often misstated) and that new Academicians give a representative example of their own work.[6] These diploma presentations, as they are called, were reviewed by the Academy's governing council and, if accepted, qualified the artist as a member of the Academy.

The Academy's second purpose was to administer a school for the teaching of art.[7] The first class, such as it was, met in November 1826. For many years, the classes of the Academy were very informal. No full-time, salaried instructors were hired until 1870, when the painter Lemuel Wilmarth was appointed instructor. Admission to the school was fairly liberal; women were admitted for the first time in 1831, and no rules, at least no published ones, limited enrollment to whites. In the early years, students spent most of their time in the "Antique" class (established in 1826), where they drew from plaster casts of classical sculptures, or in the "Life" class (established in 1837), where they sketched a human model. Members of the Academy were expected to offer their expertise free of charge on a rotating basis. As "visitors" to the Academy's studios, they would circulate among the students and critique their drawings. Work in the classroom was supplemented by a series of lectures on perspective,

anatomy, and the like. Often, "professors" were appointed in name only, evidently for honorary reasons, without ever acting in any role as teachers at the Academy school.[8] Formalization of the curriculum and the manner in which it was administered came only in the 1870s.

The third purpose of the Academy was to host annual exhibitions of contemporary American art. These exhibitions were intended to "show the state of modern art;… To furnish an opportunity for the young Artist to bring himself before the public;… To furnish a mart for the disposal of those works of modern art which may be offered for sale."[9] The importance of this function to the members of the Academy is attested by how quickly they organized the first exhibition, which opened in rented rooms on Broadway on May 13, 1826. That show contained about 179 works by thirty-two artists, including Morse, Durand, Cole, Dunlap, Washington Allston, Ithiel Towne, and Rembrandt Peale. It was not a financial success, but that fact did not deter the Academicians from their purpose, and they immediately began planning their second annual exhibition.[10]

Above: Life class, National Academy of Design School of Fine Arts, c. 1890.
Below: William St. John Harper (1851–1910), *In the National Academy of Design,* from *Harper's Weekly,* April 29, 1882.
Photographs courtesy of the National Academy.

Peter B. Wight, National Academy of Design, Twenty-Third Street and Fourth Avenue, New York City (opened 1865, demolished 1900). Courtesy of the National Academy.

Like so many of its aspects, these three functions of the Academy originated with Morse; and, as already mentioned, it was he who insisted on the inclusion of the word *national* in the Academy's title. Morse felt that not to include it would "be taking one below the American Academy."[11] The word helped to insure that artists and the general public did not think of the National Academy as simply a branch of the older institution. In its early years, however, the Academy was national only in a theoretical sense. Early constitutional rules established a regional bias that was impossible to ignore and difficult to change. Foremost among these was the rule, in effect for the first forty-five years of the Academy's existence, that required an artist to be a resident of New York City in order to be eligible for full membership in the Academy. Abetting this rule was another, in effect until the early twentieth century, that required all potential nominees to membership to have participated in the Academy's annual exhibition in the year of nomination. Since it was more difficult, logistically, for non–New Yorkers to submit works for consideration for the annual exhibitions, this rule reinforced the effect of the first. Together, they made it difficult if not impossible for non–New Yorkers to participate in the functions of the

Academy. To help rectify this, the Academy's first constitution established a category of honorary membership to which nonresident professional artists and even so-called amateurs (nonartists) could be elected. By 1830, thirty men and women had been elected to this category. They resided in cities such as Boston (for example, Washington Allston), Rome (Horatio Greenough), Philadelphia (Rosalba Peale), and London (Charles Robert Leslie), and included several art lovers and collectors, such as Thomas H. Perkins of Boston, Philip Hone of New York, and Basil Hall of London.[12]

Despite this effort, the regional bias of some of the Academy's rules was apparent and did not go unnoticed. The author of an article published in 1827 in the *North American Review* felt that the Academy was not living up to a title that implied "a public institution, founded and supported by the nation." The National Academy, he wrote, was "simply a society of artists in the City of New-York, organized for the purposes of exhibition and instruction."[13] Morse thought that this protest was "trifling" and rebutted by saying that "the Catalogue of the 64 members of the Academy will show nearly all the most eminent names of the Artists in the United States, not from New-York alone, but from Philadelphia, Boston, Washington, and Charleston."[14] Strictly speaking, he was correct, but he was including the Honorary Members in his count, thereby allowing him to claim those other cities as being within the geographical scope of the Academy.

The regional limitation on membership was finally changed when the Academicians adopted a new Constitution, amended in 1869 and published the following year. The stipulation that new Academicians must be "professional Artists only, residents of the City of New York or its vicinity" was deleted.[15] The effects of this amendment were not immediate, however, and meaningful changes in the geographical makeup of the membership were slow in coming. No nonresidents were elected to the Academy in 1870; and the following year only three out of the eleven artists nominated were from places other than New York.[16] In fact, of the thirty-five members to be elected to the Academy during the 1870s, only about seven lived outside the New York area. The proportion was even smaller during the 1880s, when only four of forty-six new members were nonresidents. In fact, 1888 was an especially fruitful year for new members, in both the quantity (ten) elected and quality (Robert Blum, William Merritt Chase, and Augustus Saint-Gaudens were all elected that year); but not one of the ten was from out of town.

The situation for nonresidents improved somewhat in the 1890s, when ten out of forty-five new Associates gave addresses that were not in New York. Even so, most of these new members lived close to the city—Frederic Remington was in New Rochelle, New York; William St. John Harper was in East Hampton on Long Island; and George Inness, Jr., and Lawrence Earle lived in Montclair, New Jersey. Slightly farther afield, new Associate member Cecilia Beaux was a resident of Philadelphia. Only one new member elected during the 1890s, John Singer Sargent, was listed as living "abroad."

Six of the artists in the current exhibition were members of the National Academy. Although most of these were elected to membership while they resided in the East, they were, thanks to the constitutional amendment of 1869–70, permitted to maintain the full privileges of membership and to reap the rewards of the status it conveyed after they moved to California.[17]

The first of these to be admitted into the Academy was Paul Dougherty, who became an Associate National Academician in 1906. Admittedly, his admission was achieved in an unusual way; that is, he and a number of other artists were accepted into the Academy when the Society of American Artists, to which they belonged, merged with the Academy in 1906. The Academicians affirmed their trust in Dougherty's artistic worth by electing him to full National Academician the next year, an understandable action since Dougherty had been participating in the Academy's exhibitions since 1898.[18] He remained a fairly active participant in the Academy's annual exhibitions over the next two decades, sending paintings to almost all of them from 1901 until 1918, when he made an extended trip to Europe. A painting of his named *The Twisted Ledge* was in the Academy's winter show of 1907 and is presumably the canvas with that title that is in the current exhibition (plate 54).[19] The Academy honored Dougherty by presenting him with four awards, including the coveted Benjamin Altman Prize for landscape painting, which he won in 1918.[20] In addition, Dougherty's paintings received favorable critical notice at the Academy's annuals. For example, his "steady vision" and his ability to depict "the simplicity of grandeur" impressed one reviewer of the annual of 1906. That same year, another critic, writing for the *New York Sun,* compared his painting *Land and Sea* with Winslow Homer's *Gulf Stream,* 1899 (The Metropolitan Museum of Art, New York), which was in the same exhibition. Homer's painting, the writer believed, was "not so impressive as Paul Dougherty's

big marine on the opposite wall. That picture is not a set composition, neither does it deal in the anecdote, grisly or sentimental, but it grips you by its sincerity, its power and its superior order of workmanship."[21]

Colin Campbell Cooper was primed for election to the National Academy by his academic training at the Pennsylvania Academy of the Fine Arts in Philadelphia and at the Académie Julian in Paris. The honor came on the Associate level in 1908, and he was elevated to full Academician in 1913. Cooper first showed his work at the Academy in the annual exhibition of 1891, and as a participant in almost every annual exhibition from 1904 until his death in 1937, he was among the most active exhibitors there during those decades. Interestingly, this activity did not abate after he moved to California in 1921. Most of the paintings that Cooper showed at the Academy were of the type for which he is best known: cityscapes, which usually contained identifiable, often famous, buildings, especially those of New York City. One of the first works he sent to the Academy was a view of Trinity Church, and he went on to show paintings of New York landmarks such as Grand Central Station and the New York Public Library, and of New York sites such as the Bowling Green

Colin Campbell Cooper, c. 1900. Courtesy of Sherrill Seely Henderson and the estate of Colin Campbell Cooper.

and Columbus Circle. Several of his paintings were illustrated in the Academy's annual exhibition catalogues; for example, *The Temple of Art: San Francisco,* a result of his inspirational trip to San Francisco in 1915, was illustrated in the catalogue for the winter exhibition of 1916. Cooper was also active at the Academy as a juror of selection and awards in several years between 1911 and 1922.

William Ritschel, who first went to California in 1911, was made an Associate of the Academy in 1910 and advanced to full Academician in 1914. Of the six Academicians represented in the current exhibition, he sent the highest number of paintings to the Academy's exhibitions (Cooper was a close second). Ritschel's work first appeared there in 1905, when he showed a painting from the years he spent in Holland, and the canvases he sent to the annuals in subsequent years reflected his many travels in Europe and the United States. The first of his paintings with an identifiable California setting to be seen at the Academy was *Monterey Coast: California,* which he sent to the winter exhibition of 1912. This painting was illustrated in the catalogue of the show, one of only eighteen works to be so honored.[22] Ritschel sent canvases to almost every Academy exhibition, both its annuals and its winter shows, until the year before his death. Almost all of those he sent after 1912 were of California subjects. In fact, although the statistics have not been gathered in any systematic way, it is probably safe to say that Ritschel sent more California paintings to exhibitions at the National Academy than did any other artist. One of his western scenes, *Rocks and Breakers: Pacific Coast,* won him the Andrew Carnegie Prize at the winter exhibition of 1913, and during the 1920s, several of his paintings were selected for purchase under the terms governing the Academy's Henry Ward Ranger Fund.[23]

William Wendt, who was made an Associate of the Academy in 1912, began participating in its annual exhibitions in 1905 when he sent a view of Montecito, a town just south of Santa Barbara, California. The painting, which was executed in an impressionistic manner, was selected for illustration in the catalogue of that show. Wendt did not show again at the Academy until 1911, when he sent two paintings, at least one of which, *Sierra Madre,* was of a California scene. Presumably, the success of that work helped spur his nomination for membership in the Academy early the next year. His *There Is No Solitude, Even in Nature,* which is in the current exhibition (plate 55), was also in the Academy's winter show of 1914. Although Wendt never received an award from the Academy and was never elected to full National Academician status, he continued to participate in its annual and winter exhibitions. A total of twenty-three of his paintings appeared there from 1905 until his death in 1946. Most of these were scenes of California and included *California Coast,* shown at the Academy in 1916, and *The Patriarchs of the Grove,* which was there in 1921.[24] Another, *Day of Sunshine,* was selected from the Academy's annual of 1926 for purchase with the Academy's Henry Ward Ranger Fund.[25]

Of the six artists in the present exhibition who became members of the Academy, Armin Hansen was the only one to have been born in California. Like Wendt, Hansen selected a California picture, *Salmon Trawlers: Monterey,* 1918 (Monterey Peninsula Museum of Art), as his debut painting at the Academy. It was shown there in 1919. The next year, a painting of his named *Boy with Cod* won the First Julius Hallgarten Prize at the Academy,[26] and he remained an especially active exhibitor there throughout the 1920s. Most of the works he sent to the exhibitions were, characteristically, of the sea and of fisherfolk. In 1927, his *Harbor Bar* was selected for illustration in the catalogue of the Academy's annual, and in 1925 his *Storm Birds* was purchased from the Academy's annual of 1925 with the Henry Ward Ranger Fund.[27] That honor undoubtedly helped his election to Associate National Academician the following year; he achieved full National Academician status in 1948.

Armin Hansen. Courtesy of the Oakland Museum of California.

PLATE 55

William Wendt (1865–1946)

There Is No Solitude, Even in Nature, 1906

Oil on canvas, 34 x 36 inches

The Joan Irvine Smith Collection

The last of the artists in this exhibition to be elected to the Academy was Arthur Hill Gilbert, who was made an Associate in 1930.[28] He was not especially active in the Academy's annuals, participating sporadically, mostly in the 1920s and 1930s.[29] In 1929, however, he won two awards at the Academy: the Second Julius Hallgarten Prize for his *Old Oak Monterey,* shown in the annual exhibition, and the J. Francis Murphy Memorial Prize for his *Near Monterey,* which was in the autumn show. The latter was further honored by being selected for purchase through the Henry Ward Ranger Fund.[30] Undoubtedly, Gilbert's achievement at the Academy that year prompted his nomination, too. It also attracted the attention of the press, even inspiring *The American Magazine of Art* to publish an article about Gilbert with the two award-winning paintings as illustrations.[31]

Of course non-Academicians could and did participate in the Academy's exhibitions. Of all the artists represented in the current exhibition, Theodore Wores was the first to have a painting shown at the Academy. That was in 1881; but he did not show again until 1891, when he sent three paintings with Japanese themes. He sent works for each year from 1895 to 1899, but then his participation ceased.

Charles Reiffel was one of the most active of the non-Academicians in this exhibition to have works accepted into the Academy's annuals. From 1910 to 1933, he participated in thirteen annual and winter exhibitions.[32] Most of the paintings that he sent were done in Connecticut; but from 1929 to 1933, he showed western scenes executed in Arizona and California. Likewise, Maurice Braun sent

Guy Rose painting in Giverny, 1890. Courtesy of Roy C. Rose and the Rose Family Photo Collection.

paintings with California subjects to eight of the Academy's exhibitions during the 1910s. In that same decade, Channel Pickering Townsley's work appeared in the annuals of 1912 and 1913 and in the winter exhibitions of 1912 and 1914. E. Charlton Fortune had five works selected for various Academy exhibitions during the next decade, and Guy Rose's paintings appeared at the Academy sporadically beginning in 1910. In that year and again in 1911 Rose sent paintings from Giverny, France, where he was living and working. The only California picture by him to appear in an Academy annual was his *Rocks and Sea: Point Lobos.* It was seen there in 1923 and has returned to the Academy in the current exhibition (plate 56). Similarly, Alson S. Clark participated in the Academy's shows only a few times, in 1906, 1907, and 1916.

Several other artists in the current exhibition sent paintings only once to the Academy. Undoubtedly, they were hindered by distance, by lack of need to market their work in the East, or both. These artists were George K. Brandriff (who showed at the Academy in 1933), Benjamin Brown (1920), Jean Mannheim (1913), Hanson Puthuff (1912), Matteo Sandona (1920), Donna Schuster (1914), and Karl Yens (1918).

As the twentieth century advanced, paintings and sculptures by Californians, and by artists from other states, appeared with increasing regularity in the Academy's New York venue. Recognition of the Academy's efforts to make itself more "national" was at least occasionally noticed in the press. A writer for *The American Magazine of Art,* whose article on Arthur Hill Gilbert was mentioned above, put it nicely. She noticed that the recognition the Academy had given Gilbert "seems a significant gesture that the Academy has no prejudices, but is vitally interested in western art and is awake to the appreciation of talent wherever it exists, irrespective of the locality in which it manifests itself."[33]

PLATE 56

Guy Rose (1867–1925)

Point Lobos, c. 1918

Oil on canvas, 24 x 29 inches

Joan Irvine Smith Fine Arts, Inc.

Notes

WILLIAM H. GERDTS
IMAGES OF "THE LAND OF SUNSHINE":
CALIFORNIA IMPRESSIONISM

Many scholars, collectors, dealers, and friends have contributed to this essay, far too numerous to mention separately. I must, however, single out certain individuals. As always, Nancy Moure has fielded my constant queries with a combination of sage advice and good cheer, queries which, over these long years of importuning, would have turned off many another colleague. Despite the unwarranted urgency of my request, Ilene Susan Fort, curator of American art at the Los Angeles County Museum of Art, and her assistant, Gwen O'Bryan, have come through with a ream of photocopies which were vital to my research and writing. Janice Driesbach, the curator at the Crocker Art Gallery in Sacramento, has now, as in the past, been generous as friend and mentor. In San Diego, I have so often called upon Martin E. Petersen, former curator at the San Diego Museum of Art, and the late Bruce Kamerling of the San Diego Historical Society that the results of their generosity are certainly present here. Mary Murray, assistant curator at the Monterey Peninsula Museum of Art, has been most generous in regard to that institution's holdings of papers concerning Euphemia Charlton Fortune. W. Douglas Hartley has been extremely helpful in sorting out the complexities of Jean Mannheim's early career. Phyllis Hattis and Johanna Raphael Sibbett have been unfailing over the years in providing me with information on Joseph Raphael, one of the most fascinating of all of the California Impressionists. Kevin Starr, state librarian of California, has been a supportive and enthusiastic colleague.

My greatest debts are fivefold. Alfred Harrison, Jr., of The North Point Gallery, and his assistant director, Jessie Dunn-Gilbert, have responded positively to all my calls upon their time, efforts, and energies; they have been so generous that I have wondered, if I'd asked Alfred and Jessie just to turn over all their incomparable research library to me, whether they might not do so—or at least copy it all! They are the best, and words really *do* fail me in offering acknowledgment. Dr. A. Jess Shenson and his brother, the late Ben Shenson, have supported this and all my investigations into California and regional art, extending far beyond our mutual interest in the art and career of Theodore Wores. I owe a tremendous debt of gratitude to my research assistants, especially Deborah Frizzell and Maggie Stenz, who have braved the rigors and vagaries of the New York Public Library—and other archival repositories—in locating often obscure articles and other references needed both for information and verification. And my wife, Abigail, has offered both consultation and wit in reaction to questions ranging from meaningful terminology to innumerable points of wording and usage, such as the hyphenation of "vis-à-vis," "turn-of-the-century," and the like, along with the separation and/or closure for "wild flowers" (wildflowers?) "brushstrokes" (brush strokes?), and about half the rest of the dictionary.

Finally, my deepest gratitude is due to Joan Irvine Smith and Jean Stern for inviting me to participate in this project, and to author the present essay. I have been a tremendous admirer of the California Impressionists since my first involvement with the topic in my 1980 book *American Impressionism*. Thus, it has always been my goal, one shared by Mrs. Smith and Jean, to bring California Impressionism to New York City. Fortunately, my good friends and colleagues Annette Blaugrund, director, and David Dearinger, curator, of the National Academy Museum have joined in our enthusiasm for the project. I am deeply honored to be included in this distinguished company.

1. C. R. Pattee, "The Land of Sunshine," *Land of Sunshine* 1 (June 1894), p. 13. "The Land of Sunshine" was also the title of an article by Henry Kingman that appeared in *World Today* 8 (February 1905), pp. 171–177, though some of Kingman's photographic illustrations—"Tent City, Coronado Beach," "General View of Los Angeles," and "Oil Wells in the Heart of Los Angeles"—would seem to have denied his basic laudatory premise.

2. *Land of Sunshine* was published under that title through 1901; it continued from 1902 renamed *Out West*, indicating Lummis's growing involvement with the preservation of the Indian and Hispanic culture and archaeology of the Southwest, reflected in his instrumental role in the founding of the Southwest Museum in 1907.

3. Some of the following material is a much-abbreviated version of a section of my essay "California Impressionism in Context" that appears in William H. Gerdts and Will South, *California Impressionism* (New York: Abbeville Press, 1998).

4. Vickery was the brother-in-law of Frederick Keppel and agent for the New York art gallery of Keppel & Company. His activities were noted and praised by Alfred Trumbull in *The Collector* 5 (February 1, 1894), p. 103.

5. I have located catalogues for the three Vickery-sponsored shows. For that in support of the Polyclinic, where works by Degas and Pissarro were shown, see "Art and Charity," *San Francisco Chronicle,* November 4, 1891, p. 12; courtesy of Alfred Harrison, Jr., The North Point Gallery, San Francisco. Harrison's contributions to my research here, as in all my writing on California art, have been indispensable.

6. J[ohn] A. Stanton, "Impressions of the Art Display," *Overland Monthly* 23 (April 1894), p. 404.

7. Arthur F. Mathews, "In the Fine-Arts Building," *Californian* 5 (March 1894), p. 410.

8. Lesley Martin, "Paintings at the Mid-Winter Fair," *The Wave,* March 24, 1894, p. 11; courtesy of Alfred Harrison, Jr., The North Point Gallery, San Francisco. In actuality, neither McCormick nor Peixotto appears to have displayed French subjects, which, among the California exhibitors, were only shown by Stanton, Eva Withrow, and perhaps Elizabeth Curtis O'Sullivan and Ruth E. Benjamin.

9. "Rare Exhibit at Local Art Gallery: Collection of Interesting Water Colors by Maurice B. Prendergast, the Boston Impressionist," *San Francisco Chronicle,* May 13, 1900, p. 11.

10. George P. West, "Secluded S.F. Painter Revealed as State's Most Famous Artist," *San Francisco Examiner,* March 28, 1925, quoted by Nancy Boas and Marc Simpson in "Pastoral Visions at Continent's End: Painting of the Bay Area 1890 to 1930," in *Facing Eden: 100 Years of Landscape Art in the Bay Area* (San Francisco: Fine Arts Museums of San Francisco, 1995), p. 44.

11. Theodore Steele, "In the Far West," 1903, typescript of a lecture delivered at the Portfolio Club in Indianapolis, Archives of American Art, Smithsonian Institution, Washington, D.C., p. 10.

12. Scholars have discussed and argued the applicability of the term *Impressionism* to the work of many of the artists included in this study. I am here using the term in its broadest meaning, and especially in a formal sense involving a concern for light, rich colorism, and painterly brushwork. Some writers have preferred the term *plein air,* but this implies works painted out-of-doors, and actually many Impressionist pictures, those by such French artists as Claude Monet included, were at least partially studio productions. Serious scholarly study of this phase of California art begins with three achievements. First, there are the tremendously significant studies published by Nancy Dustin Wall Moure, beginning with her catalogue *Los Angeles Painters of the Nineteen-Twenties* (Claremont, Calif.: Pomona College Gallery, 1972) and followed by her *Publications in Southern California Art* (Glendale, Calif.: Dustin Publications, 1975 to present). Second, there was the catalogue published by The Oakland Museum, *Impressionism: The California View* (Oakland: The Oakland Museum, 1981). Third, there was the important pair of volumes edited by Ruth Lilly Westphal, *Plein Air Painters of California: The Southland* and *Plein Air Painters of California: The North* (Irvine, Calif.: Westphal Publishing, 1982 and 1986, respectively); these are hereinafter cited as "Westphal, ed., *The Southland*" and "Westphal, ed., *The North.*" For a perceptive overview of the scholarship generated over the last twenty-five years, see Jean Stern, "The California Impressionist Style in Perspective," in Susan Landauer and Jean Stern, *California Impressionism* (Irvine, Calif., and Athens, Ga.: The Irvine Museum and Georgia Museum of Art, 1996), pp. 78–84.

13. Nancy Moure, *Painting and Sculpture in Los Angeles, 1900–1945* (Los Angeles: Los Angeles County Museum of Art, 1980), p. 11.

14. Alma May Cook, "Wm. Wendt Called 'Painter Laureate' of California," *Los Angeles Herald-Express,* March 25, 1939.

15. For instance, see Westphal, ed., *The Southland,* p. 171. This designation is discussed in Charlotte Berney, ed., "Thinking About William Wendt," *Antiques & Fine Art* 7 (December 1989), pp. 94–95. The bibliography focusing specifically on Wendt is fairly extensive, but see especially Charles Francis Browne, "Some Recent Landscapes by William Wendt," *Brush and Pencil* 6 (September 1900), pp. 257–263; Everett Carroll Maxwell, "Art," *The Graphic,* June 28, 1913; Mabel Urmy Seares, "William Wendt," *American Magazine of Art* 7 (April 1916), pp. 232–235; Ellis Prentice Cole, "William Wendt at Work," *Art Student* 1 (Fall 1916), pp. 236–240; Antony Anderson et al., *William Wendt and His*

Work (Los Angeles: Stendahl Galleries, 1926); Fred Hogue, "William Wendt," *Los Angeles Times,* April 22, 1929, II, p. 4; Arthur Millier, "Our Artists in Person No. 2—William Wendt, A. N. A.," *Los Angeles Times,* July 6, 1930, III, p. 12; John Alan Walker, "William Wendt, 1865–1946," *Southwest Art* 4 (June 1974), pp. 42–45; Nancy Dustin Wall Moure, *William Wendt 1865–1946* (Laguna Beach, Calif.: Laguna Beach Museum of Art, 1977); Westphal, ed., *The Southland,* pp. 170–175; Museum Studies Graduate Certificate Program, *In Praise of Nature: The Landscapes of William Wendt* (Long Beach, Calif.: University Art Museum, California State University, Long Beach, 1989); John Alan Walker, *Documents on the Life and Art of William Wendt (1865–1946), California's Laureate of the Paysage Moralisé* (Big Pine, Calif.: John Alan Walker, 1992).

16. John E. D. Trask, "The Department of Fine Arts at the Panama-Pacific International Exposition," in *California's Magazine* 2 (San Francisco: California's Magazine Company, 1916), vol. 2, p. 88.

17. Mildred McLouth, "William Wendt—An Appreciation," *Museum Graphic* 1 (November 1926), p. 54.

18. William A. Griffith, "Foreword," quoting a letter written by Wendt in the spring of 1898 from California, in *William Wendt Retrospective Exhibition* (Los Angeles: Los Angeles County Museum, 1939).

19. On this interpretation of Wendt's work, see Walker, *Documents on Wendt.*

20. Antony Anderson, "Art and Artists," *Los Angeles Times,* July 7, 1912 [?], III, p. 22.

21. Museum Studies Program, *In Praise of Nature,* p. 49.

22. See especially the essays by Michael P. McManus, "A Focus on Light," and Joachim Smith, "The Splendid Silent Sun: Reflections on the Light and Color of Southern California," in Patricia Trenton and William H. Gerdts et al., *California Light 1900–1930* (Laguna Beach: Laguna Art Museum, 1990), pp. 13–18 and 61–92, respectively.

23. For Puthuff, see George Wharton James, "Hanson Puthuff and His Work," *Arroyo Craftsman* 1 (October 1909), pp. 31–37; Arthur Millier, "Our Artists in Person No. 13—Hanson Puthuff," *Los Angeles Times,* September 21, 1930, III, p. 23; Everett Carroll Maxwell, "Painters of the West—Hanson Puthuff," *Progressive Arizona* 11 (September 1931), pp. 10–11 (in which *Monarch of the Malibu* is reproduced); *Hanson Puthuff, Hanson Duvall Puthuff, the Artist, the Man, 1875–1972; An Autobiography with Correspondence and Notes* by Louise Puthuff (Costa Mesa, Calif.: Spencer Printing Service, n.d. [c. 1974]); Westphal, ed., *The Southland,* pp. 84–89; Janet B. Dominik, "Artist, Hanson Puthuff," *Art of California* 2 (October/November 1989), pp. 27–31.

24. Fred Hogue, "The God of the Mountains," *Los Angeles Times,* May 22, 1927, III, p. 36.

25. Charles F. Lummis, "The Mother Mountains," *Land of Sunshine* 3 (August 1895), p. 119.

26. Hogue, "The God of the Mountains."

27. Maurice Braun, for instance, exhibited his *Yosemite Evening* at the California Liberty Fair held in Los Angeles in October 1918; two years earlier, Colin Campbell Cooper painted Yosemite after visiting the Panama-Pacific and Panama-California expositions in San Francisco and San Diego, respectively, though this was prior to his taking up permanent residence in Santa Barbara. In addition, Alfred Mitchell painted in Yosemite in 1934, and both Theodore Wores and Karl Yens also painted Yosemite.

28. For Payne, see Antony Anderson and Fred S. Hogue, *Edgar Alwyn [sic] Payne and his Work* (Los Angeles: Stendahl Galleries, 1926); S. Fred Hogue, "The Art of Edgar Alwyn [sic] Payne," *Los Angeles Times,* May 18, 1926, II, p. 4; Hogue, "The God of the Mountains"; Martin E. Petersen, "Edgar Payne," *Artists of the Rockies and the Golden West* 6 (Summer 1979), pp. 52–57; Westphal, ed., *The Southland,* pp. 158–163; Charlotte Berney, "Edgar Alwin Payne and the Grandeur of California," *Antiques & Fine Art* 3 (October 1986), pp. 18–20; Nancy Moure, *Edgar Payne 1882–1947* (Los Angeles: Goldfield Galleries, 1987); Rena Neumann Coen, *The Paynes, Edgar and Elsie: American Artists* (Minneapolis: Payne Studios, 1987). Also, see Payne's own book originally published in 1941, *Composition of Outdoor Painting,* 4th edition (Minneapolis: Payne Studios, 1988), with Sierra Divide as frontispiece.

29. For Elmer Wachtel, see "Wachtel and His Work," *Land of Sunshine* 4 (March 1896), pp. 168–172; Florence Williams, "Elmer Wachtel: An Appreciation," *International Studio* 67 (January 1919), pp. xcvii–xcviii; Antony Anderson, *Elmer Wachtel: A Brief Biography* (Los Angeles, n.p., 1930); Westphal, ed., *The Southland,* pp. 112–119.

30. Elmer Wachtel, "Western Landscape," *Western Art!* 1 (April 1914), p. 21. This judgment was confirmed a decade and a half later by Arthur Millier, "Growth of Art in California," in Frank J. Taylor, *Land of Homes* (Los Angeles: Powell, 1929), p. 334.

31. Edgar Arthur Hunt, "The Wright Criterion," *Out West* 43 (April 1916), p. 161.

32. "Wachtel and his Work," *Land of Sunshine* 4 (March 1896), p. 171.

33. For Marion Wachtel, see Arthur Millier, "Our Artists in Person No. 34—Marion Kavanagh Wachtel," *Los Angeles Times,* November 8, 1931, III, p. 16; Westphal, ed., *The Southland,* pp. 112–119; Janet Dominik, "Marion Kavanagh Wachtel," *Art of California* 1 (October/November 1988), pp. 48–53.

34. The term was introduced by Merle Armitage in the *West Coaster,* September 1, 1928, as quoted by Nancy Dustin Wall Moure in "Impressionism, Post-Impressionism, and the Eucalyptus School in Southern California," in Westphal, ed., *The Southland,* pp. 11–12. Elmer Wachtel also painted the eucalyptus, as did Edgar Payne, Guy Rose, Alson S. Clark, Maurice Braun, and Joseph Kleitsch among the artists in the present exhibition, as well as Paul Grimm, Douglas Parshall, and Orrin White.

35. Arthur Millier, "The 'Eucalyptus' School," *Los Angeles Times,* September 16, 1928, III, p. 17, in which these painters were judged not only "harmless," but to be "laying the ground-work for a really genuine indigenous Southern California art."

36. Millier, "Our Artists in Person No. 34—Marion Kavanagh Wachtel," *Los Angeles Times,* November 8, 1931, III, p. 16.

37. Redmond's *California Landscape* (Jonathan Club, Los Angeles) was exhibited at the Louisiana Purchase Universal Exposition in St. Louis in 1904; the work inspired the comment that Redmond's "wonder is color, he is known as a bold colorist; he is not afraid of painting the colors he can see and he sees more than the ordinary human being" ("Granville Redmond Still Winning Honors as an Artist," *Deaf-Mutes Journal,* June 1, 1905).

38. Antony Anderson, "Art and Artists," *Los Angeles Times,* July 7, 1907, VI, p. 2.

39. The most thorough study of Redmond is Mary Jean Haley, "Granville Redmond: A Triumph of Talent and Temperament," in *Granville Redmond* (Oakland: The Oakland Museum, 1988), pp. 1–34; Haley's essay is based on "Granville Redmond" (unpublished) by Mildred Abronda. See also Everett Carroll Maxwell, "Art and Drama Department," *West Coast Magazine* 13 (December 1912), pp. 347–350; Arthur Millier, "Our Artists in Person No. 24—Granville Redmond," *Los Angeles Times,* March 22, 1931, III, pp. 28, 30; Nancy Moure, "Five Los Angeles Artists in the Collection of the Los Angeles County Museum of Art," *Southern California Quarterly* 57 (Spring 1975), pp. 42–51; Westphal, ed., *The Southland,* pp. 90–93; Mildred Abronda, "Granville Redmond: California Landscape Painter," *Art & Antiques* 5 (November/December 1982), p. 51; Mildred Abronda, "Granville Redmond," *Art of California* 1 (December/January 1989), pp. 44–50.

40. Millier, "Our Artists: Redmond," p. 28.

41. Millier, ibid., compares the artist's repetitious poppy pictures with Camille Corot's feathery tree paintings.

42. See, for instance, Grace Hortense Tower, "California's State Flower," *Overland Monthly* 39 (May 1902), pp. 882–889.

43. Charles F. Lummis, "The Carpet of God's Country," *Out West* 22 (May 1905), pp. 306–317; reference here is specifically to pp. 307–308. See also the earlier Bertha F. Herrick, "California Wild Flowers," *The Californian* 3 (December 1892), pp. 3–15.

44. Arnold V. Stubenrauch, "The California Home Garden, and How to Make It," *Country Life in America* 1 (January 1902), p. 96.

45. Sarah-Louise Faustman, "William Franklin Jackson (1850–1936), a Biography," 1984, typescript, Archives, Crocker Art Gallery, Sacramento.

46. Margaret Marshall Doyle, "Studies by Yard Gathered for View," *San Francisco Call,* June 5, 1910, p. 41; courtesy of Alfred Harrison, Jr., The North Point Gallery, San Francisco.

47. Faustman, "William Franklin Jackson," pp. 10–11.

48. "Spring Exhibition at the Institute of Art," *San Francisco Call,* May 2, 1897, p. 19; courtesy of Alfred Harrison, Jr., The North Point Gallery, San Francisco.

49. This painting was originally exhibited at the First Annual Art Salon, held in San Francisco in November 1903. See "First Annual Art Salon Opens This Afternoon," *San Francisco Chronicle,*

November 11, 1903, p. 9; see also "Painters' and Sculptors' Display is a Triumph for Local Men," *San Francisco Call,* November 12, 1903, p. 5; both articles courtesy of Alfred Harrison, Jr., The North Point Gallery, San Francisco.

50. "Wild Gardens of California Interpreted by John M. Gamble," *California Southland* 10 (March 1928), pp. 12–13. For Gamble, see also Antony Anderson, "Art and Artists," *Los Angeles Times,* February 12, 1911, III, p. 18; Westphal, ed., *The North,* pp. 74–79.

51. For lengthy discussions of the earliest recognition of Impressionism in Southern California, see the essays in Gerdts and South, *California Impressionism.*

52. Antony Anderson, "Art and Artists," *Los Angeles Times,* December 31, 1911, III, p. 13. That these artists were not only recognized as Impressionists but also admired as such was suggested the following year, in Anderson's review of an exhibition of the California Art Club: "What is more the modern impressionism of Helena Dunlap and Jack Gage Stark is not looked at askance" (Anderson, "Art and Artists," *Los Angeles Times,* November 24, 1912, III, p. 18). Stark appears to be the first to have enjoyed this identification; Anderson had reviewed his show at the Blanchard Gallery in Los Angeles in November of 1909, under the title "Pictures by an Impressionist," and noted that "our young impressionist has used pure color, purples and greens, all through his beautiful 'Sur la Marne.'…" (Antony Anderson, "Art and Artists," *Los Angeles Times,* November 26, 1909, III, p. 15).

53. Anderson, "Art and Artists," *Los Angeles Times,* December 31, 1911.

54. Alma May Cook, "Frieseke's Latest Pictures on Exhibition in Los Angeles," unidentified clipping; courtesy of Nicholas Kilmer.

55. The definitive study of Rose is by Will South, *Guy Rose, American Impressionist* (Oakland and Irvine, Calif.: The Oakland Museum and The Irvine Museum, 1995). The other most significant publications on and by Rose are Guy Rose, "At Giverny," *Pratt Institute Monthly* 6 (December 1897), p. 81; Antony Anderson and Earl Stendahl, *Guy Rose: Paintings of France and America* (Los Angeles: Stendahl Galleries, 1922); Rose V. S. Berry, "A Painter of California," *International Studio* 80 (January 1925), pp. 332–337; Antony Anderson and Peyton Boswell, *Catalogue of the Guy Rose Memorial* (Los Angeles: Stendahl Galleries, 1926); Westphal, ed., *The Southland,* pp. 94–99; Janet Dominik, "Guy Rose—American Impressionist," *Antiques & Fine Art* 4 (December 1986), pp. 36–41; Ilene Susan Fort, "The Cosmopolitan Guy Rose," in Trenton and Gerdts et al., *California Light,* pp. 93–112; Ilene Susan Fort, "The Figure Paintings of Guy Rose, *Art of California* 4 (January 1991), pp. 46–50.

56. *Girl in a Wickford Garden, New England* (Sotheby's, New York, June 6, 1997 sale, lot 19); *Lady Sewing Amongst Trees (In the Garden)* (Butterfield & Butterfield, San Francisco and Los Angeles, June 11, 1997 sale, lot 2712).

57. S. Fred Hogue, "Guy Rose," *Los Angeles Times,* March 7, 1926, II, p. 4.

58. Antony Anderson, "Guy Rose in Pasadena," *Los Angeles Times,* March 21, 1915, III, p. 17.

59. Antony Anderson, "Paintings by Guy Rose," *Los Angeles Times,* February 14, 1915, III, p. 15. Rose had already been painting the California coastline, perhaps as early as the end of 1914, for he showed at the Steckel Gallery his *Pacific Coast* and *On the Rocks,* presumably the pictures Anderson referred to here as "a few seascapes, the first Guy Rose has ever painted, his impressions of the Pacific."

60. Antony Anderson, in his review of Rose's Battey Gallery show in "Of Art and Artists," *Los Angeles Times,* January 7, 1917, III, p. 2.

61. Hunt, "*The Wright Criterion,*" p. 161.

62. Antony Anderson, reviewing Rose's first one-person show at the Los Angeles Museum of History, Science, and Art, in "Art and Artists," *Los Angeles Times,* February 20, 1916, III, p. 4.

63. A few depictions from the model, indoors, date from Rose's California years. His best-known figure painting of this period is *The Leading Lady,* 1915 (The Buck Collection), a portrait of Miss Lucretia del Valle as Señora Josefa Yorba, when she appeared in John Steven McGroarty's *Mission Play* of 1912, performed annually at the Mission San Gabriel. See Antony Anderson, "Portrait of Miss Del Valle," *Los Angeles Times,* June 13, 1915, III, p. 15.

64. Rider appears to have maintained his ties in Chicago throughout the 1920s, and it is possible that he settled in Los Angeles later than 1924. Some sources suggest that he first appeared

in the region in 1928 and only settled there in 1931.

65. For Sorolla in Chicago, see the article by another of the Spanish painter's students, Gordon Stevenson, "Sorolla in Chicago and in Spain," *New York Times Book Review and Magazine,* August 19, 1923, pp. 3, 25. Sorolla, in turn, thought tremendously highly of American art. See Harriet Monroe, "Sorolla Admits America's Supremacy in Art," *Chicago Tribune,* April 16, 1911, IX, p. 7. Thus, it would seem natural that he would be receptive to American followers such as Rider.

66. See "Bibliography of Arthur G. Rider (1886–1975)," typescript, n.d., Orr's Gallery, San Diego.

67. For Rider, see H. L. E., "A Colorful Painter," *The Palette & Chisel* 1 (June 1924), pp. 1, 3; Robert Bethea, "Arthur Grover Rider," research project typescript, 1991, Los Angeles; courtesy of Phil Kovinick and Marian Yoshiki-Kovinick.

68. For Miller, see Marie Louise Kane, *A Bright Oasis: The Paintings of Richard E. Miller* (New York: Jordan-Volpe Gallery, 1997); for his year in California, see pp. 49–53. For Miller's presence and impact in California, see three articles by Mabel Urmy Seares: "Richard Miller in Pasadena," *Los Angeles Graphic,* September 9, 1916, p. 4; "Richard Miller in Pasadena," *Pasadena Star-News,* November 22, 1916, p. 5; "Richard Miller in a California Garden," *California Southland* 5 (February 1923), pp. 10–11.

69. P[eter] C[harles] Remondino, M.D., "California as a Health Resort," *The Californian* 4 (October 1893), pp. 681–684. Remondino had just authored *The Mediterranean Shores of America: Southern California: Its Climatic, Physical, and Meteorological Conditions* (Philadelphia: F. A. Davies, 1892).

70. J. Torrey Connor, "The Summerland of America," *Munsey's Magazine* 8 (December 1892), pp. 271–275.

71. Walter Lindley, M.D., "California's Climate," *The Californian* 1 (October 1891), p. 60. Lindley had previously collaborated with Dr. Joseph Widney on California of the South (New York: D. Appleton and Company, 1888).

72. Norman Bridge, M.D., "The Invalid in Southern California," *Land of Sunshine* 3 (June 1895), p. 25.

73. Kingman, "The Land of Sunshine," pp. 175–176.

74. Sonia Wolfson, "Art and Artists," *California Graphic,* April 16, 1927, p. 6.

75. For Frost, see "Blue Mountains and the Art of John Frost," *California Southland* 6 (March 1924), pp. 10–11; Henry M. Reed, *The A. B. Frost Book* (Rutland, Vt.: Charles E. Tuttle, 1993), pp. 107–111, 127–139. John Frost has until recently been one of the most overlooked among the California Impressionists. His production may have been reduced owing to problems of health and his limited stay in the region.

76. "John Frost Shows Recent Landscapes," *Los Angeles Times,* February 7, 1926, III, p. 32.

77. The principal studies of Clark are by Jean Stern: *Alson S. Clark* (Los Angeles: Petersen Publishing, 1983); and "Alson Clark: An American at Home and Abroad," in Trenton and Gerdts et al., *California Light,* pp. 113–136. See also Elizabeth Whiting, "Painting in the Far West: Alson Clark, Artist," *California Southland* 3 (February 1922), pp. 8–9; M[abel] U[rmy] S[eares], "Alson Skinner Clark, Artist," *California Southland* 9 (March 1927), pp. 28–29; "A Unique Monument to Old California" [the Carthay Circle Murals], *American Magazine of Art* 18 (January 1927), pp. 23–25; "The First National Bank of Pasadena, California, and First-Trust & Savings Bank of Pasadena, California," *California Southland* 11 (January 1929), pp. 18–19; John Palmer Leeper, "Alson S. Clark (1876–1949)," *Pasadena Art Institute Bulletin* 1 (April 1951), pp. 15–19; Westphal, ed., *The Southland,* pp. 52–57.

78. Probably in 1917, Rose wrote to William Macbeth, his New York dealer, that he had sold more work than any other local artist (Rose to Macbeth, April 5 [1917?], Macbeth Gallery papers, Archives of American Art, Smithsonian Institution, Washington, D.C., roll 2628).

79. Arthur Millier, the leading art critic in Los Angeles in the late 1920s, did distinguish between them in 1929, clearly voicing his favoritism when he wrote that Rose was "almost more a French Impressionist than an American painter," and deeming Wendt "the man who has most truthfully pictured Southern California" (Arthur Millier, "Growth of Art in California," in Taylor, *Land of Homes,* pp. 334–335).

80. Laguna Beach began to gain not only local but national celebrity around 1920. See Neeta Marquis, "Laguna: Art Colony of the Southwest," *International Studio* 70 (March 1920), pp. xxvi–xxvii;

Jessie A. Selkinhaus, "The Laguna Beach Art Colony," *Touchstone* 8 (January 1921), pp. 250–255; W. W. Robinson, "The Laguna Colony," *California Southland* 6 (July 1924), p. 10.

81. The most recent study of activities at Laguna Beach is Susan M. Anderson and Bolton Colburn, "Painting Paradise: A History of the Laguna Beach Art Association 1900–1930," in *Impressions of California: Early Currents in Art 1850–1930* (Irvine, Calif.: The Irvine Museum, 1996), pp. 109–133. See also Anna A[lthea] Hills, "The Laguna Beach Art Association," *American Magazine of Art* 10 (October 1919), pp. 459–463; Marquis, "Laguna: Art Colony"; Selkinhaus, "The Laguna Beach Art Colony"; W. W. Robinson, "The Laguna Art Colony," *California Southland* 6 (July 1924), p. 10; Thomas Kenneth Enman and Ruth Westphal, "Earliest Days of the Laguna Beach Art Colony," in Westphal, ed., *The Southland*, pp. 122–127; Robert M. Frash, "A Regional Response to the Impressionist Challenge," *California History* 63 (Summer 1984), pp. 252–255; Janet Blake Dominik, *Early Artists in Laguna Beach: The Impressionists* (Laguna Beach, Calif.: Laguna Art Museum, 1986); Nancy Dustin Wall Moure and Joanne L. Ratner, *A History of the Laguna Art Museum 1918–1993* (Laguna Beach: Laguna Art Museum, 1993); Nancy Dustin Wall Moure and Joanne L. Ratner, "Laguna Art Museum: The Seventy-Fifth Anniversary," *American Art Review* 5 (Spring 1993), pp. 132–139, 165.

82. Merle and Mabel Ramsey, *Pioneer Days of Laguna Beach* (Laguna Beach, Calif.: Hastie Printers, 1967), pp. 64–65.

83. Harry Noyes Pratt, "The Eucalyptus," *Overland Monthly* and *Out West Magazine* 82 (July 1924), p. 316.

84. South, *Guy Rose*, p. 66, and p. 83, n.154.

85. "The Sea Coast of Southern California," *Land of Sunshine* 2 (December 1894), p. 1.

86. Beatrice de Lack Krombach, "Sixth Annual Exhibition of the California Art Club at Exposition Park Museum," *The Graphic*, October 9, 1915, p. 6. The painting received national recognition through illustration in a Chicago magazine: Everett Carroll Maxwell, "Development of Landscape Painting in California," *Fine Arts Journal* 34 (March 1916), p. 140.

87. John Gutzon Borglum, "An Artist's Paradise," *Land of Sunshine* 2 (May 1895), p. 106.

88. "An Art Center for Los Angeles," *California Southland* 2 (November 1920), p. 11.

89. For Smith, see Neeta Marquis, "Jack Wilkinson Smith," *International Studio* 69 (December 1919), pp. lxxiv-lxxvi; "Jack Wilkinson Smith: California Artist," *Arrowhead Magazine* (March 1923), pp. 8–9; Lee Shippey, "Lee Side o' L.A.," *Los Angeles Times*, November 21, 1929, II, p. 7; Arthur Millier, "Our Artists in Person No. 15—Jack Wilkinson Smith," *Los Angeles Times*, October 5, 1930, III, pp. 22, 24; Everett Carroll Maxwell, "Jack Wilkinson Smith Constructive Artist," *Overland Monthly* 90 (October 1932), pp. 237–238; Westphal, ed., *The Southland*, pp. 106–111.

90. For Cuprien, see *The Art of F. W. Cuprien* (Los Angeles: Kanst Art Gallery, n.d. [c. 1914]); Westphal, ed., *The Southland*, pp. 134–137.

91. Yens appears to have eluded serious criticism, except for contemporary exhibition reviews. To my knowledge, the only substantial article is Everett C. Maxwell, "Art," *The Graphic*, July 27, 1912, p. 9.

92. For Hills, see Antony Anderson, "Art and Artists," *Los Angeles Times*, November 16, 1913, III, p. 6; Arthur Millier, "Our Artists in Person No. 29—Anna A. Hills," *Los Angeles Times*, June 7, 1931, III, p. 16; *Anna A. Hills* (Long Beach, Calif.: California State University, Long Beach, 1976); Westphal, ed., *The Southland*, pp. 144–147.

93. Antony Anderson, "Of Art and Artists," *Los Angeles Times*, January 22, 1922, III, p. 45.

94. I am tremendously indebted to W. Douglas Hartley, Norman, Illinois, for the chronology of Mannheim; Dr. Hartley has prepared a manuscript on the life and art of Jean Mannheim and has accumulated a great deal of material on the artist. Published sources on Mannheim include Antony Anderson, "Art and Artists," *Los Angeles Times*, November 12, 1911, III, p. 21; Everett Carroll Maxwell, "The Art of Jean Mannheim," *Overland Monthly* 91 (October 1933), pp. 125, 127; Westphal, ed., *The Southland*, pp. 78–93.

95. The major study of Kleitsch is Patricia Trenton, "Joseph Kleitsch: A Kaleidoscope of Color," in Trenton and Gerdts et al., *California Light*, pp. 137–156. See also "The Editor," [James William Pattison], "The Art of Joseph Kleitsch," *Fine Arts Journal* 37 (June 1919), pp. 46–52; Fred Hogue, "A Hungarian Artist," *Los Angeles Times*, June 25, 1928, II, p. 4; Westphal, ed., *The Southland*, pp. 152–157.

96. Charles Francis Saunders, "California," in Alice B. Lockwood, ed., *Gardens of Colony and State* (New York: Charles Scribner's Sons, 1934), vol. 2, p. 394.

97. Ibid., pp. 391–402.

98. This is not to say that the cultivation of formal gardens was not of great concern to Californians. For an overview of California garden design, see David C. Streatfield, "Where Pine and Palm Meet: The California Garden as a Regional Expression," *Landscape Journal* 4 (Fall 1985), pp. 61–73.

99. Charles Howard Shinn, "Spring Flowers of California," *Overland Monthly* n.s. 11 (April 1888), p. 417.

100. For Brown, see Mabel Urmy Seares, "California as a Sketching Ground," *International Studio* 43 (April 1911), pp. 121–132; Edna Gearhart, "Benjamin Brown of Pasadena," *Overland Monthly* 82 (July 1924), pp. 124–126; Rose V. S. Berry, "A Patriarch of Pasadena," *International Studio* 81 (May 1925), pp. 123–126; E[dna] Gearhart, "Brothers Brown: California Painters and Etchers," *American Magazine of Art* 20 (May 1929), pp. 283–289; Arthur Millier, "Our Artists in Person No. 17—Benjamin C. Brown," *Los Angeles Times*, October 9, 1930, III, pp. 14, 22; Westphal, ed., *The Southland*, pp. 44–47. See also the compendium by John Alan Walker, *Benjamin Chambers Brown (1865–1942): A Chronological and Descriptive Bibliography* (Big Pine, Calif.: John Alan Walker, 1989).

101. See the definitive study by May Brawley Hill, *Grandmother's Garden: The Old-Fashioned American Garden 1865–1915* (New York: Harry N. Abrams, 1995). Hill deals specifically with California gardens in pages 201–212.

102. "In the Studios," *American Art News* 14 (April 29, 1916), p. 7.

103. For the Santa Barbara art colony at just the time Cooper moved there, see L. W. Wilson, "Santa Barbara's Artist Colony," *American Magazine of Art* 12 (December 1921), pp. 411–414; for a more recent assessment, see Gloria Rexford Martin, "Then and Now," *Antiques & Fine Art* 9 (November/December 1991), pp. 85–93.

104. The bibliography on Cooper is fairly extensive. For his California years, see James M. Hansen, *Colin Campbell Cooper* (Santa Barbara: n.p., 1981); Tina Goolsby, "Colin Campbell Cooper," *Art & Antiques* 6 (January/February 1983), pp. 56–63; Westphal, ed., *The North*, pp. 58–63.

105. Van Gogh's *The Sower;* see Jean Stern, *The Paintings of Franz A. Bischoff* (Los Angeles: Petersen Publishing, 1980), n.p.

106. The two major studies of Bischoff are both by Jean Stern: *The Paintings of Franz A. Bischoff;* and "Franz Bischoff: From Ceramist to Painter," in Trenton and Gerdts et al., *California Light*, pp. 157–170. See also Westphal, ed., *The Southland*, pp. 38–43; Janet B. Dominik, "Franz Bischoff," *Art of California* 2 (April/May 1989), pp. 12–17.

107. Ed Ainsworth, *Painters of the Desert* (Palm Desert, Calif.: Desert Printers, 1960), p. 55.

108. For Lauritz, see Arthur Millier, "Our Artists in Person No. 30—Paul Lauritz," *Los Angeles Times*, July 5, 1931, III, p. 12; John Hilton, "Artist Who Grinds His Own Pigments," *Desert Magazine* (March 1941), p. 22; Ed Ainsworth, "Paul Lauritz: The Man Who Paints the Desert's Spirit," *Palm Springs Villager* (May 1957), n.p.; Ainsworth, *Painters of the Desert,* pp. 52–58; Westphal, ed., *The Southland,* pp. 74–77.

109. Millier, "Our Artists—Lauritz."

110. For Coburn and his urban imagery, see Bradley J. Delaney, *Frank Coburn (1862–1938): An Early Los Angeles Painter* (San Diego: Orr's Gallery, 1991). A few other Los Angeles paintings are known by the Impressionists, such as Paul Lauritz's *Old Los Angeles, 1922* (Mr. and Mrs. Peter Ochs) and Sam Hyde Harris's *Old Los Angeles* (see Ruth Westphal and Jean Stern, *The Paintings of Sam Hyde Harris (1889–1977)* [Beverly Hills, Calif.: Petersen Publishing, 1980], p. 35), but these tend to avoid or downplay the sense of metropolitan modernism.

111. See William H. Gerdts, *Impressionist New York* (New York: Abbeville Press, 1994).

112. See, for instance, the discussion of such hostelries as the Hotel Coronado in San Diego, the Cliff House in San Francisco, and the Del Monte Hotel in Monterey (this last was soon to become a venue for many artists but not the subject of their brushes), in A. J. Wells, "California Summer Resorts," *Out West* 19 (July 1903), pp. 115–127.

113. For the interpretation of this distinct facet of American Impressionism, see the study by Lisa N. Peters, *American Impressionist Images of Suburban Leisure and Country Comfort* (Carlisle, Penn.: Trout Gallery, Dickinson College, 1997).

114. For Hinkle, not included in the present exhibition, see Arthur Millier, "Our Artists in Person

No. 38—Clarence K. Hinkle," *Los Angeles Times,* June 4, 1933, II, p. 4; *Clarence Hinkle 1880–1960* (Santa Barbara: Santa Barbara Museum of Art, 1960); 45th Anniversary Exhibit: *Clarence Hinkle 1880–1960* (Laguna Beach, Calif.: Laguna Beach Art Association, 1963); Raymond-Callison Gallery, *Clarence Keiser Hinkle (1880–1960): A Selection of His Paintings* (Stockton, Calif.: University of the Pacific, 1978); Westphal, ed., *The Southland,* pp. 70–77. Born on a ranch outside of Sacramento, Hinkle was one of the few native Californians among the Southern California Impressionists. He worked in San Francisco from 1912–17, in Los Angeles from 1917–30, and in Laguna Beach from 1931–35; after 1935 he was in Santa Barbara. Hinkle's painting combines aspects of Impressionism with Cézanne-influenced strategies of Post-Impressionism.

115. For Bischoff and Smith together, see Jean Stern, *The Paintings of Bischoff,* p. 169. Smith studied with Robert Henri in New York and moved to Los Angeles in 1920. After Bischoff's death and the stock market crash, both in 1929, Smith abandoned painting and became an interior decorator.

116. The most notable pictures of harbors filled with fishing boats by a California artist were created by Edgar Payne, but these were European scenes of Concarneau, Brittany, and on the Adriatic, near Venice, which Payne visited beginning in 1923.

117. For Hunt, see Westphal, ed., *The Southland,* pp. 148–151. For the location here, I am indebted to the entry by Nancy Moure in *A Time and Place: From the Ries Collection of California Painting* (Oakland: The Oakland Museum, 1990), p. 80.

118. For Harris, see Westphal and Stern, *The Paintings of Harris;* Westphal, ed., *The Southland,* pp. 64–69.

119. For Brandriff, see Arthur Millier, "Our Artists in Person No. 26—George Brandriff," *Los Angeles Times,* April 19, 1931, III, pp. 10, 26; Everett Carroll Maxwell, "Painters of the West—George K. Brandriff," *Progressive Arizona* 11 (October 1931), pp. 16–17, 20; Frank Ankebrand, Jr., "Notes on Vineland Artists, 1861–1940," *Vineland [New Jersey] Historical Association Bulletin* 25 (January 1940), pp. 24–26; Westphal, ed., *The Southland,* pp. 128–133.

120. See Bolton Colburn, "George Kennedy Brandriff," in *75 Works: 75 Years Collecting the Art of California* (Laguna Beach, Calif.: Laguna Art Museum, 1993), p. 49.

121. Lummis began his investigation and championing of the Missions soon after he arrived in California in 1885. See "The Old Missions," *Drake's Magazine* 7 (March 1889). He also is almost certainly the author of "The Landmarks Club," *Overland Monthly* 23 (September 1905), pp. 257–264. For Lummis himself, see Edwin R. Bingham, *Charles F. Lummis: Editor of the Southwest* (San Marino, Calif.: Huntington Gallery, 1955); Kevin Starr, *Americans and the California Dream, 1850–1915* (New York: Oxford University Press, 1973), pp. 396–401; Turbese Lummis-Fiske and Keith Lummis, *Charles F. Lummis: The Man and His West* (Norman, Okla.: University of Oklahoma Press, 1975).

The extensive literature on the Missions begins with Helen Hunt Jackson's *Glimpses of California and the Missions* (1883; new edition, Boston: Little, Brown, 1902); it was first published a year before her influential novel, *Ramona: A Story* (Boston: Roberts Brothers, 1884). See also the important volume by Lummis's major challenger, George Wharton James, *In and Out of the Old Missions* (Boston: Little, Brown, 1905). Carey McWilliams has estimated that "not a year has passed since 1900 without the publication of some new volume about the Missions" (Carey McWilliams, *Southern California: An Island on the Land* [1946; new edition, Layton, Utah: Gibbs Smith, 1973], p. 77). For other early accounts, see Frances Fuller Victor, "Studies of the California Missions.—I, II III," *The Californian* 5 (May 1882), pp. 389–405; 5 (June 1882), pp. 514–525; 6 (July 1882), pp. 15–26 (published before H. H. Jackson's book); and two articles by Laura Bride Powers entitled "The Missions of California," in *The Californian* 2 (September 1892), pp. 547–556, and *The Californian* 4 (July 1893) pp. 142–157. For the time of the Impressionists, see Vernon J. Selfridge, *The Miracle Missions* (Los Angeles: Grafton Publishing, 1915). For more modern descriptions and assessments, see Paul C. Johnson, ed., *The California Missions* (Menlo Park, Calif.: Lane Book Company, 1965); Starr, *Americans and the California Dream;* Davis Dutton, ed., *Missions of California* (New York: Ballantine Books, 1972); and especially James J. Rawls, "The California Mission As Symbol and Myth," *California History* 71 (Fall 1992), pp. 342–361.

122. See, for instance, "Ruins of the Franciscan Missions in California," *Century* 26 (June 1883), pp. 199–215; Henry W. Henshaw, "Missions and Mission Indians of California," *Popular Science Monthly* 37 (August 1890), pp. 465–485; John T. Doyle, "The Missions of Alta California," *Century* 41 (January 1891), pp. 289–402; Torrey Connor, "Among the Old Missions of California," *Chautauquan* 22 (November 1895), pp. 185–192; George Wharton James, "The Franciscan Mission Buildings of California," *The Craftsman* 5 (January 1904), pp. 321–335. Attitudes toward the Missions and their restoration changed very rapidly toward the end of the century. Doyle, for instance, in January 1891, concluded that each "stands there today, magnificent, even in its ruins" ("The Missions of Alta California," p. 402), while two years later, in July 1893, Powers suggested "preserving from further disintegration the crumbling sanctuaries" ("The Missions of California," p. 157).

123. For a complete study of the pictorial images of the Missions, see Jean Stern, Gerald J. Miller, Pamela Hallan-Gibson, and Norman Neuerburg, *Romance of the Bells: The California Missions in Art* (Irvine, Calif.: The Irvine Museum, 1995). For the Pre-Impressionist period, see George Watson Cole, "Missions and Mission Pictures: A Contribution Towards an Iconography of the Franciscan Missions of California," *News Notes of California Libraries* 5 (July 1910), pp. 390–412.

124. Pamela Hallan-Gibson, "Mission San Juan Capistrano," in Stern et al., *Romance of the Bells,* pp. 64–69.

125. Beatrice de Lack Krombach, "Art," *The Graphic,* January 16, 1915, p. 13; Townsley's career and art has so far escaped scholarly examination.

126. Eunice T. Gray, "Chase Summer Art School," *American Art News* 13 (October 17, 1914), p. 2.

127. *California's Magazine* 2, vol. 1, p. 21ff.

128. Nancy Dustin Wall Moure, "The California Art Club to 1930," *Impressions of California: Early Currents,* p. 94. Moure suggests here that, in the 1915 annual, figure and portrait paintings almost equaled the number of landscapes, but this doesn't seem to be true, though the proportional change from 1911 is indeed striking. My own calculation is that among the seventy-nine works shown, twenty-six paintings were probably portraits and figure studies, and forty-one were landscapes. Of course, titles can be misleading, and some of the landscapes may have included fairly prominent figures.

129. Arthur Millier, "An Age of Innocence: Southern California Art in the Twenties," in Moure, *Los Angeles Painters of the Nineteen-Twenties,* n.p.

130. Trenton, "Joseph Kleitsch," p. 148; for a reproduction of the 1922 *Oriental Shop,* see p. 143.

131. Antony Anderson, "Art and Artists," *Los Angeles Times,* December 6, 1914, pp. 5, 6.

132. For Schuster, see the essay by Leonard R. de Grassi in *Donna Norine Schuster 1883–1953* (Downey, Calif.: Downey Museum of Art, 1977); Westphal, ed., *The Southland,* pp. 100–105; Roberta Gittens, "Donna Schuster," *Art of California* 4 (May 1991), pp. 16–20; Patricia Trenton and Roberta Gittens, "Donna Norine Schuster," *Southwest Art* 22 (February 1993), pp. 68–74, 132.

133. Meta Cressey appears to have so far eluded scholarly study. For information on her and her husband, Bert, see the compilation of photocopied material amassed by Robert Simpson, now deposited at the Los Angeles County Museum of Art. I am tremendously grateful to Ilene Susan Fort, curator of American art, and her associate, Gwen O'Bryan, for their assistance here. See also Antony Anderson, "Art and Artists: The Cressey Studio," *Los Angeles Times,* July 5, 1914, III, p. 11. For Bert Cressey, see Arthur Millier, "Our Artists in Person No. 37—Bert Cressey," *Los Angeles Times,* March 13, 1932, III, p. 24.

134. The "conservative" Progressives working in Southern California in the later 1910s and the 1920s have not received the attention directed to either the Impressionists or the later American Scene painters, Surrealists, and Modernists. See, however, Susan M. Anderson, *California Progressives 1910–1930* (Newport Beach, Calif.: Orange County Museum of Art, 1996); for the definition quoted here, see p. 10.

135. Arthur Millier, "Art," *Los Angeles Times,* March 13, 1927, III, p. 28.

136. M[abel] Urmy Seares, "California as Presented by Her Artists," *California Southland* 6 (June 1924), p. 9.

137. For Vysekal, see Luvena Buchanan, "Edouard A. Vysekal, Painter," *Czechoslovak Review* 8 (June 1924), pp. 157–159; Sonia Wolfson, "Two Ironic Romanticists," *The Argus* 4 (October 1928), pp. 3, 14; Arthur Millier, "Our Artists in Person No. 4—Edouard Vysekal," *Los Angeles Times,* July 20, 1930, III, p. 12.

138. For an overall view of the leading landscape painters of San Diego, see Martin E. Petersen, *Second Nature: Four Early San Diego Landscape Painters* (San Diego and Munich: San Diego Museum of Art and Prestel-Verlag, 1991).

139. Susan Landauer, "Impressionism's Indian Summer," in Landauer and Stern, *California Impressionism,* p. 18.

140. For a Theosophical interpretation of Braun's art, see Reginald Poland, "The Divinity of Nature in the Art of Maurice Braun," *The Theosophical Path* 34 (May 1928), pp. 473–476; and, by Braun himself, "Theosophy and the Artist," *The Theosophical Path* 14 (January 1918), pp. 7–13, and "What Theosophy Means To Me," *Theosophical Path* 35 (October 1928), pp. 367–368.

141. Joachim Smith, "The Splendid Silent Sun," p. 89.

142. Antony Anderson, "Of Art and Artists," *Los Angeles Times,* November 15, 1914, III, p. 10.

143. "Maurice Braun, Landscapist," *Western Art!* 1 (June/July/August 1914), p. 27. The literature on Braun is fairly extensive. In addition to the articles previously cited, see "Landscapes of Maurice Braun," *Western Art* 1 (April 7, 1916), pp. 10–11; Esther Mugan Bush, "A Master Brush which Breathes Its Inspiration from Point Loma," *Santa Fe Magazine* 11 (August 1917), pp. 13–21; "A Master-Brush of Point Loma," *The Theosophical Path* 14 (January 1918), pp. 13–18; Hazel Boyer, "The Homecoming of Maurice Braun," *Southwest Magazine* 1 (March 1924), p. 7; Hazel Boyer, "A Notable San Diego Painter," *California Southland* 6 (April 1924), p. 12; Helen Comstock, "Painter of East and West," *International Studio* 80 (March 1925), pp. 485–488; "Maurice Braun: Painter," *San Diego Magazine* 4 (December/January 1951/52), pp. 13–16, 43–44; Martin E. Petersen, "Maurice Braun: Master Painter of the California Landscape," *The Journal of San Diego History* 23 (Summer 1977), pp. 20–40; Westphal, ed., *The Southland,* pp. 186–191; Martin E. Petersen, "Profile: Artist, Maurice Braun," *Art of California* 2 (August/September 1989), pp. 44–53; Petersen, *Second Nature,* pp. 24–35.

144. Braun, "Theosophy and the Artist," p. 7.

145. For Mitchell, the primary study is Thomas R. Anderson, *Sunlight and Shadow: The Art of Alfred R. Mitchell, 1888–1972* (San Diego: Museum of San Diego History, 1988). See also Martin E. Petersen, "Alfred R. Mitchell, Pioneer Artist in San Diego," *Journal of San Diego History* 19 (Fall 1973), pp. 42–50; Westphal, ed., *The Southland,* pp. 198–203; Petersen, *Second Nature,* pp. 36–45.

146. For Reiffel, see Arthur Millier, "Charles Reiffel, American Landscape Painter," *The Argus* 3 (July–August 1928), p. 176; Eileen Dwyer, "The Art of Charles Reiffel," *The Argus* 4 (April 1929), p. 20; Fine Arts Society of San Diego, *Charles Reiffel: A Memorial Exhibition of His Paintings* (San Diego: Fine Arts Gallery, 1942); Westphal, ed., *The Southland,* pp. 204–208; Martin E. Petersen, "Success at Mid-Life: Charles Reiffel, 1862–1942, San Diego Artist," *Journal of San Diego History* 31 (Winter 1985), pp. 24–39; Petersen, *Second Nature,* pp. 46–55; Martin E. Petersen, "Charles Reiffel," *Art of California* 4 (July 1991), pp. 34–40.

147. Millier, "Charles Reiffel."

148. Beatrice de Lack Kromback, "The San Diego Awards," *The Argus* 1 (August 1927), p. 33; the short-lived San Francisco publication *The Argus* (1927–29) appears to have been especially appreciative of Reiffel's art.

149. Martin E. Petersen, "Contemporary Artists of San Diego," *Journal of San Diego History* 16 (Fall 1970), pp. 3–10.

150. Charles Reiffel, "The Modernistic Movement in Art," *The Modern Clubwoman* (January 1930), p. 4.

151. Arthur Millier, "The Art Temperaments of Northern and Southern California Compared," *The Argus* 1 (August 1927), p. 32.

152. Though there is no definitive study of Wores, the bibliography on him is quite extensive, but the works published deal especially with his years in Japan. See Lewis Ferbraché, *Theodore Wores: Artist in Search of the Picturesque* (San Francisco: privately published, 1968); Joseph A. Baird, Jr., *Theodore Wores—The Japanese Years* (Oakland: The Oakland Museum, 1976); Gary A. Reynolds, "A San Francisco Painter, Theodore Wores," *American Art Review* 3 (September–October 1976), pp. 101–117; Michael Preble, *Theodore Wores 1859–1939* (Huntsville, Ala.: Huntsville Museum of Art, 1980); Westphal, ed., *The North,* pp. 172–177; Jan N. Thompson, "Theodore Wores," *Art of California* 3 (May 1990), pp. 16–24; William H. Gerdts and Jan Newstrom Thompson, *Theodore Wores: An American Artist in Meiji Japan* (Pasadena, Calif.: Pacific Asia Museum, 1993). The finest publication

of reproductions of Wores's paintings is in *Japanese: The Art of Theodore Wores* (Tokyo: Asahi Shimbun, 1986), in which a number of the artist's later plum- and almond-blossom paintings are reproduced, complementing those of cherry blossoms painted earlier in Japan.

153. Theodore Wores, "An Artist's Tale," *Women's City Club Magazine* (March 1938), quoted in Ferbraché, *Theodore Wores: Artist in Search of the Picturesque,* pp. 57–58.

154. Anna Cora Winchell, "Artists and Their Work," *San Francisco Chronicle,* October 17, 1920.

155. *San Francisco Call,* October 21, 1920.

156. Ferbraché, *Theodore Wores: Artist in Search of the Picturesque,* p. 58.

157. For the sociological implications of this theme in California and, indeed, in American Impressionist painting, see Bram Dijkstra, "The High Cost of Parasols: Images of Women in Impressionist Art," Trenton and Gerdts et al., *California Light,* pp. 33–52. Such images, however, were not nearly so plentiful in California Impressionism as they were in the work of eastern or expatriate American artists.

158. Surprisingly, given both Raphael's tremendous accomplishment and his current esteem, there has been no in-depth modern consideration of his art or career. However, the artist's daughter, Johanna Raphael Sibbett, together with Dr. Phyllis Hattis, is currently involved in a major study of Raphael, complete with a catalogue raisonné. Otherwise, see Gene Hailey, ed., *California Art Research* (San Francisco: Federal WPA Project, 1937), vol. 5, pp. 31–43; *An Exhibition of Rediscovery: Joseph Raphael, 1872–1950,* introduction by Theodore M. Lilienthal (San Francisco: California Historical Society, 1975); Anita Ventura Mozley, "Joseph Raphael: Impressionist Paintings and Drawings," typescript essay and catalogue information for an exhibition held at the Stanford University Museum of Art, 1980; Emke Raassen-Kruimel, *Joseph Raphael, 1869–1950* (Laren, the Netherlands: Singer Museum, 1982); Westphal, ed., *The North,* pp. 160–165.

159. *Oakland Tribune,* April 15, 1916, quoted in "Joseph Raphael Chronology," p. 4; courtesy of Dr. Phyllis Hattis.

160. Raphael to Albert Bender, Special Collections, Mills College Library, Oakland.

161. The art exhibitions held at the Del Monte Hotel garnered considerable publicity in the local press in their time. See two articles by Josephine Blanch, curator of the Del Monte Gallery: "The Del Monte Gallery," *Western Art!* 1 (June/July/August 1914), p. 34; and "The Del Monte Art Gallery," *Art & Progress* 5 (September 1914), pp. 387–392. In an article dealing almost exclusively with the Tonalist artists resident there, Blanch christened Monterey "The 'Barbizon' of California: Some Interesting Studios There," *Overland Monthly* 50 (July 1907), pp. 63–68.

162. Betty Hoag McGlynn, *Carmel Art Association: A History* (Carmel-by-the-Sea, Calif.: Carmel Art Association, 1987), pp. 5–13.

163. For the artistic presence in Monterey, see the catalogues of two exhibitions held at the Monterey Peninsula Museum of Art: *Helen Spangenberg, Yesterday's Artists on the Monterey Peninsula* (Monterey, Calif.: Monterey Peninsula Museum of Art, 1976); *Monterey: The Artist's View, 1925–1945* (Monterey, Calif.: Monterey Peninsula Museum of Art, 1982). See also Betty Lochrie Hoag, *Del Monte Revisited* (Carmel, Calif.: Carmel Museum of Art, 1969); Barbara J. Klein, "The Carmel Monterey Peninsula Art Colony: A History," *American Art Review* 8 (September–October 1996), pp. 110–117.

164. Harvey L. Jones, *Twilight and Reverie: California Tonalist Painting: 1890–1930* (Oakland: The Oakland Museum, 1995).

165. Ellen Dwyer Donovan, "California Artists and Their Work," *Overland Monthly* 51 (January 1908), p. 33.

166. Morgan's work was noted and praised in connection with a reception she gave at her Carmel studio in the summer of 1910. See Doyle, "Studies by Yard Gathered for View."

167. For Morgan, see "M. de Neale Morgan, Water-Colorist," *Western Art!* 1 (June/July/August 1914), p. 25; Eleanor Taylor Houghton, "A Woman Painter," *Overland Monthly* 83 (February 1925), pp. 62–63, 91; Westphal, ed., *The North,* pp. 120–125; Betty Hoag McGlynn, "By the Sea: M DeNeale Morgan and E. Charlton Fortune," *Antiques & Fine Art* 7 (January/February 1990), pp. 84–90; *Six Early Women Artists: A Diversity of Styles* (Carmel, Calif.: Carmel Art Association, 1991), pp. 76–91.

168. Antony Anderson, "Art and Artists," *Los Angeles Times,* October 8, 1911, III, p. 18. Morgan's

predilection for the cypress-tree motif continued throughout her career. See, for instance, Josephine Mildred Blanch, "California Artists in Force at Del Monte Gallery," *The Carmelite,* October 22, 1931, p. 5, which states: "De Neale Morgan chooses as her motif almost always the Monterey cypresses so in her picture, 'Early Morning, Monterey Coast,' is shown her intimate knowledge of this subject."

169. "Unusual Merit Attaches to Exhibit of San Francisco Art Association," *San Francisco Call,* November 20, 1903, p. 16; courtesy of Alfred Harrison, Jr., The North Point Gallery, San Francisco.

170. Blanch, "California Artists in Force," p. 35.

171. Hailey, ed., *California Art Research,* vol. 12, p. 61.

172. Merle Schipper, "E. Charlton Fortune: Light, Color, and the Sea," in Robert E. Brennan and Merle Schipper, *Color and Impressions: The Early Work of E. Charlton Fortune* (Monterey: Monterey Peninsula Museum of Art, 1990), p. 49.

173. Anna Cora Winchell, "Artists and Their Work," *San Francisco Chronicle,* December 19, 1920, p. 57.

174. The major study of Fortune is Brennan and Schipper, *Color and Impressions;* Brennan, now deceased, wrote a lengthy unpublished biography of Fortune. See also [Jeanne B. Salinger], "Paintings by Charlton Fortune," *The Argus* 2 (November 1927), p. 68; Hailey, ed., *California Art Research,* vol. 12, pp. 54–76; Westphal, ed., *The North,* pp. 68–73; Janet B. Dominik, "E. Charlton Fortune," *Art of California* 2 (August/September 1989), pp. 54–58. The Monterey Peninsula Museum of Art holds a significant archive on the artist; among the material is Fortune's 1967

"Autobiography," which has proved useful in the present essay. My thanks to Mary Murray, the Assistant Curator at the Museum, for her efforts on my behalf.

175. The bibliography on Nelson is scarce; see Westphal, ed., *The North,* pp. 126–131. I am grateful to Gilbert T. Vincent of the New York State Historical Association in Cooperstown, who has perceptively noted that Samuel Nelson, a Supreme Court Justice in the mid-nineteenth century, was an important resident of Cooperstown and had descendants living in California; Bruce Nelson may have been one of them, and been drawn back to the ancestral hometown.

176. Major studies of Hansen are Raymond L. Wilson, "The Graphic Art of Armin Hansen," in Anthony R. White, *The Graphic Art of Armin C. Hansen: A Catalogue Raisonné* (Los Angeles: Hennessey & Ingalls, 1986); Anthony R. White and Charlotte Berney, *Armin Hansen: The Jane and Justin Dart Collection* (Monterey, Calif.: Monterey Peninsula Museum of Art, 1993). See also Harry Noyes Pratt, "Three California Painters," *American Magazine of Art* 16 (April 1925), pp. 199–204; Josephine Blanch, "Armin Hansen Painter of the Sea," *Game and Gossip* 1 (February 1927), pp. 22–23; Aline Kistler, "Armin Hansen Etcher of the Sea," *Prints* 5 (November 1934), pp. 1–9; Hailey, ed., *California Art Research,* vol. 9, pp. 104–137; "Dean of Western Painters," *Western Woman* 11 (October/November/December 1944), pp. 3–4; Marjorie Warren, "Portraits: Armin Hansen Painter of the Sea," *What's Doing Magazine* 1 (September

1946), pp. 22–23, 49; "Armin Hansen: He Paints the Sea," *Spectator* (Carmel), February 18, 1954, pp. 3, 8; Westphal, ed., *The North,* pp. 86–91; *Our First Five National Academicians* (Carmel, Calif.: Carmel Art Association, 1989), n.p.

177. Hansen earned the dubious designation of the "Winslow Homer of the West." See Helen Spangenberg, *Yesterday's Artists on the Monterey Peninsula,* p. 61. Even more questionable is the reference to him as "California's 'Remington'" (*Monterey, The Artist's View,* p. 23), which probably drew upon Laura Bride Powers, "Painter Folk Put Forth Most Worthy Work" *San Francisco Call,* September 10, 1905, p. 19; courtesy of Alfred Harrison, Jr., The North Point Gallery, San Francisco.

178. *Making Port* is a more dynamic version of Hansen's *Towboat Ahoy,* sold at auction at Butterfield & Butterfield, San Francisco, *Selected California Paintings,* October 14, 1987, lot 2092.

179. "Armin Hansen: He Paints the Sea," *Spectator,* p. 8.

180. For Ritschel, see Thomas H. Parkhurst, "Little Journeys to the Homes of Great Artists," *Fine Arts Journal* 33 (October 1915), pp. 294–297; De Witt Lockman, "William Ritschel," interviews, March 11–19, 1926, manuscript at New-York Historical Society, New York; Christine Turner Curtis, "Painters and Sculptors of the West: William Ritschel, California's Painter of the Sea," *California Southland* 9 (August 1926), pp. 10–11; Arthur Millier, "William Ritschel and Others in the South," *The Argus* 5 (March 1929), p. 5; "California Artists," *Pictorial California and the Pacific* 5 (May 1930),

pp. 18–19; Westphal, ed., *The North,* pp. 166–171; Janet B. Dominik, "William Ritschel, N. A.," *Art of California* 2 (February/March 1989), pp. 20–27; *Our First Five National Academicians,* n.p.

181. *William Ritschel, N. A. Memorial Exhibition* (Carmel: Carmel Art Association, 1949), n.p.

182. Dominik, "William Ritschel," p. 22.

183. John Frederick Harley, Jr., "Ritschel Is Dean of Marine Painters," *Peninsula Herald* (Monterey), November 1, 1946.

184. Rose's initial visit to Carmel was reported in "Pine Needles," *Carmel Pine Cone,* August 1, 1918, p. 1. His return the next year was noted in "Pine Needles," *Carmel Pine Cone,* July 24, 1919, p. 1. On October 23, the column reported that an article, "Among the Pines at Carmel by the Sea," written by Guy Rose's artist-writer wife, Ethel, was published in *California Southland* that month; see Ethel Rose, "Among the Pines at Carmel-by-the-Sea," *California Southland* 1 (October/November 1919), pp. 21–22. For the 1920 visit, see "Pine Needles," *Carmel Pine Cone,* October 7, 1920, p. 1.

185. Antony Anderson reported on Rose's plans in "In the Realm of Art: Pictures by Guy Rose," *Los Angeles Times,* June 30, 1918, III, p. 6.

186. Rose, "Among the Pines at Carmel," p. 21.

187. Antony Anderson, "Art and Artists: Landscapes by Guy Rose," *Los Angeles Times,* May 15, 1921, III, p. 2.

188. Berry, "A Painter of California," p. 334.

189. For Gilbert, see Josephine Mildred Blanch, "Arthur Hill Gilbert," *American Magazine of Art* 21 (October 1930), pp. 579–581; K. Aflund, "Arthur Hill Gilbert Now Showing in S.F.," *Peninsula Herald* (Monterey), November 1, 1946; "Recipient of High Honors," *Western Woman* 13, nos. 2–3 (1951), pp. 20–21; Moure, "Five Los Angeles Artists," pp. 38–42; *Our First Five National Academicians,* n.p.

190. *A Time and Place,* entry on Gilbert by Nancy Moure, p. 70.

191. Ameen Rihani, "The Marines of Paul Dougherty," *International Studio* 73 (April 1921), p. lv. Even early in his career, one writer reviewing a Dougherty show at the Macbeth Gallery noted that "Dougherty bids fair to become the successor to Winslow Homer" ("Art Notes," *Sun* [New York], February 12, 1909, p. 6). In the early twentieth century, Dougherty was often grouped with Frederick J. Waugh, Emil Carlsen, Alexander Harrison, and Charles Woodbury as the major heirs to Homer (and to a lesser degree, William Trost Richards). See Anna Seaton-Schmidt, "Some American Marine Painters," *Art and Progress* 2 (November 1910), pp. 3–8; Birge Harrison, "Recent Tendencies in Marine Painting," *Scribner's Magazine* 49 (April 1911), pp. 469–477; George Alfred Williams, "Art in America. V: American Sea Painters," *Woman's Home Companion* 38 (August 1911), pp. 4–5. See also the section on "Winslow Homer and the Painters of the Sea" in the one general American art survey authored by a Californian, Eugen Neuhaus, *The History and Ideals of American Art* (Stanford, Calif.: Stanford University Press, 1931), pp. 293–314, where Homer is followed by Waugh, Carlsen, Woodbury, and, not surprisingly (given the geographic bias of the author), Dougherty, Hansen, and Ritschel. Ritschel was also mentioned in Charles H. Caffin, "American Painters of the Sea," *Critic* 43 (December 1903), pp. 548–559, just before Dougherty appeared on the national scene. Ritschel and Dougherty were cited together in a review of the 1913 Winter Exhibition of the National Academy of Design (W. H. De B. Nelson, "The National Academy of Design: Winter Exhibition," *International Studio* 51 [February 1914], p. clxxxiii), and later both figured in the comprehensive survey by William Howe Downes, "American Painters of the Sea," *American Magazine of Art* 23 (November 1931), pp. 360–374, published just at the time Dougherty settled in California. Though the source is not known and the statement thus unsupported, Downes, after noting that "second only to Winslow Homer in the delineation of surf are Paul Dougherty and Frederick Waugh," went on to comment that "Dougherty and Waugh need fear no rivals. Winslow Homer was characteristically generous in his praise of these younger colleagues of his. He said, in substance, that there would be no cause for mourning when his time came to lay down his brush forever, so long as such worthy successors were there to carry on" (p. 374). For a contemporary assessment of Homer's followers as painters of figureless coastal dramas, see Bruce Robertson, *Reckoning with Winslow Homer: His Late Paintings and Their Influence* (Cleveland: Cleveland Museum of Art, 1990), pp. 44–62.

192. Nancy Hale and Fredson Bowers, eds., *Leon Kroll: A Spoken Memoir* (Charlottesville, Va.: University Press of Virginia, 1983), p. 15.

193. Edwin A. Rockwell, "Paul Dougherty—Painter of Marines: An Appreciation," *International Studio* 36 (November 1908), pp. iii–xi; William B. M'Cormick, "Paul Dougherty: Rebel to Classification," *Arts and Decoration* 8 (April 1918), pp. 251–254, 274; Rihani, "The Marines of Paul Dougherty"; A[bel] G. Warshawky, "Pictures Are Poems of Color, Movement," *Peninsula Herald* (Monterey), November 1, 1946; Mahonri Sharp Young, "The Crest of the Wave," in *Paul Dougherty A Retrospective Exhibition* (Portland, Me.: Portland Museum of Art, 1978); Westphal, ed., *The North,* pp. 64–67; Mary Carroll Nelson, "Essay," (reprinted from *Southwest Profile* 1 [September/October 1986]), *Paul Dougherty 1877–1947* (Hickory, N.C.: Hickory Museum of Art, 1988); *Our First Five National Academicians,* n.p.

194. "Mahonri Young Paul Dougherty Macbeth Gallery," *Art News* 29 (February 28, 1931), p. 12.

195. Rockwell, "Paul Dougherty," p. iv, in which the picture was noted as "a study in perspective of rock forms."

196. *Sun* (New York), "Academy Exhibition. Second Notice," December 23, 1907, p. 4.

197. Arthur Millier, "New Developments in Southern California Painting," *American Magazine of Art* 27 (May 1934), p. 241.

198. Mabel Urmy Seares, "A California School of Painters," *California Southland* 3 (February 1921), p. 10. The question was asked again three years later: "Many, many times of late have we heard the phrase 'California school of art' and just as often the derisive but interested query, 'What do you mean—"California art"?' Is there really a type of painting or branch of art peculiar to and characteristic of this section of the country?" ("A School of California Painting Is Taking Its Place in World of Art," *California Graphic,* February 23, 1924, p. 14).

1. Minutes, National Academy of Design, January 14, 1826.

2. Primary documentation of the history of the National Academy resides in the archives of the Academy at its headquarters in New York. Notable among these sources are the minutes of the Academy's governing council, the records of the Academy's school, and the catalogues of the Academy's annual exhibitions, of which there is a complete set from 1826 to the present. The standard published sources on the history of the Academy are Thomas S. Cummings, *Historic Annals of the National Academy of Design* (New York, 1861); and Eliot Clark, *History of the National Academy of Design 1825–1953* (New York: Columbia University Press, 1954).

3. Morse's opinions about the necessity of art in a civilized society are expressed in a series of lectures he delivered in New York in 1826. These are reprinted in Samuel F. B. Morse, *Lectures on the Affinity of Painting with Other Fine Arts,* Nicolai Cikovsky, Jr., ed. (Columbia and London: University of Missouri Press, 1983).

4. Quotes in Paul Staiti, "Ideology and Politics in Samuel F. B. Morse's Agenda for a National Art," *Samuel F. B. Morse: Educator and Champion of the Arts in America* (New York: National Academy of Design, 1982), p. 23.

5. Morse could use the word *design* in the title because, to him and his contemporaries, it referred to the traditional fine arts: painting, sculpture, and architecture. By the turn of the century, however, the word had lost its older meaning and was beginning to cause some confusion as to the purpose of the Academy. The Academicians made an attempt to deal with that confusion in 1937 by passing a resolution to drop the word in common references to the Academy. That resolution was never really enforced, however, and it was not until 1997 that the issue was again brought before the organization's governing council. In that year, the council voted to begin proceedings by which the name would officially and legally be changed to simply "The National Academy."

6. Because of the regulations, the Academy now owns one of the largest collections of American art in the world.

7. To date, the most thorough discussion of the history of the Academy's school during the nineteenth century is by Lois Fink in Lois Marie Fink and Joshua C. Taylor, *Academy: The Academic Tradition in American Art* (Washington, D.C.: Smithsonian Institution Press, 1975), pp. 29–85.

8. For example, Horatio Greenough was named professor of sculpture in each academic year from 1829 to 1836. Since he was in Europe during that entire period, he obviously could not have been teaching at the Academy.

9. "Preface," *The Exhibition of the National Academy of Design* (New York, 1827), p. 2.

10. The vagaries of financial condition and artistic style have yet to stymie the intentions of the Academicians. To date, they have hosted 172 annual exhibitions.

11. Minutes, National Academy of Design, January 14, 1826.

12. "Officers and Members of the National Academy of Design," *The Exhibition of the National Academy of Design* (New York, 1830), p. 5.

13. Quoted in Cummings, *Historic Annals,* p. 45.

14. Quoted in ibid., p. 56.

15. *Constitution of the National Academy of Design* (New York, 1870), p. 5.

16. For the purposes of this essay, residency has been determined by consulting each artist's address as given in the Academy's annual exhibition catalogue for the year of his or her election. In actuality, however, the numbers of nonresidents elected may be slightly higher than those given here. Artists sometimes listed the addresses of their New York studios or of their dealers in the Academy's catalogues when in fact they lived elsewhere. A good example of this is William Ritschel, who, for his listing in the Academy's catalogues, continued to give a New York address until 1923, long after his move to California in 1911.

17. An indication that membership in the Academy meant something to the citizens of California during the first half of this century is seen in events surrounding a special exhibition held in 1931 to bring financial stability to the new Carmel Art Association in Carmel, California. Both at the time and later, it was proudly announced that several National Academicians, including William Ritschel and Armin Hansen, organized that exhibition. The artists assumed, evidently correctly, that their status as Academicians would gain them respect for their actions. This was reiterated in 1937 when the Los Angeles Art Association mounted

the exhibition *National Academy Painters in California*. It featured the work of Arthur Hill Gilbert and Armin Hansen, among others. In 1989, the Carmel Art Association presented *Our First Five National Academicians*, which included paintings by Ritschel, Hansen, Gilbert, Paul Dougherty, and Howard Smith.

18. The catalogues for the Academy's annuals through 1950 have been indexed. These indexes were published in three stages. The latest, and most useful for the period covered in this essay, is Peter Hastings Falk, ed., *The Annual Exhibition Record of the National Academy of Design 1901–1950* (Madison, Conn.: Sound View Press, 1990).

19. Dougherty also served on juries for Academy exhibitions seventeen times between 1909 and 1928.

20. The award carried a stipend of one thousand dollars. Dougherty won it for his painting *Bottallack Cove.*

21. Quoted in *Paul Dougherty: Land and Sea* (Hickory, N.C.: Hickory Museum of Art, 1988), n.p. In 1933, Dougherty's *Heavy Sea* was purchased from the Academy's annual exhibition with the Ranger Fund. Still administered by the Academy today, this fund was established by the bequest of the painter and National Academician Henry Ward Ranger (1858–1916) for the purchase of paintings from the Academy's annual exhibitions. Once thus acquired, the works are distributed to museums around the country on extended loan. Following the artist's death, the paintings can be claimed by the Smithsonian Institution, Washington, D.C., for the nation's collection.

22. This was out of a total of 511 paintings and sculptures that were in the exhibition.

23. Ritschel's paintings purchased with the Ranger Fund were *Evening Tide, California,* purchased in 1920, and *Sunlit Shores, California* and *The Enchanted Pool,* both of which were purchased in 1926 and presented to the Minneapolis Society of Fine Art. All three of these paintings eventually went to the Smithsonian Institution.

24. The portrait that Wendt presented to the National Academy on his election to membership was painted by Jean Mannheim, who is also represented in the current exhibition. The painting was shown at the Academy's annual exhibition of 1913.

25. In 1926, the painting was sent to the Malson Public Library, Malson, Massachusetts, and in 1956, it went to the Smithsonian.

26. For an unknown reason, the painting was not listed in the catalogue; but the roster of prize winners at the front of the catalogue identified Hansen as the winner of the First Hallgarten Prize. At least one source identified the honored painting as *Boy with Cod,* which, at the time, was in the collection of the Los Angeles County Museum. See "Armin Hansen," *Game and Gossip* (February 1927), p. 22.

27. The painting was presented by the Academy to the Norfolk Society of Art, Norfolk, Virginia. In 1967, it went to what is now the National Museum of American Art, Smithsonian Institution.

28. The Academy's permanent collection includes of portrait of Gilbert by Edward J. Finley Timmons (1882–1960), who apparently was married to Gilbert's sister Marjorie. Like Gilbert, Timmons was a member of the Carmel Art Association. Gilbert gave the painting to the Academy when he was elected as an Associate.

29. In the Academy's winter exhibition of 1928, he showed *Duneland: Monterey,* a work that shared its subject matter and presumably its style with *Land of Gray Dunes, Monterey,* in the current exhibition.

30. In accordance with the terms of Ranger's bequest, the painting was given by the Academy to a museum, in this case the Springville Art Center of the Rockies in Springville, Utah.

31. Josephine Mildred Blanch, "Arthur Hill Gilbert," *The American Magazine of Art* 21 (October 1930), pp. 578–581.

32. In the Academy's winter exhibition of 1918, Reiffel showed a painting titled simply *Summer,* which may be the work with that title in the current exhibition (pl. 38).

33. Blanch, "Arthur Hill Gilbert," p. 580.

CHECKLIST OF THE EXHIBITION

Franz A. Bischoff (1864–1929)
Peonies, c. 1912
Oil on canvas, 30 x 40 inches
Joan Irvine Smith Fine Arts, Inc.

Franz A. Bischoff (1864–1929)
San Juan Capistrano Mission Yard, c. 1922
Oil on canvas, 24 x 30 inches
The Joan Irvine Smith Collection

George K. Brandriff (1890–1936)
Cannery Row, Newport Beach, c. 1928
Oil on board, 14 x 18 inches
The Irvine Museum

Maurice Braun (1877–1941)
San Diego Countryside with River, c. 1925
Oil on canvas, 30 x 40 inches
Joan Irvine Smith Fine Arts, Inc.

Benjamin Brown (1865–1942)
The Joyous Garden, c. 1910
Oil on canvas, 30½ x 40½ inches
Joan Irvine Smith Fine Arts, Inc.

Alson S. Clark (1876–1949)
The Weekend, Mission Beach, 1924
Oil on canvas mounted on board,
25¼ x 32 inches
The Irvine Museum

Alson S. Clark (1876–1949)
Ruins of the Chapel, San Juan Capistrano, 1919

Oil on board, 31 x 25 inches
Joan Irvine Smith Fine Arts, Inc.

Colin Campbell Cooper (1856–1937)
Pergola at Samarkand Hotel, Santa Barbara,
c. 1921
Oil on canvas, 29 x 36 inches
Joan Irvine Smith Fine Arts, Inc.

Meta Cressey (1882–1964)
Under the Pepper Tree, c. 1927
Oil on canvas, 36¾ x 40½ inches
Joan Irvine Smith Fine Arts, Inc.

Frank Cuprien (1871–1948)
An Evening Symphony
Oil on canvas, 18 x 26 inches
Joan Irvine Smith Fine Arts, Inc.

Paul Dougherty (1877–1947)
The Twisted Ledge
Oil on canvas, 34 x 36 inches
Joan Irvine Smith Fine Arts, Inc.

E. Charlton Fortune (1885–1969)
Study of Monterey Bay, c. 1918
Oil on canvas, 12 x 16 inches
The Irvine Museum

John Frost (1890–1937)
The Flowering Desert, 1922
Oil on canvas, 27 x 32 inches
Joan Irvine Smith Fine Arts, Inc.

John Frost (1890–1937)
The Pool at Sundown, 1923
Oil on panel, 24 x 28 inches
Joan Irvine Smith Fine Arts, Inc.

John Gamble (1863–1957)
Santa Barbara Landscape
Oil on canvas, 24 x 36 inches
Joan Irvine Smith Fine Arts, Inc.

Arthur Hill Gilbert (1894–1970)
Land of Gray Dunes, Monterey
Oil on canvas, 32 x 40 inches
The Irvine Museum

Armin Hansen (1886–1957)
Making Port
Oil on canvas, 30 x 32 inches
The Joan Irvine Smith Collection

Armin Hansen (1886–1957)
The Farmhouse, 1915
Oil on canvas, 30 x 36 inches
The Irvine Museum

Sam Hyde Harris (1889–1977)
Todd Shipyards, San Pedro, c. 1925
Oil on canvas, 20 x 23 inches
The Irvine Museum

Anna Hills (1882–1930)
*The Spell of the Sea (Laguna Beach, Near Moss
Point),* 1920

Oil on canvas, 30 x 40 inches
Joan Irvine Smith Fine Arts, Inc.

Thomas Hunt (1882–1938)
Untitled (Los Angeles Harbor)
Oil on canvas, 28 x 31 inches
The Irvine Museum

William F. Jackson (1850/1851–1936)
Radiant Valley
Oil on canvas, 20 x 30 inches
Joan Irvine Smith Fine Arts, Inc.

Joseph Kleitsch (1882–1931)
Bougainvillea, Mission San Juan Capistrano,
1923
Oil on canvas, 30 x 24 inches
Joan Irvine Smith Fine Arts, Inc.

Joseph Kleitsch (1882–1931)
The Oriental Shop, 1925
Oil on canvas, 32 x 26 inches
Joan Irvine Smith Fine Arts, Inc.

Paul Lauritz (1889–1975)
Poinsettias, c. 1925
Oil on canvas, 32 x 36 inches
The Irvine Museum

Jean Mannheim (1862–1945)
Arch Beach, Laguna Beach
Oil on canvas, 34 x 39 inches
The Irvine Museum

Alfred Mitchell (1888–1972)
In Morning Light, 1931
Oil on Masonite, 44 x 56 inches
The Irvine Museum

Mary DeNeale Morgan (1868–1948)
Cypress at Monterey
Watercolor and gouache, 18½ x 24½ inches
Joan Irvine Smith Fine Arts, Inc.

Bruce Nelson (1888–1952)
The Summer Sea, 1915
Oil on canvas, 30 x 40 inches
The Irvine Museum

Edgar Payne (1883–1947)
Sycamore in Autumn, Orange County Park,
c. 1916
Oil on board, 32 x 42 inches
Joan Irvine Smith Fine Arts, Inc.

Edgar Payne (1883–1947)
The Sierra Divide, 1921
Oil on canvas, 24 x 28 inches
Joan Irvine Smith Fine Arts, Inc.

Hanson Puthuff (1875–1972)
Monarch of the Malibu
Oil on canvas, 32 x 40 inches
Joan Irvine Smith Fine Arts, Inc.

Joseph Raphael (1869–1950)
Market of St. Catherine, Bruxelles, c. 1911

Oil on panel, 7 x 7 inches
The Irvine Museum

Granville Redmond (1871–1935)
Nocturne
Oil on canvas, 30 x 40 inches
Joan Irvine Smith Fine Arts, Inc.

Granville Redmond (1871–1935)
California Landscape with Flowers
Oil on canvas, 32 x 80 inches
The Irvine Museum

Charles Reiffel (1862–1942)
Summer
Oil on canvas, 34 x 37 inches
Joan Irvine Smith Fine Arts, Inc.

Arthur G. Rider (1886–1975)
The Spanish Boat, c. 1921
Oil on canvas, 35 x 41 inches
Joan Irvine Smith Fine Arts, Inc.

Arthur G. Rider (1886–1975)
Mission Garden, San Juan Capistrano, c. 1929
Oil on canvas, 22 x 20 inches
Joan Irvine Smith Fine Arts, Inc.

William Ritschel (1864–1949)
Purple Tide, c. 1915
Oil on canvas, 36 x 40 inches
The Joan Irvine Smith Collection

Guy Rose (1867–1925)
Provençal Olive Orchard (In the Olive Orchard)
Oil on canvas, 15 x 18 inches
The Joan Irvine Smith Collection

Guy Rose (1867–1925)
Laguna Eucalyptus, c. 1916
Oil on canvas, 40 x 30 inches
The Irvine Museum

Guy Rose (1867–1925)
Incoming Tide, c. 1917
Oil on canvas, 24 x 29 inches
The Joan Irvine Smith Collection

Guy Rose (1867–1925)
Indian Tobacco Trees, La Jolla
Oil on canvas, 24 x 29 inches
The Joan Irvine Smith Collection

Guy Rose (1867–1925)
Point Lobos, c. 1918
Oil on canvas, 24 x 29 inches
Joan Irvine Smith Fine Arts, Inc.

Guy Rose (1867-1925)
San Gabriel Road, c. 1919
Oil on canvas, 24 x 29 inches
Joan Irvine Smith Fine Arts, Inc.

Matteo Sandona (1881–1964)
In Her Kimono

Oil on canvas, 35 ¼ x 28 ½ inches
Joan Irvine Smith Fine Arts, Inc.

Donna Schuster (1883–1953)
On the Beach, c. 1917
Oil on canvas, 29 x 29 inches
The Irvine Museum

Jack Wilkinson Smith (1873–1949)
Crystal Cove State Park, 1923
Oil on canvas, 52 x 70 inches
Joan Irvine Smith Fine Arts, Inc.

Channel P. Townsley (1867–1921)
Mission San Juan Capistrano, 1916
Oil on canvas, 32 x 40 inches
Joan Irvine Smith Fine Arts, Inc.

Edouard Vysekal (1890–1939)
Joy, 1917
Oil on canvas, 46 x 35 inches
The Irvine Museum

Elmer Wachtel (1864–1929)
Golden Autumn, Cajon Pass
Oil on canvas, 22 x 30 inches
Joan Irvine Smith Fine Arts, Inc.

Marion Kavanagh Wachtel (1876–1954)
Landscape with Oak Trees
Watercolor and pastel, 20 x 16 inches
Joan Irvine Smith Fine Arts, Inc.

William Wendt (1865–1946)
There Is No Solitude, Even in Nature, 1906
Oil on canvas, 34 x 36 inches
The Joan Irvine Smith Collection

William Wendt (1865–1946)
The Silent Summer Sea, 1915
Oil on canvas, 40 x 50 inches
Joan Irvine Smith Fine Arts, Inc.

William Wendt (1865–1946)
Ranch in the Valley, c. 1928
Oil on canvas, 30 x 40 inches
Joan Irvine Smith Fine Arts, Inc.

Theodore Wores (1859–1939)
A Saratoga Road
Oil on canvas, 44 x 24 inches
Joan Irvine Smith Fine Arts, Inc.

Theodore Wores (1859–1939)
A Hillside in Saratoga
Oil on canvas, 44 x 24 inches
Joan Irvine Smith Fine Arts, Inc.

Karl Yens (1868–1945)
America the Beautiful, 1918
Oil on canvas, 40 x 50 inches
The Irvine Museum

Biographies

of the Artists

PLATE 57

John Frost (1890–1937)
The Pool at Sundown, 1923
Oil on panel, 24 x 28 inches
Joan Irvine Smith Fine Arts, Inc.

Franz A. Bischoff

Born January 14, 1864, in Bomen, Austria
Died February 5, 1929, in Pasadena, California

Franz Bischoff began his artistic training at a craft school in Bomen, Austria. A precocious student, he went to Vienna in 1882 for further training in painting, design, and ceramic decoration. In 1885, he came to the United States and obtained employment as a painter in a ceramic factory in New York City. He moved to Pittsburgh, then Fostoria, Ohio, and finally Dearborn, Michigan, continuing to work as a porcelain painter.

Bischoff became one of the foremost porcelain painters of his day and founded the Bischoff School of Ceramic Art in Detroit and in New York. He formulated and manufactured many of his own colors, participated in exhibitions and won awards, and earned a reputation as "king of the rose painters."

He first visited California in 1900 and, finding the climate and scenery appealing, began to make plans to move his family to San Francisco. However, the earthquake of April 1906 persuaded him to reconsider, and instead he moved his family to the Los Angeles area. In 1908 he built a studio-home along the Arroyo Seco in South Pasadena that included a gallery, a ceramic workshop, and a painting studio. In 1912 Bischoff took an extended tour of Europe, where he studied the works of the Old Masters and the Impressionists.

Once in California, Bischoff turned to landscape in addition to continuing his flower paintings and his porcelain work. Through the 1920s, he painted the coastal areas of Monterey and Laguna Beach, the Sierra Nevada Mountains, and the desert near Palm Springs. Some of his most charming works were painted in the small central California village of Cambria. In 1928 he and his friend John Christopher Smith traveled to Utah, where they painted in Zion National Park.

Bischoff exhibited with the California Art Club and the Laguna Beach Art Association. In 1924 he received the Huntington Prize, an annual award given for the most popular painting at the California Art Club exhibition. His porcelain works were exhibited at the 1893 World's Columbian Exposition in Chicago and at the 1904 Louisiana Purchase Universal Exposition in St. Louis.

George Kennedy Brandriff

Born February 13, 1890, in Millville, New Jersey
Died August 14, 1936, in Laguna Beach, California

George Brandriff was introduced to art in childhood by his uncle, William Kennedy, a watercolorist. He worked briefly as a piano salesman both in his hometown and in California, where he moved in 1913. A year later he enrolled in the College of Dentistry at the University of Southern California, Los Angeles. In 1918 he opened a dentistry practice in Hemet.

While continuing his dentistry career, Brandriff enjoyed painting in his spare time, and in 1923 he started taking art lessons with Anna Hills and Carl Oscar Borg in Laguna Beach. He also studied on weekends with Jack Wilkinson Smith. He soon developed friendships with the artists

Edgar and Elsie Payne, Hanson Puthuff, William Wendt, Arthur Hill Gilbert, Clarence Hinkle, and William Griffith, and he received guidance and critiques from all of them.

In 1927 Brandriff built a studio in Laguna Beach, which he used on a part-time basis. A year later he closed his dentistry practice and moved to Laguna with the aim of becoming a full-time, professional painter. His subjects included landscapes, seascapes, still lifes, figure studies, and harbor scenes. He painted in California, Arizona, and in Europe, which he visited in 1929.

Brandriff was an active member of the California Art Club and the Painters of the West, beginning in 1925. He also served as president of the Laguna Beach Art Association from 1934 until his death, which came in 1936 by suicide, caused by concern over his cancer. A brilliant painter who started late and died young, he garnered a number of awards, including a Silver Medal from the Painters of the West in 1929 and a Second Prize from the California State Fair, Sacramento, in 1930.

MAURICE BRAUN

Born October 1, 1877, in Nagy, Bittse, Hungary
Died November 7, 1941, in San Diego, California

Maurice Braun immigrated to the United States with his family when he was four years of age. An exceptional talent, he copied works of art at the Metropolitan Museum and in 1897 enrolled in classes at the National Academy of Design. He spent three years there and then studied under William Merritt Chase for an additional year. In 1902 he went to Europe, visiting Austria, Germany, and Hungary, the country of his birth.

Returning in 1903 to New York, Braun soon earned a reputation as a figure and portrait painter. However, his interest in landscape painting led him to move to California. In 1910 he opened a studio on Point Loma in San Diego. He became an active member of the art community there and in 1912 founded the San Diego Academy of Art. One of his most important pupils was Alfred R. Mitchell. Braun was also active in art circles in San Francisco and Los Angeles, exhibiting with the California Art Club, at Kanst Galleries, and with the Laguna Beach Art Association.

In 1921 Braun returned to the East and established studios in New York City and in Connecticut at Silvermine and the art colony in Old Lyme. After a few years he returned to San Diego, but from 1924 to 1929 he spent part of each year in the East. In 1929 he joined nine other artists in forming the Contemporary Artists of San Diego.

Braun was affiliated with the Theosophical Society, whose tenets included a transcendentalism, and Theosophy had a profound influence on his art. His paintings were expressions of nature's moods rather than simply descriptions of the landscape.

Braun enjoyed a national reputation, and his paintings were exhibited in Chicago, Philadelphia, Pittsburgh, and New York City. A one-artist show was held at Milch Galleries in New York in 1915, the same year that he received a Gold Medal at the Panama-California Exposition in San Diego. Other prizes included the Hallgarten Prize, National Academy of Design, New York, 1900, and a purchase award from the Witte Memorial Museum, San Antonio, Texas, in 1929.

BENJAMIN CHAMBERS BROWN

Born July 14, 1865, in Marion, Arkansas
Died January 19, 1942, in Pasadena, California

Benjamin Brown studied at the St. Louis School of Fine Arts. In 1886 he made a trip to California with his parents, who were considering moving to Pasadena. While in California he made numerous pencil sketches of landmarks. He returned to St. Louis and continued his studies; then he opened his own art school in Little Rock and specialized himself in portraiture.

In 1890 Brown traveled to Europe with his friends, the artists William A. Griffith and Edmund H. Wuerpel. In Paris he studied at the Académie Julian for one year. He returned to the United States, and subsequently moved to Pasadena, in 1896. He painted portraits, but finding few patrons, began to paint landscapes as well.

Brown was active with many of the developing art societies in Southern California. He was also an etcher and, along with his brother, Howell (1880–1954), founded the Print Makers Society of California, which sponsored annual international print exhibitions for many years.

Brown had patrons both in California and in the East. He was a member of the American Federation of Arts, the California Art Club, the

California Society of Printmakers, and the Pasadena Society of Artists. He received numerous awards, including a Bronze Medal, Lewis and Clark Exposition, Portland, 1905; a Silver Medal at the Alaska-Yukon-Pacific Exposition, Seattle, 1909; and a Bronze Medal for etching, Panama-Pacific International Exposition, San Francisco, 1915.

ALSON SKINNER CLARK

Born March 25, 1876, in Chicago, Illinois
Died March 23, 1949, in Pasadena, California

Alson S. Clark enrolled in Saturday classes at the Art Institute of Chicago in 1887 at the age of eleven. He also received private tutoring from a German painter while visiting Europe with his family a few years later. After completing his public school education, he studied at the Art Institute from November 1895 through March 1896. Not satisfied with the teaching methods there, he left for New York City, where he enrolled in the newly formed school of William Merritt Chase.

Late in 1898 Clark went to Paris, where he enrolled in the Académie Carmen, the atelier of James McNeill Whistler. He remained there for about six months. He traveled around France and to Holland and Belgium. He continued his studies in Paris at the Académie Delecluse and with Alphonse Mucha. In 1901, Clark's painting *The Violinist* was accepted at the Paris Salon.

Clark returned to the United States and early in 1902 opened a studio in Watertown, New York. Newly married, he returned to Paris that fall, and he and his wife then divided their time between France and the United States until the outbreak of the First World War. Clark exhibited at the Art Institute of Chicago, which held a one-artist show in January 1906. His works from this period—including figural works, especially studies of his wife Medora, as well as landscapes, city scenes, and interiors—reflect the influence of Whistler.

On a summer trip in France in 1907, Clark began to lighten his palette to the higher key of his first teacher, Chase. The change in his style toward an Impressionist method was reinforced during a trip to Spain in 1909 and was seen in his work thereafter. In October and November of 1910 he visited Giverny, where he saw Lawton Parker, an old classmate; Frederick Frieseke; and Guy Rose.

Clark traveled throughout Europe and the United States. In 1913, on his way to Paris, he stopped in Panama and decided to undertake the project of recording the construction of the Panama Canal. Eighteen of those paintings were exhibited at the Panama-Pacific International Exposition in San Francisco in 1915.

The Clarks returned to America upon the beginning of World War I. After the United States entered the war, Clark enlisted in the Navy and was sent to France to work as an aerial photographer. Clark visited California in the winter of 1919 for reasons of health; then, in January 1920, he decided to remain, acquiring a house and studio along the Arroyo Seco in Pasadena. He renewed his acquaintance with Guy Rose, who had returned to California in 1914. In 1921 Clark began teaching at the Stickney Memorial School of Art, along with Rose. Attracted to the southwestern landscape, Clark made numerous painting trips in California and in Mexico. He sent works for exhibition to New York and Chicago, was represented in Los Angeles by Stendahl Galleries, and also received mural commissions.

Clark received many awards, including a Bronze Medal, Louisiana Purchase Exposition, St. Louis, 1904; the Martin B. Cahn Prize, Art Institute of Chicago, 1906; a Bronze Medal, Panama-Pacific International Exposition, 1915; the Grand Prize, Southwest Museum, Los Angeles, 1923; the Huntington Prize, California Art Club, 1924; and a First Prize, Pasadena Art Institute, 1933.

COLIN CAMPBELL COOPER

Born March 8, 1856, in Philadelphia, Pennsylvania
Died November 6, 1937, in Santa Barbara, California

Colin Campbell Cooper attended the Pennsylvania Academy of the Fine Arts, beginning in 1879. In 1886 he went to Europe, first painting in Holland and Belgium before moving on to Paris. In Paris he studied at the Académie Julian, the Académie Delecluse, and the Académie Viti.

After his return to the United States in 1895, Cooper taught watercolor painting at the Drexel Institute in Philadelphia for three years. He returned to Europe in 1898, traveling and painting in Holland, Italy, and Spain and developing a reputation as a painter of the great architecture of Europe. He continued to be interested in the interpretation of architecture after his return to the United

States in 1902, and he painted a series of Impressionist cityscapes of New York, Philadelphia, and Chicago. Over the next several years he continued his European sojourns, and in 1913 went to India.

Cooper spent the winter of 1915 in Los Angeles and in the spring of 1916 visited San Diego. In January 1921 he established permanent residency in Santa Barbara and, during the 1920s, served as dean of the School of Painting at the Santa Barbara School of the Arts. He made another trip to India and visited England, France, and Spain in 1923.

Cooper was elected to the National Academy of Design as an Associate in 1908 and gained Academician status in 1913. He was a member of the Philadelphia Watercolor Club, the American Watercolor Society, the National Arts Club, the New York Society of Painters, the New York Watercolor Club, the California Art Club, the San Diego Art Guild, and the Santa Barbara Art Club.

He won a number of awards, among them the W. T. Evans Prize, American Watercolor Society, 1903; the Sesnan Medal, Pennsylvania Academy of the Fine Arts, 1904; a Silver Medal, International Fine Arts Exposition, Buenos Aires, 1910; a Gold Medal in oils and a Silver Medal in watercolor, Panama-Pacific International Exposition, San Francisco, 1915; and the Hudnut Prize, New York Watercolor Club, 1918.

META CRESSEY

Born May 3, 1882, in Cleveland, Ohio
Died May 4, 1964, in Los Angeles, California

Meta Cressey was one of the earliest Modernist artists in Los Angeles. Born Meta Gehring, she came from a wealthy family, and upon the death of her father, she and other members of the family shared a generous trust fund. She studied art at the Cleveland School of Art and in New York with William Merritt Chase and Frank Vincent Dumond. She was a proficient sketcher and practiced ceramic decoration, excelling in flower painting on porcelain.

In 1911, she enrolled at the National Academy school in New York and took classes with Robert Henri. There, she met Bert Cressey (1883–1944), an art student from the Los Angeles area. In the summer of 1912, Bert and Meta accompanied Henri on a painting trip to Spain. After five months there, the party disbanded; Meta returned to New York but Bert stayed in Paris, sharing a studio with Thomas Skinner, another student from Henri's class. The following year, Bert returned to the United States and joined Meta and her family in Cleveland, where the couple was married, on May 19, 1913.

They moved to Bert's home, in Compton, and built a studio-home on five acres of the family farm. In 1917 Meta and Bert Cressey were among a small group of artists who founded the Los Angeles Modern Art Society, which also included Helena Dunlap (1876–1955), Edgar Keller (1868–1932), Henrietta Shore (1880–1963), and Karl Yens. The society held nonjuried invitational shows, featuring modern works by local as well as foreign artists.

Meta Cressey was a member of and frequent exhibitor at the California Art Club. In 1927, she showed *Under the Pepper Tree* (Joan Irvine Smith Fine Arts, Inc.) at the Painters and Sculptors Annual Exhibition at the Los Angeles Museum.

FRANK WILLIAM CUPRIEN

Born August 23, 1871, in Brooklyn, New York
Died June 21, 1946, in Laguna Beach, California

Frank Cuprien attended art classes at the Cooper Union and the Art Students League in New York City. He later studied in Philadelphia with Carl Weber and also received criticism from the noted marine painter William Trost Richards, who would become a major influence.

Cuprien completed his education with several years of study in Europe: in Munich with Karl Raupp and in Paris at the Académie Julian. In addition, he studied music—voice and piano— at the Royal Conservatories in Munich and Leipzig, from which he graduated in 1905.

Returning to the United States, he first went to Florida and the Gulf of Mexico. He then settled in Waco, Texas, where he taught at Baylor University. Around 1912 he moved to California, living first in Santa Monica and then on Catalina Island. In 1914 he built a studio-home, which he called "The Viking," in Laguna Beach. He became one of the leading artists of the community and in 1918 helped to found the Laguna Beach Art Association, of which he served as president from 1921 to 1922. A master of seascapes, Cuprien was often voted the popular prize in the Laguna

Beach Art Association exhibitions during the 1920s and 1930s.

Cuprien garnered a number of awards during his career. Among them were a First Prize, Fifth Annual Cotton Exhibition, Galveston, Texas, 1913; a Silver Medal, Panama-California Exposition, San Diego, 1915; and a Bronze Medal, California State Fair, Sacramento, 1919.

PAUL DOUGHERTY
Born September 6, 1877, in Brooklyn, New York
Died January 9, 1947, in Palm Springs, California

Trained as a lawyer, Paul Dougherty passed the New York State Bar examination and practiced law briefly before deciding to study art. He studied with Robert Henri at the Art Students League of New York. After a study tour through Europe, Dougherty returned to America in 1905 and settled on the coast of Maine. There, he focused on the heroic coastline and painted magnificent views of the rocks and waves. His reputation as an artist was fixed by 1907, when he was elected a full member of the National Academy of Design, having been admitted as an Associate the previous year.

Dougherty is known for his majestic views of the coast, which often show tremendous waves battering against the rocks. In his later years, he began to seek a change of climate. In 1928 he made the first of several visits to Arizona, and in 1931 he moved to the Monterey area and continued to paint the sea. Sometimes it is difficult to differentiate his eastern from his western seascapes.

Chronic health concerns caused him to spend winters in Palm Springs, where he died in 1947.

EUPHEMIA CHARLTON FORTUNE
Born January 15, 1885, in Sausalito, California
Died May 15, 1969, in Carmel, California

E. Charlton Fortune was born in California but was sent to Scotland at the age of twelve to be educated at a convent school in Edinburgh. She subsequently enrolled in the Edinburgh College of Art and then spent a year studying at St. John's Wood School of Art in London. In 1905 she returned to California and enrolled in the California School of Design in San Francisco. Around 1907 she went to New York to study at the Art Students League. At the time she was an aspiring portrait painter, but meeting William Merritt Chase influenced her toward landscape.

In 1910 Fortune began a two-year stay in England and Scotland, during which she visited France for the first time. After her return to Northern California, she took an active part in local art circles, exhibiting her work at several galleries. In the summer of 1914, she persuaded William Merritt Chase to teach at the Carmel Summer School. The popularity of Impressionism and Chase's teaching style were apparent, as over one hundred and fifty students attended his classes.

Fortune established a studio-home around 1914 in Monterey, where she taught plein-air classes. In 1921 she again went to Europe, and during the next several years divided her time between London, Cornwall, Paris, Cannes, and St. Tropez. In 1924 a painting of the harbor at St. Ives, Cornwall, earned her a Silver Medal at the Paris Salon.

She returned to Monterey in the spring of 1927. The following year Fortune founded the Monterey Guild, a group of ten artists who produced handmade pews, chancels, candelabra, and other such items for Roman Catholic churches. She remained devoted to the guild for the rest of her life.

Fortune was a member of the California Art Club, the San Francisco Art Association, the Monterey Guild, the Society of Scottish Artists, and the Liturgical Arts Society. Her awards included a Silver Medal, Panama-Pacific International Exposition, San Francisco, 1915; a Silver Medal, Panama-California International Exposition, San Diego, 1916; the Walter Prize, San Francisco Art Association, 1921; the aforementioned Silver Medal, Société des Artistes Français, 1924; and a First Prize, California State Fair, Sacramento, 1930.

JOHN FROST
Born May 14, 1890, in Philadelphia, Pennsylvania
Died June 5, 1937, in Pasadena, California

John Frost was introduced to art by his father, Arthur B. Frost (1851–1928), a well-known American illustrator. When the family moved to Paris, John and his older brother, Arthur B. Jr., took classes at the Académie Julian under Jean-Paul Laurens. Young John worked with the American Impressionist Richard Miller in Paris from 1906 to 1908 and remained a close friend of the painter, visiting Miller often at his house in Giverny. In Europe, both brothers contracted tuberculosis, a disease that would take both their lives. John spent two years in a sanitorium in Switzerland.

The Frost family went back to New York in 1915 after the outbreak of World War I, and John worked as an illustrator. In 1919 the family moved to Pasadena, seeking a warm, dry climate to diminish the lingering effects of John's tuberculosis.

Frost admired the works of the Impressionists and painted in that style all his life. The artist Guy Rose was a lifelong painting and fishing companion of Arthur B. Frost, Sr., and John Frost's style was strongly influenced by Rose's work. Furthermore, Frost had met Alson S. Clark while painting in France, and after Frost, Clark, and Rose were all living in Pasadena, their friendship became a significant factor in each of their styles.

John Frost was a member of the California Art Club, the Painters and Sculptors Club of Los Angeles, and the Pasadena Society of Artists. He won prizes at the Southwest Museum in 1921, 1922, and 1923, and a Gold Medal at the Painters and Sculptors Club Exhibition in 1924.

JOHN MARSHALL GAMBLE

Born November 25, 1863, in Morristown, New Jersey

Died April 7, 1957, in Santa Barbara, California

John Gamble entered the San Francisco School of Design in 1886, studying there under Emil Carlsen and Virgil Williams. In 1890 he went to Paris to study at the Académie Julian and the Académie Colarossi. He returned to San Francisco in 1893 to begin his professional career.

His paintings of California wild flowers earned him a national reputation. When asked how he came to specialize in that subject, he said that he saw the flowers simply as patches of color: "I liked the way they designed themselves across the field."

The San Francisco earthquake and fire of 1906 destroyed his studio, and he lost the complete inventory of his work except for three paintings that were with an art dealer. By the end of the year, Gamble made the decision to move to Los Angeles to be near his close friend, the artist Elmer Wachtel. A brief stopover in Santa Barbara persuaded him to relocate to that idyllic community on the coast. He became an active member of the arts community and served on the Santa Barbara Architectural Board of Review, acting as color advisor for new construction.

Gamble was a member of the American Federation of Arts, the Foundation of Western Artists, the San Francisco Art Association, and the Santa Barbara Art Association. In 1909 he received a Gold Medal at the Alaska-Yukon-Pacific Exposition, Seattle.

ARTHUR HILL GILBERT

Born June 10, 1894, in Mt. Vernon, Illinois

Died April 28, 1970, in Stockton, California

Arthur Gilbert was educated at Northwestern University and at the United States Naval Academy in Annapolis. After his military service, he came to California, in 1920, and began his art studies. He enrolled at the Otis Art Institute and continued his training by taking classes in Paris and London.

Gilbert moved to Monterey in 1928 and became well known for his paintings of the picturesque trees, dunes, and rugged coastline. In 1930, one of his paintings won the Second Hallgarten Prize in the annual exhibition at the National Academy of Design, while in another Academy show his painting *Near Monterey* both won the Murphy Prize and was purchased through the Ranger Fund. That year the artist was elected an Associate member of the National Academy.

In his later years, Gilbert moved to a ranch near Stockton, where he died in 1970.

ARMIN CARL HANSEN

Born October 23, 1886, in San Francisco, California

Died April 23, 1957, in Monterey, California

As a child, Armin Hansen received tutoring in art from his father, the artist Hermann Wendleborg Hansen (1854–1924), who was known for his paintings of the American western frontier. The younger Hansen then studied at the California School of Design under Arthur Mathews from 1903 to 1906.

In 1906 he went to Germany, where he studied for two years under the Impressionist Carlos Grethe at the Royal Academy in Stuttgart. During his time in Germany, Hansen visited Munich and Paris and traveled to Holland and Belgium.

Around 1908 he went to Nieuwpoort on the coast of Belgium, where he painted scenes of the life of North Sea fishermen. For the next few years he painted there and at the seaport town of Oostend while working occasionally as a deckhand. His love for the sea would be reflected in his work for his entire career.

Hansen returned to the United States in 1912 and taught for several months at the University of California at Berkeley. The next year he moved to Monterey, where he became an active member of the art community and a mentor to young artists. He became known for his marine paintings and etchings that recorded the activities of that bustling fishing community. In 1918 his privately held classes were incorporated into the California School of Fine Arts as the Monterey Summer School. Hansen was made director and instructor for landscape classes. His influence on aspiring artists was profound, and former students refer to the period of the 1920s in Monterey as the "golden era" for both artistic and social activities.

Hansen exhibited widely in California, in the eastern United States, and in Europe. He helped to found the Carmel Art Association and held memberships in the California Society of Etchers, the Salmagundi Club (New York), the San Francisco Art Association, and the Société Royale des Beaux-Arts, Brussels. Elected to the National Academy of Design in 1926, he gained full Academician status in 1948. Hansen's numerous awards included a First Prize, International Exposition,

Brussels, 1910; a Silver Medal, Panama-Pacific International Exposition, San Francisco, 1915; a Purchase Prize, San Francisco Art Association, 1916; Gold Medals in drawing and in painting, San Francisco Art Association, 1919; the First Hallgarten Prize, National Academy of Design, New York, 1920; the Ranger Fund Purchase Prize, National Academy of Design, 1925; and a Gold Medal, Painters of the West, 1925.

Sam Hyde Harris

Born February 2, 1889, in Brentford, England
Died May 30, 1977, in Alhambra, California

Sam Hyde Harris immigrated to the United States with his family in 1904 and settled in Los Angeles. While studying in the evenings at the Art Students League and at the Cannon Art School with F. Tolles Chamberlin, Stanton MacDonald-Wright, and Hanson Puthuff, he pursued a career as a commercial artist in advertising. In 1913 he spent six months in Europe, where he was inspired by the light and atmospheric effects in the works of the English masters John Constable and Joseph M. W. Turner.

After returning to Los Angeles, Harris continued his successful commercial-art career, designing advertisements and posters for the Southern Pacific, Union Pacific, and Santa Fe railroads. One of his best-known assignments was designing the windmill logo for Van De Kamp's Bakeries; it is still used today. All the while, on weekends, he continued to paint elegant, light-filled studies of farms and vistas in the San Gabriel Valley.

During the 1920s Harris studied privately with Puthuff, taking painting trips with him to the deserts of California and Arizona. He also painted with Jean Mannheim and Edgar Payne. He liked to paint in the rural environs of Pasadena and San Gabriel as well as in the city of Los Angeles. During the 1930s he painted harbor scenes in San Pedro, Sunset Beach, and Newport Beach. In the 1940s and 1950s, after he retired, he often painted in the desert with James Swinnerton.

Harris was a member of the California Art Club, the Painters and Sculptors Club, and the Laguna Beach Art Association. He received a Special Award from the California Art Club in 1941 and a Silver Medal from the Painters and Sculptors Club in 1944.

Anna Althea Hills

Born January 28, 1882, in Ravenna, Ohio
Died June 13, 1930, in Laguna Beach, California

Anna Hills received her education at Olivet College in Michigan, the Art Institute of Chicago, and the Cooper Union in New York City. She worked with Arthur Wesley Dow for two years. She then went to Europe, where she studied at the Académie Julian and traveled and painted in Holland and England, where she studied with John Noble Barlow.

She returned to the United States and moved to Los Angeles around 1912. A year later she relocated to Laguna Beach, where she became a founding member of the Laguna Beach Art Association in 1918. She became an indefatigable leader of that group, serving as president from 1922 to 1925 and from 1927 to 1930, the period during which the group raised the funds necessary to build their permanent gallery on Cliff Drive. A highly respected teacher, Hills promoted the visual arts through lectures and the organization of special exhibits that circulated among Orange County public schools.

Originally a figure painter, Hills turned to the landscape after her move to California. In addition to the Laguna Beach Art Association, Hills held memberships in the California Art Club and the Washington Water Color Club. Among her awards were a Bronze Medal, Panama-California Exposition, San Diego, 1915; a Bronze Medal, California State Fair, Sacramento, 1919; and the Landscape Prize, Laguna Beach Art Association, 1922 and 1923.

THOMAS LORRAINE HUNT

Born February 11, 1882, in London, Ontario, Canada
Died April 17, 1938, in Santa Ana, California

Thomas Hunt studied with his father, the Canadian artist John Powell Hunt, and later with Hugh Breckenridge at the Pennsylvania Academy of the Fine Arts and in Gloucester, Massachusetts. Settling in Cleveland, Ohio, Hunt worked in construction and painted in his spare time. In 1924 he came to California and lived in Hollywood and in San Bernardino. In 1927 he established himself in Laguna Beach and actively participated in local exhibitions.

Hunt gradually evolved from Impressionism to a distinctive and unique form of Post-Impressionism. His mature works concentrate on color and the surface plane of the painting. They are characterized by almost flat areas of vivid color arranged in representational patterns, resulting in bold, dramatic canvases that celebrate color. He was uncommonly Modernistic for the period in which he worked.

WILLIAM FRANKLIN JACKSON

Born in 1850 or 1851, in Council Bluffs, Iowa
Died January 9, 1936, in Sacramento, California

William F. Jackson came west with his family as a boy of twelve. He lived in Sacramento until about 1875, when he enrolled in the California School of Design in San Francisco. There he studied under Virgil Williams and Benoni Irwin.

Jackson returned to Sacramento in 1880 and opened a studio. In 1884 he became the curator of the newly founded Crocker Art Gallery and director of its art school. He remained in those positions until his death.

A close friend and painting companion of William Keith, Jackson traveled widely in California, painting majestic landscapes of rolling hills with poppies and lupines. He exhibited at the California State Fair in 1880 and in 1901, when he was awarded a Gold Medal, and served on the Art Commission of the 1915 Panama-Pacific International Exposition, San Francisco.

JOSEPH KLEITSCH

Born June 6, 1882, in Nemet Szent Mihaly, Hungary (present-day Romania)
Died November 16, 1931, in Santa Ana, California

While in his teens, Joseph Kleitsch was apprenticed to a sign painter, but he left after about eighteen months to open his own studio as a portrait painter. Around 1901 he immigrated to Germany and then to the United States, settling in Cincinnati, Ohio. Around 1905 he moved to Denver, where he painted portraits of prominent businessmen. About 1907 he was in Hutchinson, Kansas, but after only a short time, he relocated to Mexico City, residing there between 1907 and 1909. Sometime in 1909 he moved to Chicago.

In 1912 Kleitsch gained recognition for commissioned portraits of Mexican President Francisco Madero and his wife. Well established as a portrait painter, he joined the Palette and Chisel Club and began participating in local exhibitions with the Club and at the Art Institute of Chicago around 1914. He started to paint interior scenes with figures, which were often placed in front of a window. He received high praise for these works and was compared favorably to the Spanish artist Joaquin Sorolla as well as to Rembrandt.

In 1920 Kleitsch moved to Southern California, establishing residency in Laguna Beach. He was already acquainted with artists who had preceded him, such as Edgar Payne. Again he established himself as a portrait painter—his main source of income—but also began to include landscape and still lifes in his oeuvre. He was a bold colorist, employing a bravura brushstroke. He especially enjoyed painting in and around Laguna Beach, whose charms he knew would soon succumb to real estate development.

In 1925 Kleitsch went to Europe, visiting France and Spain, where he painted portraits and landscapes. He returned to California in November 1927 and continued to paint in Laguna until his untimely death at the age of forty-nine.

Kleitsch held memberships with the Chicago Society of Artists, the Laguna Beach Art Association, the Palette and Chisel Club of Chicago, and the Painters and Sculptors Club, which he cofounded in 1923 with Grayson Sayre. The numerous awards that he garnered during his career included a Gold Medal, Palette and Chisel Club; a Silver Medal, Painters and Sculptors Club; a First Prize, California State Fair; and a First Prize and Figure Prize, Laguna Beach Art Association.

PAUL LAURITZ

Born April 18, 1889, in Larvik, Norway
Died October 31, 1975, in Glendale, California

Paul Lauritz studied as a youth at the Larvik Art School in the town of his birth. At the age of sixteen he immigrated to eastern Canada, then worked his way west and settled in Portland, Oregon, where he found commercial art work. Lured by tales of Alaskan gold, he traveled to that remote region, where he painted dramatic mountain scenes. While there, he befriended the artist Sydney Laurence and exhibited with him.

In the latter part of 1919, Lauritz moved to Los Angeles and opened a studio. He began teaching at the Chouinard School of Art in 1928 and later also taught at Otis Art Institute. He was a member of the Los Angeles Municipal Art Commission for six years, during which time he helped to organize the first municipal art exhibitions.

Lauritz specialized in landscape work and painted along the coast from Laguna Beach to Monterey, in the High Sierra, and in the deserts of California, Nevada, and Mexico. He returned to his native Norway in 1925, and in 1928, he received a special commission from the king.

Lauritz was an active member of the Laguna Beach Art Association, the Painters and Sculptors Club, and the California Art Club, of which he served two years as president. He also held memberships in the Salmagundi Club, New York, and the Royal Society of Art in England. His awards included a Purchase Prize, San Diego Museum of Art, 1928; a First Prize, California State Exposition, 1922, 1923, 1924; and a First Prize, California Art Club, 1947, 1949, 1950, 1952, 1953.

JEAN MANNHEIM

Born November 18, 1862, in Kreuznach, Germany
Died September 6, 1945, in Pasadena, California

Jean Mannheim studied in Paris at the Académie Delecluse, the Académie Colarossi, and the Académie Julian. In 1881 he came to the United States, residing with his sister in Chicago, and while there earned a living as a portrait painter. Each summer, he returned to Europe to continue his art studies.

Around 1903 Mannheim began teaching in London at the Brangwyn School of Art, operated by Frank Brangwyn. He returned to the United States two years later, settling briefly in Denver, where he taught at the Denver Art School. Mannheim moved to Los Angeles in 1908, opened a studio in the Blanchard Building, and began teaching in his own school. He built a studio-home on the Arroyo Seco in Pasadena. After the death of his wife in 1910, he worked primarily out of his home in order to care for his young daughters. His work is characterized by exceptional portraits and figural paintings, as well as landscapes painted throughout California.

An active participant in the Los Angeles area art community, Mannheim was a founding member of the California Art Club and the Laguna Beach Art Association. He was also a member of the Pasadena Art Club and the Long Beach Art Association. Among the awards he received were a Gold Medal, Alaska-Yukon-Pacific Exposition, Seattle, 1909; Gold and Silver Medals, Panama-California Exposition, San Diego, 1915; and a First Prize, London School of Art.

ALFRED R. MITCHELL

Born June 18, 1888, in York, Pennsylvania
Died November 9, 1972, in San Diego, California

Alfred Mitchell came to California in 1908, settling in San Diego where, in 1913, he began to study at the San Diego Academy of Art under Maurice Braun. His talents were acknowledged just two years later when he received a Silver Medal at the Panama-California Exposition in San Diego. Encouraged by Braun, Mitchell decided to return to his native Pennsylvania in 1916 and enroll in the Pennsylvania Academy of the Fine Arts, where he was influenced by Daniel Garber and Edward Redfield. In 1920 Mitchell was awarded the Cresson European Traveling Scholarship, which allowed him to spend the summer of 1921 in England, France, Italy, and Spain.

Upon completion of his studies, Mitchell returned to San Diego and became an active member of the art community. He played a leading role in the formative years of the Fine Arts Gallery of San Diego, and in 1929 he was a founding member of the Associated Artists of San Diego; he was also a member of the La Jolla Art Association.

Mitchell's early works are impressionistic, reflecting his tutelage under Braun, Garber, and Redfield. His later works, however, are more strongly realistic, reflecting his admiration for the work of Thomas Eakins.

Mitchell received many awards in addition to those previously mentioned. Among them were the Edward Bok Philadelphia Prize, Pennsylvania Academy of the Fine Arts, 1920; the Leisser Farnham Prize, San Diego, 1927; the Highest Award, Laguna Beach Art Association, 1940; and both a First Prize and a Purchase Prize, San Diego Art Institute Annual, 1960.

MARY DeNEALE MORGAN

Born May 24, 1868, in San Francisco, California
Died October 10, 1948, in Carmel, California

Mary DeNeale Morgan studied privately under William Keith and, during the period 1884–95, at the California School of Design under Virgil Williams, Emil Carlsen, Amédée Joullin, and Arthur F. Mathews

In 1896 she opened a studio in Oakland, which she maintained until 1907, when she moved to Carmel. In 1914, she attended William Merritt Chase's plein-air summer school in Carmel. She served as director of the Carmel School of Art from 1917 to 1925 and was a founding member of the Carmel Art Association in 1927.

One of the best loved and most influential of Carmel's art teachers, Morgan specialized in views of the Carmel-Monterey coastline, frequently showing sand dunes and cypress trees. She worked in oil, tempera, watercolor, and pastel.

ERNEST BRUCE NELSON

Born June 13, 1888, in Santa Clara County, California
Died 1952 in New York City

Bruce Nelson studied civil engineering at Stanford University beginning in 1905. There, he met Robert B. Harshe, who was head of the Art Department, and after three years he transferred his interests to architecture. After leaving Stanford Nelson worked for an architectural firm in San Francisco. He then went to New York and enrolled in the Art Students League. He also attended the Woodstock Summer School under Birge Harrison. He returned to San Francisco in 1912 and began exhibiting, immediately receiving positive criticism.

In the summer of 1913, Nelson opened a studio in Pacific Grove, where he offered private and group classes. He continued to exhibit his paintings in San Francisco and Los Angeles. Nelson served in the Army Camouflage Corps during World War I; after his discharge in 1918, he went to Cooperstown, New York, where he painted murals at the home of James Fennimore Cooper. It is believed that he then moved to New York City, where he died in 1952.

Alma May Cook predicted in the *Los Angeles Tribune* (May 17, 1914) that Nelson would some day take a high place in the annals of American art. Yet, mysteriously, the last exhibition record for him appeared in 1924. During his short career he was accorded a one-artist show at the opening of the Oakland Art Gallery (now the Oakland Museum of California) in 1916, and he received a Silver Medal at San Francisco's Panama-Pacific International Exposition in 1915 for *The Summer Sea* (The Irvine Museum).

EDGAR ALWIN PAYNE

Born March 1, 1883, in Washburn, Missouri
Died April 8, 1947, in Hollywood, California

Edgar Payne was essentially a self-taught artist. He left home around 1902 at the age of nineteen, and he traveled for a number of years throughout the South, the Midwest, and in Mexico, taking various jobs as a house painter, sign painter, scenic painter, and portrait and mural artist. In 1907 he settled in Chicago, where he enrolled in a portraiture class at the Art Institute of Chicago, but left after only two weeks. At this time he began landscape painting in the form of murals and small easel works. He exhibited with the Palette and Chisel Club, from which he sold some of his paintings.

Payne visited California in 1909 and spent some time painting in Laguna Beach. He also stopped in San Francisco, where he met his future wife, the artist Elsie Palmer (1884–1971). He visited California a second time in 1911 and married Elsie in Chicago in November 1912. They lived in Chicago until 1917, during which time they became well established in that city's art community. Payne exhibited at the Art Institute as well as the Palette and Chisel Club. He continued with his mural work and made annual trips to California.

In the summer of 1917, Payne accepted a significant commission for murals in the Congress Hotel in Chicago. The job was huge, requiring over eleven thousand square feet of canvas. To produce these murals, Payne rented an old factory in Glendale, California, where the murals were painted. In 1918, when the project was completed, the Paynes moved to Laguna Beach. Edgar Payne became active in the art colony there and in 1918 was a founding member and first president of the Laguna Beach Art Association.

Payne was an ceaseless traveler and painted throughout California, Arizona, and New Mexico, as well as in Canada. No locale was too remote, and he spent a great deal of time in the High Sierra Mountains, living for weeks at his elaborate campsites. Payne Lake, high in these mountains, is named in his honor. In the summer of 1922, the Paynes went to Europe, painting for a two-year period in France, Switzerland, and Italy. His favorite painting locations were the Alps and in the fishing ports. His painting of Mont Blanc entitled *The Great White Peak* received an honorable mention at the Paris Salon in the spring of 1923.

After their return to the United States in the fall of 1924, the Paynes spent some time in Chicago, then returned to Laguna Beach. Over the next several years they lived in California, Connecticut, and New York and made painting trips to the California Sierras, Utah, and New Mexico. In 1928 another trip was made to Europe, where Payne painted in the harbors of Chioggia and Brittany. He continued to paint the California Sierra Nevada Mountains, a subject that earned him national renown.

In 1946, Payne was diagnosed with cancer. His wife, Elsie, from whom he had separated in 1932, closed her own studio and moved back in with Edgar at his Seward Street house. She nursed him through his final months until his death on April 8, 1947.

The perpetuation of Edgar Payne's memory became the life mission of his widow. She did this by organizing a large number of exhibitions of his paintings. In 1952, Elsie, who was also a sculptor, created a bronze relief plaque of her husband for the Laguna Beach Art Museum.

Payne was a member of the California Art Club, the Painters and Sculptors of Southern California, the Chicago Art Club, the Palette and Chisel Club of Chicago, and the Salmagundi Club in New York City. His works were exhibited in Chicago and New York. His awards included the Martin B. Cahn Prize, Art Institute of Chicago, 1921; a Gold Medal, California Art Club, 1925; and the Ranger Fund Purchase Award, National Academy of Design, 1929. His book *Composition of Outdoor Painting*, published in 1941, is now in its fifth printing.

HANSON DUVALL PUTHUFF

Born August 21, 1875, in Waverly, Missouri
Died May 12, 1972, in Corona del Mar, California

Hanson Puthuff attended the University of Denver Art School, graduating in 1893 at the age of eighteen. He studied at the Chicago Academy of Fine Arts, and for a brief period he worked as a mural painter before returning to Denver in 1894. There he found employment designing posters for an advertising firm.

In 1903, Puthuff moved to Los Angeles, where he continued his profession of painting billboard posters. He also began to paint easel works, which he first exhibited in 1905. *Los Angeles Times* art critic Antony Anderson gave the show a favorable review, and the two men became friends. Together they founded the Art Students League in Los Angeles.

Puthuff went to Chicago in 1906 and worked as a scene painter and participated in local art exhibitions. He returned to Los Angeles the following year and began to devote more time to his painting. He was a founding member of the

California Art Club and was also a member of the Laguna Beach Art Association, the Pasadena Society of Artists, and the Painters and Sculptors Club.

In the 1920s Puthuff painted dioramas for the Los Angeles Museum of History, Science, and Art. He gave up his commercial career in 1926 to concentrate all his time on his easel painting. Many of his works depict the environs near his home in La Crescenta. He also painted in the Sierras and in the canyons of Arizona.

Puthuff received a number of awards, including two Silver Medals, Panama-California Exposition, San Diego, 1915; a Gold Medal, California State Fair, Sacramento, 1918; a First Prize, Laguna Beach Art Association, 1920 and 1921; a Gold Medal, Painters of the West, 1927; a Silver Medal, Pacific Southwest Exposition, Long Beach, 1928; and a Purchase Prize, Chicago Galleries Association, 1931.

Joseph Raphael

Born June 2, 1869, in San Francisco, California
Died December 11, 1950, in San Francisco, California

Joseph Raphael was the first of four children of Nathan Raphael, a tailor who was born in Poland, and Elizabeth Moses Raphael, who was born in England. At the age of fifteen, he left home and went to the Arizona Territory to work in a trading post. In 1887 he returned to San Francisco and began his art studies at the San Francisco Art Association School of Design, with Arthur F. Mathews and Douglas Tilden. In 1902 he went to Paris to take classes at the Ecole des Beaux-Arts and at the Académie Julian with Jean-Paul Laurens. He excelled in class, and his paintings were accepted for exhibition at the Salon from 1904 to 1909.

In 1910, Raphael returned to San Francisco to exhibit a group of Dutch paintings at the San Francisco Institute of Art. By 1911 he had returned to Europe and settled in Uccle, a suburb of Brussels. In 1912 he sent a group of paintings to San Francisco for the first of a long series of annual exhibitions at the Hegelsen Gallery.

In August 1914, Germany invaded Belgium, and Raphael, who was in Belgium, was unable to return to the United States. His dealer continued to enter Raphael's paintings in exhibitions, including the Panama-Pacific International Exposition in San Francisco and the Panama-California Exposition in San Diego, both in 1915.

Raphael and his wife and children remained in Europe for thirty-seven years, returning to America in 1939 just prior to the outbreak of World War II. They settled in San Francisco and he maintained a home and studio there for the rest of his life.

Raphael spent the greater part of his life in Europe, yet he remains one of the most important Impressionist painters of California as his works were shown in nearly every important California art exhibition. Among his awards were a Gold Medal at the Mark Hopkins Art Institute, San Francisco, 1900; honorable mentions at the Paris Salon, 1905 and 1915; a Silver Medal, Panama-Pacific International Exposition, San Francisco, 1915; a Gold Medal, Panama-California Exposition, San Diego, 1915; and a Gold Medal, San Francisco Art Association, 1918.

Granville Richard Seymour Redmond

Born March 9, 1871, in Philadelphia, Pennsylvania
Died May 24, 1935, in Los Angeles, California

Granville Redmond (né Grenville) contracted scarlet fever at the age of two and a half, and the illness left him permanently deaf. In 1874 his family came to California, and in 1879 Redmond enrolled in what was then called the Institution for the Deaf, Dumb, and Blind at Berkeley (now called the California School for the Deaf, in Fremont). His artistic talents were recognized and encouraged by the photographer and teacher Theophilus Hope d'Estrella, who taught him drawing and pantomime. He also received sculpture lessons from the sculptor Douglas Tilden.

After graduation in 1890, Redmond enrolled in the California School of Design. In 1893, with a stipend from the Institution for the Deaf, he went to Paris, where he attended the Académie Julian. After five years in France, he returned to California and opened a studio in Los Angeles. For the next several years, he painted throughout the Los Angeles area, including Laguna Beach, Long Beach, Catalina Island, and San Pedro. He visited and painted in Northern California in 1902 and 1905.

In 1908 he relocated to Parkfield on the Monterey Peninsula, where he resumed his friendships with his former classmates from the California School of Design, Gottardo Piazzoni and Xavier Martinez. He moved to San Marco in 1910 and had a studio in Menlo Park.

In 1917 Redmond traveled to Los Angeles with Gottardo Piazzoni with the intent of auditioning for the movies. He felt that his natural skills as a pantomimist would make him an ideal actor, as all movies at the time were silent. He met Charlie Chaplin, who cast him in a small role in *A Dog's Life.* Chaplin became a close friend and gave Redmond space on his movie lot to set up a painting studio. In turn, Redmond taught Chaplin sign language. Between 1918 and 1929, Redmond had minor roles in seven Chaplin movies, and he painted throughout Southern California.

Redmond was, without question, one of California's leading landscape painters. Hampered by long periods of recurring depression, he preferred to paint in a moody, introspective style characterized by the use of dark tones of brown, gold, and olive-green, but his patrons favored cheerful paintings of rolling hills covered with golden poppies and other wild flowers. He was a member of the Bohemian Club, San Francisco, the San Francisco Art Association, the California Art Club, and the Laguna Beach Art Association. Redmond's awards included the W. E. Brown Gold Medal, California School of Design, 1891; a medal, Louisiana Purchase Exposition, St. Louis, 1904;

and a Silver Medal, Alaska-Yukon-Pacific Exposition, Seattle, 1909.

CHARLES REIFFEL

Born April 9, 1862, in Indianapolis, Indiana
Died March 14, 1942, in San Diego, California

Charles Reiffel went to work as a teenager in a clothing store in Cincinnati, a job he held for ten years. At work, he passed the time by drawing, and this interest in art led him to become a journeyman lithographer. That career took him first to New York and then to England, where he designed posters. He stayed there six years, during which time he began to paint in his spare time. Before returning to the United States, he took a nine-month leave to travel throughout Europe and North Africa, and he studied briefly at the Munich Academy under Carl Marr. The influence of the Munich School, which emphasized texture and line over subject matter, was profound.

Reiffel returned to the United States in 1904 and resided in Buffalo, New York, where he continued to work as a lithographer. He began to exhibit his paintings at the Albright-Knox Art Gallery in Buffalo and received favorable reviews. Soon other East Coast galleries and museums took note of his work.

In 1912 Reiffel moved to the artists' colony in Silvermine, Connecticut, and was a founding member of the Silvermine Artists' Guild. After several years of commuting from Silvermine to a lithography job in New York City, he resigned and became a full-time painter. In 1925 he undertook

an extensive trip through the Southwest. He headed for Santa Fe, but a storm diverted him to San Diego. Charmed by the character of the small city, he opted to remain. He became an active member of the art community there, but unfortunately his painting style was too progressive for the conservative patrons of San Diego and his paintings did not sell.

Reiffel held memberships in many arts organizations, including the California Art Club, the Chicago Galleries Association, the Cincinnati Art Club, the Laguna Beach Art Association, the Salmagundi Club (New York), the San Diego Art Guild and the Arts Club of Washington, D.C. His many awards included a Silver Medal, Art Institute of Chicago, 1917; a Gold Medal, California Art Club, 1928; a Gold Medal, Painters of the West, 1930; First Prize, John Herron Art Institute, Indianapolis, 1929; and the John C. Shaffer Grand Prize, Hoosier Salon, Indianapolis, 1938.

ARTHUR GROVER RIDER

Born March 21, 1886, in Chicago, Illinois
Died January 25, 1975, in Los Angeles, California

Arthur Rider attended the Chicago Academy of Fine Arts. In 1911, he heard a lecture by the noted Spanish artist Joaquín Sorolla, who would be a great influence on his work. He then went to Europe, where he studied at the Académie Colarossi and the Académie de la Grande Chaumiére in Paris. He spent several summers in Valencia, Spain, studying at the Werntz Academy of Fine Arts, where he befriended Sorolla.

Rider returned to Chicago, where he participated in exhibitions at the Art Institute and with the Chicago Galleries Association. After visiting California, he rented a house in Laguna Beach from 1928 to 1931, and in 1931 settled permanently in Los Angeles. He worked for Twentieth Century Fox and MGM studios, retiring at the age of eighty-four.

Rider painted throughout California and Mexico, seeking locales that reminded him of the color and light he had seen in Spain. His paintings are rich in color with intense, brilliant light. Many of his Spanish pictures depict the activities of fishermen on the beach in Valencia and their boats with the single, white billowing sail.

Rider held memberships in the Palette and Chisel Club, the Chicago Galleries Association, the California Art Club, the Painters and Sculptors Club, and the Laguna Beach Art Association. He was awarded a Purchase Prize, Art Institute of Chicago, 1923; a Second Prize, California State Fair, Sacramento, 1936; a First Prize, California Art Club, 1940; and a First Prize, Painters and Sculptors Club, 1954.

WILLIAM FREDERICK RITSCHEL
Born July 11, 1864, in Nuremberg, Germany
Died March 11, 1949, in Carmel, California

As a youth William Ritschel spent several years as a sailor before entering the Royal Academy of Design in Munich, where he studied under Friedrich August von Kaulbach and Karl Raupp. His twin passions of art and the sea combined to make marine painting the primary focus of his work. After completing his studies, he traveled and painted extensively throughout Europe for a number of years, showing his work in exhibitions in Berlin, Munich, and Paris.

In 1895 Ritschel immigrated to the United States and settled in New York. He continued to participate in art exhibitions and received strong praise for his work. Sometime after 1909 he moved to California. In 1918 he purchased land high on a bluff overlooking the Pacific Ocean in Carmel Highlands and constructed a castlelike stone house based on a fifteenth-century Basque design. Dubbed by the artist "The Castle," the house afforded impressive views of the ocean below.

His passion for the sea lured Ritschel to the South Seas, where he painted in 1921 and 1922. He also went to Capri and Asia in 1924 and made a trip around the world in 1926. He filled his studio-home with many objects and sculptures collected on his trips. His paintings of the sea in its many moods and of man's relationship to it brought him high praise in Europe as well as in the United States where he was called the "dean of American marine painters."

Ritschel was elected an Associate of the National Academy of Design in 1910 and a full Academician in 1914. He was also a member of the American Watercolor Society, the Salmagundi Club, the San Francisco Art Association, the Academy of Western Painters, and the Carmel Art Association. His numerous awards included the Carnegie Prize, National Academy of Design, New York, 1913; a Gold Medal, Panama-Pacific International Exposition, San Francisco, 1915; Ranger Fund purchases, National Academy of Design, 1921 and 1926; the Harris Prize, Art Institute of Chicago, 1923; and an honorable mention, Paris Salon, 1926.

GUY ROSE
Born March 3, 1867, in San Gabriel, California
Died November 17, 1925, in Pasadena, California

Guy Rose attended the California School of Design in 1886 and 1887 and studied under Virgil Williams and Emil Carlsen. In 1888 he went to Paris and enrolled in the Académie Julian. He was an exceptional student who won every award the school offered and soon found his paintings accepted for the annual Paris Salon exhibitions.

In 1894 Rose experienced a bout of lead poisoning that forced him to abandon oil painting. He returned to the United States in the winter of 1895 and began a career as an illustrator. He also taught drawing and portraiture at the Pratt Institute in Brooklyn. He gradually regained his health and returned to oil painting around 1897.

In 1899 he returned to Paris, where he continued to do illustrations for *Harper's Bazaar* and other American magazines. Rose was greatly influenced by Claude Monet, and in 1904 Rose and his wife, Ethel, settled in Giverny, becoming members of the small American art colony there. He associated with the artists Richard Miller, Lawton Parker, and Frederick Frieseke. In 1910, Frieseke, Miller, Parker, and Rose exhibited in New York as "the Giverny group."

Rose returned permanently to the United States in 1912 and lived for a time in New York. He moved to Pasadena at the end of 1914 and became active in local art circles, serving for several years on the board of trustees of the Los Angeles Museum of History, Science, and Art. He became the director of the Stickney Memorial School of Fine Arts in Pasadena and persuaded Richard Miller to teach at the school in 1916.

Rose painted primarily in the southern part of the state until about 1918, at which time he began to spend summers in Carmel and Monterey. He developed a serial style of painting similar to that of Monet, in which the same scene would be depicted at different times of day.

Rose was a member of the California Art Club and the Laguna Beach Art Association. Three one-artist exhibitions were held for him at the Los Angeles Museum, in 1916, 1918, and 1919. He was represented in Los Angeles by Stendahl Galleries and in New York by William Macbeth. Among his awards were a Bronze Medal, Pan-American Exposition, Buffalo, 1901; a Silver Medal, Panama-Pacific International Exposition, San Francisco, 1915; and the William Preston Harrison Prize, California Art Club, 1921. He was disabled by a stroke in 1921, four years before his death.

MATTEO SANDONA

Born April 15, 1881 or 1883, in Schio, Italy
Died November 7, 1964, in San Francisco, California

Italian born, Matteo Sandona came to the United States in 1894 and settled with his family in Hoboken, New Jersey. Two years later, he went back to Italy to take art classes in Verona and Paris. Sometime about 1900, he returned to America and studied at the National Academy of Design in New York.

In 1901 Sandona moved to San Francisco. There, he joined a group of disaffected young artists who protested the exhibition policies of the conservative San Francisco Art Association. These artists, including Gottardo Piazzoni, Xavier Martinez, and Peter Neilson, formed the California Society of Artists. An exceptional portrait painter, Sandona also excelled in figure studies and still lifes. A consistent prize winner in exhibitions, he was asked to serve on the international jury of awards for the 1915 Panama-Pacific International Exposition in San Francisco.

Sandona's works can be seen in the National Museum of American Art, Washington, D.C., and in San Francisco at the M. H. de Young Memorial Museum, the California Palace of the Legion of Honor, the San Francisco Museum of Modern Art, and the Bohemian Club. His awards included a Silver Medal, Lewis and Clark Exposition, Portland, 1905; and a Silver Medal, California State Fair, Sacramento, 1917.

DONNA NORINE SCHUSTER

Born January 6, 1883, in Milwaukee, Wisconsin
Died December 27, 1953, in Los Angeles, California

Donna Schuster attended the School of the Art Institute of Chicago, from which she graduated with honors. She then studied in Boston at the Museum of Fine Arts School with Edmund C. Tarbell and Frank W. Benson. She went on a painting tour of Belgium in 1912 with William Merritt Chase and won the William Merritt Chase Prize.

Schuster moved to Los Angeles in 1913, and the following summer studied once again with Chase at the Carmel Summer School. In the fall of 1914, she made a series of watercolor sketches depicting the construction of the buildings for the Panama-Pacific International Exposition in San Francisco. These were later exhibited at the Los Angeles Museum of History, Science, and Art.

In 1923 she built a studio-home in the hills of Griffith Park in Los Angeles and joined the faculty of Otis Art Institute. She spent her summers at a second studio-home in Laguna Beach. In 1928 she began to study with Stanton MacDonald-Wright, and thereafter her work reflected the influence of Cubism and Expressionism.

Schuster was active in many arts organizations and held memberships in the California Art Club, the Laguna Beach Art Association, West Coast Arts, and the California Water Color Society, of which she was a founding member. She was also a member of the Group of Eight, who considered themselves Modernist in their use of rich color, expressive painting techniques, and an emphasis on the human figure. She received many awards, including a Silver Medal, watercolors, Panama-Pacific International Exposition, San Francisco, 1915; a Gold Medal, California State

Fair, Sacramento, 1919; and a Gold Medal, Painters of the West, 1924 and 1929.

JACK WILKINSON SMITH
Born February 7, 1873, in Paterson, New Jersey
Died January 8, 1949, in Monterey Park, California

Jack Wilkinson Smith and his family moved from New Jersey to Michigan in 1886. Soon thereafter, the thirteen-year-old Smith dropped out of high school, ran away to Chicago, and began his art career working as a "paint boy" in a Chicago outdoor advertising company painting shop, where Smith met the artist Gardner Symons. He also studied at the Art Institute of Chicago and was influenced by the work of his friend and painting companion William Wendt.

Smith moved to Cincinnati to work as a sketch artist with the *Cincinnati Enquirer,* and he received national recognition for his front-line sketches of battle scenes in the Spanish-American War in 1898. He studied at the Cincinnati Art Academy with Frank Duveneck and joined the Cincinnati Art Club, where he first gained exposure to serious American art.

In 1906 Smith visited California, which he called "nature's own paradise of scenic splendor and variety." He painted in Los Angeles, then traveled north to Oregon. Returning to Southern California, he established a studio-home in Alhambra in an area known as "Artists' Alley." His neighbors there included the sculptor Eli Harvey and the painter Frank Tenney Johnson. In 1923 he

helped found the Biltmore Salon, a gallery devoted to western artists. It featured the work of Smith, Johnson, Clyde Forsythe, George K. Brandriff, Carl Oscar Borg, Hanson Puthuff, and William Wendt, among others.

Smith was best known for his seascapes and mountain landscapes. His paintings of surf crashing among the rocks are unparalleled. He was a member of the California Art Club, the Sketch Club, and the Laguna Beach Art Association. His awards included a Silver Medal, Panama-California Exposition, 1915; a Gold Medal, California State Fair, 1919; and a Gold Medal, Painters of the West, 1924 and 1929.

CHANNEL PICKERING TOWNSLEY
Born January 20, 1867, in Sedalia, Missouri
Died December 2, 1921, in London, England

Channel Townsley studied art with William Merritt Chase in New York, and then in Paris at the Académies Julian and Delecluse. A teacher and administrator, he managed William Merritt Chase's summer school at Shinnecock, Long Island, before coming to California in 1914 to become director of the Stickney Memorial Art School in Pasadena, a post he held until 1918.

Townsley reorganized the curriculum at Stickney, and one of his first acts was to hire Guy Rose as an instructor. He held summer plein-air classes in Monterey in 1914 and 1916, in the manner of the Shinnecock School. When the Otis Art Institute opened in Los Angeles in 1918, Townsley became its director and left Rose in charge at

Stickney. Townsley died in London, while on leave to visit his friend, the painter Frank Brangwyn.

EDOUARD ANTONIN VYSEKAL
Born March 17, 1890, in Kutna Hora, Czechoslovakia
Died December 2, 1939, in Los Angeles, California

Edouard Vysekal (pronounced Vee'-sah-kahl) began his art training in Prague, and after coming to the United States in 1907 he continued his studies at the Art Institute of Chicago. He also took classes with Stanton MacDonald-Wright, the noted Modernist who, along with Morgan Russell, devised Synchromism, the one and only American international early Modern art style. Synchromism was a disciplined approach to painting that sought to create rhythmic movement and emotional content solely through the use of color.

In 1912 Vysekal began teaching at the Art Institute of Chicago and soon fell in love with and married one of his pupils, Luvena Buchanan (1873–1954). In 1914 the couple visited California to paint a mural commission at the Barbara Worth Hotel in El Centro. After its completion, they decided to remain in California and live in Los Angeles.

The Vysekals established a home and studio in the Hollywood Hills. Edouard taught at the Art Students League and the Otis Art Institute. At the Art Students League, Vysekal rekindled his friendship with MacDonald-Wright, who was the director at the time. Over the next twenty years,

Vysekal's style became more and more progressive, and he came to be regarded as one of California's eminent Modernists.

Vysekal is known for his vivid and bold use of color combined with a daring approach to form. His early paintings show a strong debt to Post-Impressionism, but as it developed, his technique displayed strong influences from many of the current modern trends, notably Synchromism and Cubism. He was a member of the Modern Art Society of Los Angeles and participated in exhibitions that featured California's more progressive painters.

ELMER WACHTEL

Born January 21, 1864, in Baltimore, Maryland
Died August 31, 1929, in Guadalajara, Mexico

In 1882 Elmer Wachtel came to Southern California to live with his older brother John, who was married to the sister of Guy Rose and managing the Rose family ranch, Sunny Slope. An aspiring violinist, Wachtel became first violin of the Philharmonic Orchestra in Los Angeles in 1888. He held the same position during 1893–94 with A. J. Stamm's Philharmonic Orchestra.

During this time Wachtel also pursued an interest in drawing and painting. He became active in local art circles, which included John Gutzon Borglum and J. Bond Francisco. With several other artists they founded the Los Angeles Art Association in the late 1880s. In 1895 Wachtel went to New York and enrolled in the Art Students League but, unhappy with the teaching methods, left after only two weeks. He remained in New York and received criticism from William Merritt Chase. He exhibited with the New York Water Color Society. After returning to California in 1896, he spent a brief period in San Francisco, where he exhibited with the San Francisco Art Association. He then returned permanently to Los Angeles.

Wachtel worked as a pen-and-ink illustrator for *Land of Sunshine* and *Californian* magazines. Around 1900 he went to England and Europe, studying at the Lambeth Art School in London and visiting and painting with his friend Gutzon Borglum, who was living there. He also associated with the English illustrators Fred and Tom Wilkinson. Within a few years of his return to Los Angeles, Watchtel had established a reputation as an accomplished landscape artist. William Keith sent the young artist Marion Kavanaugh to see him in 1903, and they were married in Chicago the following year.

Somewhat of an artistic maverick, Elmer Wachtel was at first a Tonalist and showed moody and poetic landscapes in dark tones. As he progressed, he accepted some of the Impressionist esthetic and brightened his palette. Many of his mature works show a more decorative and lyrical style, very reminiscent of that of Arthur F. Mathews, the San Francisco landscape and figure painter who influenced a generation of Northern California painters, although Wachtel rarely included figures in his compositions.

Elmer and Marion Kavanagh Wachtel spent the next twenty-five years as inseparable painting companions, he working in oils and she in watercolor. They traveled throughout California, the deserts of Arizona and New Mexico, and in Mexico. It was during a painting trip to Guadalajara in 1929 that Elmer Wachtel died.

Wachtel was an individualist who shunned the many arts organizations that were organized in the early 1900s. He refused to join the California Art Club at its founding in 1909. This in no way affected the esteem in which he was held by his fellow artists. One-artist exhibitions were held for him at the Los Angeles Museum of History, Science, and Art in 1915 and 1918. A memorial exhibition was held at Kanst Art Gallery in 1930. He received two awards from the San Francisco Art Association: for watercolor in 1902 and for oils in 1906.

MARION KAVANAGH WACHTEL

Born June 10, 1876, in Milwaukee, Wisconsin
Died May 22, 1954, in Pasadena, California

Marion Kavanaugh studied at the Art Institute of Chicago and in New York with William Merritt Chase. For several years she taught at the Art Institute of Chicago. She then traveled to San Francisco to study with William Keith. Keith recommended that she go to Los Angeles to see the artist Elmer Wachtel. They met in 1903 and were married the following year in Chicago. Thereafter she signed her name "Marion Kavanagh Wachtel."

Returning to Los Angeles, the couple built a studio-home in the Mt. Washington area. They remained there until 1921 when they moved to the Arroyo Seco area of Pasadena. They traveled throughout Southern California and the Southwest to paint. Originally trained as a portrait artist, Marion Wachtel painted portraits of the Hopi on a trip to Northern Arizona and New Mexico in 1908.

Perhaps so as not to compete with her husband, Wachtel worked primarily in watercolor throughout their marriage and displayed remarkable dexterity in her handling of the medium. She received high praise for her works, which are delicate, lyrical interpretations of the landscape, in a manner that shows her masterly control of tone and color.

She was elected to the New York Water Color Club in 1911, was elected an Associate of the American Water Color Society in 1912, and was a founding member of the California Water Color Society in 1921. She also held memberships in the Pasadena Society of Artists and the Academy of Western Painters. Her works were exhibited in solo exhibitions in Los Angeles as well as jointly with her husband's. One-artist exhibitions of her paintings were held at the Los Angeles Museum of History, Science, and Art in 1915 and 1917.

After her husband's death in 1929, Wachtel temporarily lost interest in painting. She resumed working about 1931, painting landscapes around her home on the Arroyo Seco, and views of the foothills of the San Gabriel Mountains and several of the Sierra Nevada Mountains; many of these are in oil paint.

WILLIAM WENDT

Born February 20, 1865, in Bentzen, Germany
Died December 29, 1946, in Laguna Beach, California

William Wendt immigrated to the United States in 1880 and settled in Chicago, where he worked in a commercial art firm. Essentially self-taught, he attended evening classes at the Art Institute of Chicago for only a brief period; dissatisfied with figure studies, he preferred painting landscapes. Wendt quickly became an active exhibitor in various Chicago art shows, winning the Second Yerkes Prize at the Chicago Society of Artists exhibition in 1893.

Wendt became friends with the artist Gardner Symons, and together they made a number of trips to California between 1896 and 1904 and, in 1898, to the art colony at St. Ives in Cornwall, England. Works from each of those trips were exhibited at the Art Institute of Chicago.

Wendt settled in Los Angeles with his wife, the sculptor Julia Bracken, in 1906. Already a successful painter, he quickly became a leading member of the art community and was a founding member of the California Art Club in 1909. He moved his home and studio to the art colony at Laguna Beach in 1912, the same year that he was elected an Associate of the National Academy of Design. He was a founding member of the Laguna Beach Art Association in 1918, and although somewhat shy and reclusive, he was Laguna's most important resident artist-teacher.

To Wendt, nature was a manifestation of God, and he viewed himself as nature's faithful interpreter. Only rarely did he include people or animals in his landscapes. He worked out-of-doors, sometimes sketching and sometimes making large, finished works. His early works reflect the feathery brushstrokes and hazy atmosphere of Impressionism. In his later works, after about 1912, he employed a distinctive blocklike brushwork that gave a solidity to his renditions of natural forms. A prolific painter, he was known as the "dean" of Southern California's landscape painters.

A regular exhibitor in Los Angeles, Chicago, and New York, Wendt received numerous awards for his works. Among these were a Bronze Medal, Pan-American Exposition, Buffalo, 1901; a Silver Medal, Louisiana Purchase Exposition, St. Louis, 1904; and a Silver Medal, Panama-Pacific International Exposition, San Francisco, 1915. In 1925 he received a Gold Medal at the Pan-American Exhibition in Los Angeles for *Where Nature's God Hath Wrought* (Los Angeles County Museum of Art).

THEODORE WORES

Born August 1, 1859, in San Francisco, California
Died September 11, 1939, in San Francisco, California

Theodore Wores was the second of seven children born to Joseph Wores and Gertrude Liebke Wores, who came to California from Hungary in 1852. Young Wores was an avid sketcher as a child and took private lessons from Joseph Harrington while still in public school.

In 1874, Wores was one of forty students to pass the entrance examination for the very first art class at the San Francisco Art Association School of Design. He studied under Virgil Williams until the summer of 1875, when he went to Munich to enroll in the Bavarian Royal Academy. There, he studied under Ludwig Loefftz and Alexander Wagner. He won several awards in the Academy, and in 1879 he went to Florence to study with Frank Duveneck.

After seven years in Europe, Wores came back to San Francisco, in 1881. He rented a studio next door to William Keith and began a long series of paintings of Chinatown. In 1885 Wores traveled to Japan, where he painted for three years. Upon his return to San Francisco, he exhibited his Japanese paintings and found immediate critical success. He followed this up by showing his works in New York and London. In 1891, he was back in San Francisco.

In 1892 Wores made a second trip to Japan, staying for two years. In 1901 he undertook a two-year tour of Hawaii, Samoa, and Spain. The San Francisco earthquake of 1906 and the resultant great fire destroyed Wores's house and studio. Undaunted, he remained in the city and began teaching at the San Francisco Art Institute. In 1913 he returned to Hawaii, and in 1915 spent two years painting in Taos, New Mexico. In 1926, he moved to Saratoga, where he converted an abandoned church into a studio and weekend retreat. He died in San Francisco, on September 11, 1939.

Wores exhibited at the St. Louis Exposition of 1895, won a Gold Medal at the Alaska-Yukon Exposition, Seattle, 1909, and a Gold Medal at the Panama-Pacific International Exposition, San Francisco, 1915. His works are in the collections of the Oakland Museum; the Palace of the Legion of Honor and the de Young Museum in San Francisco; the Monterey Peninsula Museum of Art; the Los Angeles County Museum of Art; the White House Collection; the E.B. Crocker Museum, Sacramento; the Honolulu Academy of Art; the Amon Carter Museum, Fort Worth; and the Bohemian Club, San Francisco.

Karl Julius Heinrich Yens

Born January 11, 1868, in Altona, Germany
Died April 13, 1945, in Laguna Beach, California

Karl Yens studied in Berlin with Max Koch, and in Paris with Benjamin Constant and Jean Paul Laurens. He worked as a muralist in Germany, then in Scotland. In 1901 he immigrated to the United States, where he painted murals in New York City and Washington, D.C.

In 1910 Yens moved to Southern California. He became active in the art circles in Los Angeles and Pasadena. In 1918 he moved to Laguna Beach, where he built a studio-home on the Coast Highway near Ruby Street. He was a founding member of the Laguna Beach Art Association in the summer of 1918.

Yens worked in both oil and watercolor, painting a variety of subjects, including portraits, figure works, still lifes, landscapes, and genre scenes. His style is colorful and decorative.

Yens held memberships in a number of arts organizations, including the California Art Club, the Academy of Western Painters, the California Water Color Society, the Painters and Sculptors of Los Angeles, and the San Diego Fine Arts Society. He received many awards for his work.

SELECTED BIBLIOGRAPHY

Anderson, Susan M. *Regionalism: The California View, Watercolors, 1929–1945,* exhibition catalogue. Santa Barbara: Santa Barbara Museum of Art, 1988.

Anderson, Thomas R., and Bruce A. Kamerling. *Sunlight and Shadow: The Art of Alfred R. Mitchell, 1888–1972,* exhibition catalogue. San Diego: San Diego Historical Society, 1988.

Art of California. San Francisco: R. L. Bernier, Publisher, 1916. Reprinted by Westphal Publishing, Irvine, California.

Baigell, Matthew. *The American Scene: American Painting of the 1930s.* New York: Praeger Publishing, 1974.

Baird, Joseph Armstrong, Jr., ed. *From Exposition to Exposition: Progressive and Conservative Northern California Painting, 1915–1939,* exhibition catalogue. Sacramento: Crocker Art Museum, 1981.

Brinton, Christian. *Impressions of the Art at the Panama-Pacific Exposition.* New York: John Lane, 1916.

Cahill, Holger. *American Art Today, New York World's Fair.* New York: National Art Society, 1939.

California Design 1910. Pasadena: California Design Publications, 1974.

California Grandeur and Genre: From the Collection of James L. Coran and Walter A. Nelson-Rees, exhibition catalogue. Palm Springs, Calif.: Palm Springs Desert Museum, 1991.

Carl Oscar Borg: A Niche in Time, exhibition catalogue. Palm Springs, Calif.: Palm Springs Desert Museum, 1990.

Coen, Rena Neumann. *The Paynes: Edgar and Elsie, American Artists.* Minneapolis: Payne Studios, 1988.

Color and Impressions: The Early Work of E. Charlton Fortune, exhibition catalogue. Monterey, Calif.: Monterey Peninsula Museum of Art, 1990.

Cornelius, Brother, F.S.C. *Keith: Old Master of California.* New York: G. P. Putnam's Sons, 1942.

Dominik, Janet Blake. *Early Artists in Laguna Beach: The Impressionists,* exhibition catalogue. Laguna Beach, Calif.: Laguna Art Museum, 1986.

Falk, Peter Hastings. *Who Was Who in American Art.* Madison, Conn.: Sound View Press, 1985.

Gerdts, William H. *American Impressionism,* exhibition catalogue. Seattle: Henry Art Gallery, University of Washington, 1980.

_____. *American Impressionism.* New York: Abbeville Press, 1984.

PLATE 58
Guy Rose (1867–1925)
Indian Tobacco Trees, La Jolla
Oil on canvas, 24 x 29 inches
The Joan Irvine Smith Collection

_____. *Art Across America.* 3 volumes. New York, Abbeville Press, 1990.

Granville Redmond, exhibition catalogue. Oakland: The Oakland Museum, 1988.

Hailey, Gene, ed. *Abstract from California Art Research: Monographs.* W.P.A. Project 2874, O.P. 65-3-3632. 20 volumes. San Francisco: Works Progress Administration, 1937.

Hughes, Edan Milton. *Artists in California: 1786–1940.* 2nd ed. San Francisco: Hughes Publishing, 1989.

Impressionism: The California View, exhibition catalogue. Oakland: The Oakland Museum, 1981.

Keyes, Donald D. *American Impressionism in Georgia Collections.* Athens, Ga.: Georgia Museum of Art, University of Georgia, 1993.

Laird, Helen. *Carl Oscar Borg and the Magic Region.* Layton, Utah: Gibbs M. Smith, Peregrine Smith Books, 1986.

McClelland, Gordon T., and Jay T. Last. *The California Style: California Watercolor Artists, 1929–1955.* Beverly Hills, Calif.: Hillcrest Press, 1985.

Millier, Arthur. "Growth of Art in California." In *Land of Homes* by Frank J. Taylor. Los Angeles: Powell Publishing, 1929.

Moure, Nancy Dustin Wall. *Artists' Clubs and Exhibitions in Los Angeles before 1930.* Los Angeles: Privately published, 1974.

_____. *The California Water Color Society: Prize Winners, 1931-1954: Index to Exhibitions, 1921–1954.* Los Angeles: Privately published, 1973.

_____. *Dictionary of Art and Artists in Southern California before 1930.* Los Angeles: Privately published, 1975.

_____. *Loners, Mavericks, and Dreamers: Art in Los Angeles before 1900,* exhibition catalogue. Laguna Beach, Calif.: Laguna Art Museum, 1994.

_____. *Los Angeles Painters of the Nineteen-Twenties.* Claremont, Calif.: Pomona College Gallery, 1972.

_____. *Painting and Sculpture in Los Angeles: 1900–1945,* exhibition catalogue. Los Angeles: Los Angeles County Museum of Art, 1980.

_____. *Southern California Artists: 1890–1940,* exhibition catalogue. Introduction by Carl Dentzel. Laguna Beach, Calif.: Laguna Beach Museum of Art, 1979.

_____. *William Wendt, 1865-1946,* exhibition catalogue. Laguna Beach, Calif.: Laguna Beach Museum of Art, 1977.

Nelson-Rees, Walter A. *Albert Thomas DeRome, 1885–1959.* Oakland: WIM, 1988.

Nochlin, Linda. *Realism.* New York: Penguin Books, 1971.

Orr-Cahall, Christina. *The Art of California: Selected Works of The Oakland Museum.* Oakland: The Oakland Museum Art Department, 1984.

Perine, Robert. *Chouinard: An Art Vision Betrayed.* Encinitas, Calif.: Artra Publishing, 1985.

Petersen, Martin E. *Second Nature: Four Early San Diego Landscape Painters,* exhibition catalogue. San Diego and Munich: San Diego Museum of Art and Prestel-Verlag, 1991.

South, Will, William H. Gerdts, and Jean Stern. *Guy Rose, American Impressionist.* Oakland and Irvine, Calif.: The Oakland Museum and The Irvine Museum, 1995.

Stern, Jean. *Alson S. Clark.* Los Angeles: Petersen Publishing, 1983.

_____. *Masterworks of California Impressionism: The FFCA, Morton H. Fleischer Collection.* Phoenix: FFCA Publishing Company, 1986.

_____. *The Paintings of Franz A. Bischoff.* Los Angeles: Petersen Publishing, 1980.

_____. *Palette of Light: California Paintings from The Irvine Museum,* exhibition catalogue. Irvine, Calif.: The Irvine Museum, 1995.

Stern, Jean, Janet Blake Dominik, and Harvey L. Jones. *Selections from The Irvine Museum,* exhibition catalogue. Irvine, Calif.: The Irvine Museum, 1993.

Stern, Jean, and Gerald J. Miller. *Romance of the Bells: The California Missions in Art,* exhibition catalogue. Irvine, Calif.: The Irvine Museum, 1995.

Stern, Jean, and Joan Irvine Smith. *Reflections of California: The Athalie Richardson Irvine Clarke Memorial Exhibition,* exhibition catalogue. Irvine, Calif.: The Irvine Museum, 1994.

Stern, Jean, and Ruth Westphal. *The Paintings of Sam Hyde Harris.* Los Angeles: Petersen Publishing, 1980.

Stern, Jean, et al. *Impressions of California, Early Currents in Art 1850–1930,* companion volume to KOCE-TV (PBS) video series. Irvine, Calif.: The Irvine Museum, 1996.

Tonalism: An American Experience. New York: Grand Central Art Galleries Art Education Association, 1982.

Trenton, Patricia, and William H. Gerdts. *California Light 1900–1930,* exhibition catalogue. Laguna Beach, Calif.: Laguna Art Museum, 1990.

Vincent, Stephen, ed. *O California!: Nineteenth and Early Twentieth Century California Landscapes and Observations.* San Francisco: Bedford Arts, 1990.

Westphal, Ruth Lilly. *Plein Air Painters of California: The North.* Irvine, Calif.: Westphal Publishing, 1986.

_____. *Plein Air Painters of California: The Southland.* Irvine, Calif.: Westphal Publishing, 1982.

Westphal, Ruth Lilly, and Janet Blake Dominik, eds. *American Scene Painting: California, 1930s and 1940s.* Irvine, Calif.: Westphal Publishing, 1991.

Index

Illustration pages are indicated by **bold** type.

The Irvine Museum

ALL THINGS BRIGHT & BEAUTIFUL
CALIFORNIA IMPRESSIONIST PAINTINGS
FROM THE IRVINE MUSEUM

was edited by Joseph N. Newland
and designed by Lilli Colton.
The text was composed in Minion.
5,000 casebound and 17,000
softbound copies were lithographed
in Italy by I.G.E. Musumeci
through Overseas Printing
Corporation. Production was
coordinated by Lilli Colton.
This is the first edition.